# Parenting That
# Works

# Parenting That
# Works

## Building Skills That Last a Lifetime

Edward R. Christophersen, PhD,
and Susan L. Mortweet, PhD

American Psychological Association • Washington, DC

First Printing, August 2002
Second Printing, October 2002
Third Printing, January 2007
Fourth Printing, December 2008

Published by
APA LifeTools
American Psychological Association
750 First Street, NE
Washington, DC 20002
www.apa.org

| To order | Tel: (800) 374-2721, Direct: (202) 336-5510 |
| APA Order Department | Fax: (202) 336-5502, TDD/TTY: (202) 336-6123 |
| P.O. Box 92984 | On-line: www.apa.org/books/ |
| Washington, DC 20090-2984 | E-mail: order@apa.org |

In the U.K., Europe, Africa, and the Middle East, copies may be ordered from
American Psychological Association
3 Henrietta Street
Covent Garden, London
WC2E 8LU England

Typeset in Sabon by EPS Group Inc., Easton, MD

Printer: Port City Press, Inc., Baltimore, MD
Cover Designer: Naylor Design, Washington, DC
Technical/Production Editor: Jennifer L. Macomber

The opinions and statements published are the responsibility of the authors, and such opinions and statements do not necessarily represent the policies of the American Psychological Association.

Library of Congress Cataloging-in-Publication Data
Christophersen, Edward R.
    Parenting that works : building skills that last a lifetime / Edward R. Christophersen, Susan L. Mortweet.
        p. cm.
    Includes bibliographical references and index.
    ISBN 1-55798-924-9 (alk. paper)
        1. Parenting. 2. Child rearing. I. Mortweet, Susan L. II. Title.

HQ755.8.C485 2002
649′.1—dc21
                                                                2002022841

British Library Cataloguing-in-Publication Data
A CIP record is available from the British Library.

Printed in the United States of America

# CONTENTS

# Parenting That
# Works

# INTRODUCTION

Perhaps more than at any other time in history, today's parents are concerned about the future of their children. They don't just want a child who will make the honor roll or who will get into college. They want a child who will be happy, caring, and compassionate. A child who can be assertive without being aggressive or violent. A child who can make and keep friends without succumbing to pressure to use drugs or to be overly thin. A child who has the skills to handle life's frustrations without lashing out or losing self-esteem.

How do you raise a child with such strengths? Are these qualities inherited, or can parents really have some kind of impact on how their child turns out? After 25 years of seeing children in a clinical pediatric setting, we have come to the conclusion that children act the way they do because of a complex interplay between some inherited traits, which for the most part cannot be changed, and the environment. Unfortunately, we as parents often do not know if the environment we are providing for our children will serve them well in adulthood until they are halfway through adolescence. Often this is because we parent as we were parented, without taking time to explore the extensive information now available about how best to influence our children.

Throughout this book, we take the position that from the

very beginning, we are training our children to be adults—adults with whom we would like to interact regularly, and whose company we anticipate and enjoy. In fact, we simply do not have the option of *not* training our children. Effective parenting requires that you have a long-term plan for what you want to teach your child about appropriate behavior and that you have daily interactions with your child that foster the characteristics you find important. Our basic approach in this book involves helping you use your time, energy, and introspection to decide now what skills you want your child to have in 10 years. By doing so, you can begin teaching those skills to your child during the everyday interactions that constitute parenting. We call this your "10-Year Plan." If you want a child who will help with chores, communicate with you about pressures at school, and be kind to his or her little sister, our approach will help you encourage the development of these skills in your child. If you want to raise a child who is good at sharing and at taking turns and who can cope with the frustrations that are part of everyday interactions with his or her peers, we can help you encourage the development of those skills in your child as well.

You can also use your 10-Year Plan in deciding whether a given parenting approach is helping you make progress toward your desired results. For example, if you typically purchase two of each toy to keep sibling conflict over toys to a minimum, you need to ask yourself whether you are teaching your children the important life skill of sharing, or merely avoiding the conflict that arises in day-to-day play. If you have a toddler with poor self-quieting skills and you are lying down with him at bedtime, you need to ask yourself if your child is learning essential skills that he needs to be able to initiate and maintain sleep on his own.

We emphasize the prevention of problems by helping you teach life skills when they are developmentally appropriate. Thus, the majority of this book focuses on school-age children and younger, with the assumption that preventing problems is much more manageable when your child is young. We also make suggestions for correcting behavior problems your child may already have. These suggestions are best suited for children with mild-to-moderate problems and may not be appropriate for severely oppositional children or those with special needs. We also provide guidance on when to seek professional help for your child. Nevertheless, the overriding concept of long-term strategies for building life skills in you and your child will fit a wide variety of parents and children.

This book is divided into sections on parenting skills and on child skills. Part I discusses building your skills as a parent, including encouraging appropriate behaviors in your child, providing your child with positive feedback, communicating with your child, using effective discipline strategies, and developing vital parent coping skills. Part II provides suggestions for managing your child's behavior in public, choosing toys and games for your child, and helping your child cope with divorce.

Part III discusses building your child's skills, with particular reference to self-quieting skills and independent play skills. Part IV addresses problems with bedtime, toileting, aggression, and whining and tantrums.

It is important to remember as you read this book that teaching any new skill takes time. You must be committed to trying the strategies in this book for a reasonable length of time—at least three months—and with consistent effort and mindfulness. In fact, if you use these strategies effectively, your child's behavior may initially become a little worse. This is because your child may resist your efforts to change outcomes that were predictable for her. That is a positive sign that you are on the right track and challenging your child to change her misbehaviors by minding your new rules. Rest assured, your child's initial resistance to your changing the rules is to be expected and is a necessary step for you to become a more effective parent.

Many parenting books currently on the market focus on what to do after your child is already demonstrating behavior problems. This book describes what you can do to prevent behavior problems, as well as how to address common problems, in a way that will teach your children the skills you want them to have as adults. By using the strategies suggested in this book, you can raise your child to be an adult who has good coping skills, who can interact appropriately with others, who enjoys a variety of activities, and who values his own company—in other words, the adult we would enjoy and would like to be ourselves.

# Part I

## BUILDING EFFECTIVE PARENTING SKILLS

# CHAPTER 1

# TEACHING YOUR CHILD WHAT IS IMPORTANT

How much influence does your behavior have on the behavior of your child? A tremendous amount! Your everyday behavior teaches your child what is important to you. Even with no forethought and no planning, your behavior significantly shapes the way your child will behave now and as an adult. Children learn by what they see and hear their parents do on a daily basis. For example, if your child sees you donating clothes to a homeless shelter each year, she will begin to appreciate the importance of giving back to the community, regardless whether you ever discuss it with her. If he sees you holding doors open for others and letting an older person go ahead of you in line at the grocery store, he is learning to show the same consideration to others. If she hears you talking pleasantly about your coworkers and family members, she will come to recognize and value the positive traits of others.

On the other hand, each time your child hears you and your partner arguing loudly with each other, making critical comments, or pounding your fists, he will be one step closer to arguing loudly, criticizing, and showing aggression when he is upset. If she hears you complaining on a daily basis about your job, coworkers, and responsibilities around the house, she may view her school, her interactions with others, and your requests for cooperation with chores with the same disdain.

If your child is not behaving as you would like him to, or if you are reading this book to avoid having behavior problems with your child, you can plan to systematically teach what behaviors you want your child to learn. This chapter discusses the parenting skill of teaching through modeling the behaviors you want your child to display, including social skills, language skills, problem solving, routines, and lifelong interests.

## TEACHING THROUGH MODELING SOCIAL SKILLS

You can teach your children to get along with others by modeling social behaviors and giving them plenty of opportunities to practice. To keep track of the behaviors you want to model for your child (for example, treat people with more consideration, complain less about housework), write up a "to-do" list. If you display your to-do list on the refrigerator door or bathroom mirror, you'll have a constant reminder that what you do affects how your child behaves. Then periodically rate yourself on how well you are performing each of the skills you want to model for your child. Occasionally note the progress your child is making on learning that skill as well.

Then, determine which social skills, such as sharing, your child needs to build, and plan how to provide the necessary opportunities. Do you need to invite children over to play more often? Do you need to limit the amount of toys or snacks your child is receiving to encourage cooperation? Add this plan to your to-do list.

If and when your child asks you why you are making up your list or what the list is for, you can, of course, explain to her that you are trying to get better organized or that you are trying very hard to treat the people around you better. But be careful—most parents tend to want to go into a long explanation about what they are doing. Frequent, brief descriptions that are specific to your child's questions will convey more understandable information than one lengthy discussion. Be careful to note how much time you talk about your child's skills, or lack thereof, versus giving chances for practice. Constantly talking about the importance of polite behavior, criticizing your child, and expressing your disappointment simply are not the most effective tools for teaching social behavior to children. The key is providing opportunities to practice the skills that you value.

You as a parent can have a great influence on your child's behavior by doing little more than behaving yourself and providing opportunities for your child to do the same. Modeling the behaviors of sharing, using good manners, and interacting with younger children and pets will teach your child how to positively interact with others.

Your approach to teaching your child each specific skill can involve the same five steps:

1. pointing out to your child when you do it yourself
2. finding opportunities when you can prompt the behavior in your child
3. praising your child when she engages in the behavior
4. instructing your child to engage in the behavior
5. delivering appropriate consequences for not engaging in the behavior.

## Sharing

Sharing is a skill that all parents wish their children would demonstrate. You can use the five steps listed in the previous section to encourage sharing in your child as follows:

1. *Point out times, in everyday situations, when you are sharing.* For example, if you are splitting a piece of pie with your son, say something like, "Mommy is sharing her pie with you." When you are letting another driver pull ahead of you, encouraging another shopper to check out ahead of you, or loaning a shovel to a neighbor, simply point out to your child, at the time, how you are "sharing."

2. *Find opportunities for your child to share.* The easiest way to teach a child how to share is to provide her with many, many opportunities to do so. Arrange opportunities for your child to share with you, siblings, or other children visiting your child to illustrate to your child what sharing means. For example, when eating at a fast food restaurant, empty all of the French fries onto one person's plate. That person divides the fries among everyone else's plate, saying, "I'm sharing my French fries with you." At the next visit your child can empty the fries onto her plate and share with everyone else (even if she relinquishes only the brown, crinkled ones).

Instead of giving each child a piece of toast at home, fix one piece of toast, break it, and give them each half. You can comment, "You will need to share this one before I will make more" to let them know what you are trying to teach them. You can always fix another piece of toast later for them to share. Similarly, instead of giving each child a can of soda, give them one can and two glasses or cups. When they share fairly, they both get half the treat.

If one child chooses to not share the treat, make sure the child who was willing to share gets his half but the child who refused to share does not. You can also comment, "You need to share to get your part of the treat, or you do not get anything" to reinforce the lesson about sharing. A simple trick to encourage fair division when sharing is to allow the child who did not divide the item to choose her half first. This trick will help to keep the division fair and both parties happy with the outcome.

*3. Praise your child whenever you see her sharing with you or with other children.* If you see your daughter offer to let her friend play with one of her toys or dolls, make sure you let her know that you liked the way she offered to share. Praising your child can take many different forms. You can verbally thank her or give her a hug for sharing. The important point is that she gains some type of recognition for her efforts at sharing. Some parents working on sharing post a "share card" on the refrigerator door, and they record each major incident when a child shares. Then everyone who goes to the refrigerator sees the share card.

*4. Instruct your children to ask before borrowing.* If your two boys are playing on the floor with different toys, almost inevitably one is going to want to play with something the other has. Prompt that child to ask his brother instead of simply taking it away from him. If one child nicely asks the other if he can play with a toy, you'll probably need to get involved in the situation either by reiterating the request or offering a compromise so that the child is rewarded for his efforts at appropriate attempts to share. This doesn't mean that a child always gets a toy just because he asked nicely. However, if he never gets the toy when he's asked for it nicely, he'll get discouraged and stop asking for it and go back to just taking what he wants.

You might consider using practice sessions where you plan on being with your children the entire time they are playing. Before they begin playing, tell them that this is a day when you want them to practice sharing their toys. Encourage one child to ask, nicely, to play with the toy that the other child is playing with. Then, if the second child shares, praise her. If she refuses to share, you might need to remove the toy from her possession and hand it to the other child. Although you may not see much of an improvement the first time or two that you do this, you will probably see an improvement after several practice sessions.

Children do, of course, have the right to their own toys. But this right has to be established ahead of time and handled accordingly. You can decide, with your two children, which toys belong to each and will not be shared. This can be especially important for older children, who do have a right to keep their prized possessions out of the hands of their younger siblings. They, in turn, are responsible for keeping those toys in their own personal bin instead of just leaving them out like they do their other toys. Although it is very tempting to tell an older child "just let him have it" when a younger child has her prized possession, this behavior will not teach either one of them about sharing. It may also cause hard feelings between the two children, resulting in negative behavior.

5. *Implement consequences for not complying with the rules.* If the children are fighting over a particular toy, the toy can be placed in time-out. The toy stays in time-out until both of the children are willing to share it. In this way, neither child comes out ahead by refusing to share; rather, they both lose. If you have established with your children ahead of time that they are playing with toys that must be shared, then implementing consequences such as time-out for a toy or child is appropriate. (See chapter 4 for a discussion of time-out.)

For many children, sharing doesn't come naturally. It's only after they have grown accustomed to sharing that they will find it easier to do. Thus, assist them in developing this skill by having consistent rules regarding what has to be shared and what does not, and use consequences consistently. Like most of the other skills that you have to teach your children, it will be much easier if you start out, when they are young toddlers, by making sharing an everyday part of playing. That way, there's never a time when they aren't expected to share their toys.

It is through repeated exposure, opportunities, and positive consequences that children learn concepts such as sharing. They do not learn to share by watching parents who do not model sharing but discipline the children for not sharing. Rather, children learn a particular behavior, such as sharing, by being a part of the process over and over again.


## Using Good Manners

Another social behavior you can teach using the five-step outline is the use of good manners.

*1. Point out times in everyday situations when you or others use good manners.* It is very important to model common courtesies such as saying "please" and "thank you" to your children, other family members, and strangers. From the time children are in preschool, they pay attention to your social skills and how you treat others. Parents of school-age children have a particularly heavy modeling responsibility, because school-age children are very observant. Children notice how polite Mom and Dad are to each other, how they treat other adults and other children, and whether they say nice or unpleasant things about people who are not present. There is no hiding from your child. Parents need to be constantly aware that they are setting daily examples that are very likely to be followed.

There are many naturally occurring situations when either you or another adult exhibits good manners. While you are working on good manners with your child, you will need to be vigilant of good manners, always ready to point them out. When the person who waits on you at a restaurant or at the dry cleaners is pleasant, point it out to your son. Whether it's personnel at a car service shop, a grocery store, or the preschool or school, try to identify times and places where people exhibit good manners and point these out to your child. You can even make a game out of it to see who will be the first to notice when someone is using good manners.

*2. Find opportunities when good manners are appropriate.* Before you get to the door of the school, tell your daughter that you would appreciate it if she would hold the door for you. If you are going into the principal's office, prompt your child to stand next to the principal until he looks at her and then to ask her question. You may also want to require your child to say "please" before receiving a treat or item being passed at the table and "thank you" upon receiving it. The more aware you are of your manners, the more opportunities you are likely to find to ask your child to use her good manners.

*3. Praise your child whenever he uses good manners.* You can further reinforce your child's learning of this skill by complimenting him when he is courteous to you and others. Such praise may be verbal, such as "I like it when you are so polite to strangers" or "That lady seemed very impressed that you held the door for her, what good manners!" Certainly a brief squeeze of the shoulder or smile can also tell your child that you noticed his polite behavior. We are all embarrassed when our children use a profane word or phrase that they have overheard us use in times of frustration. We are typically quick to reprimand such behavior as well. Take advantage of the fact that your child is equally as likely to mimic your polite behaviors, especially if you give him the opportunity to do so and praise him for his efforts.

*4. Instruct your child when the use of good manners would be appropriate.* For example, tell her, "This would be a good time to ask the cashier if you could please have your change back in quarters" or "Please hold the door open for that lady with all of the packages; she would appreciate your good manners." Once again, if you are aware of your manners throughout the day, you will find many chances to instruct your child when to use her manners.

*5. Implement consequences for not using good manners.* If your child orders dessert but forgets to say please, prompt him to say please. If the prompting doesn't result in his saying please, consider canceling the dessert order. Similarly, if you are at the dinner table at home and your child doesn't say please after your prompting, then don't pass the item he wanted. By focusing on situations when your child wants something when trying to establish good manners, you are more likely to receive cooperation than in situations where he is not as interested. For example, prompting a child to ask his teacher to "please give me my makeup homework" may not be as effective to encourage good manners as requiring him to say please before he receives the candy he is requesting at the store.

How long should parents be willing to prompt children before expecting them to exhibit good manners? A long time! We don't have a problem with parents prompting their children for a year or two before ever expecting the children to exhibit good manners without any prompting. Of course, if your child holds a door for someone without being prompted or carries a bag of groceries without being asked, make sure to praise her for doing so.

## Interacting With Younger Children and Pets

One final example of how teaching social skills in steps can be used to teach children how to get along with others is in the area of handling younger children, siblings, and pets. If you would like your older child to be able to interact appropriately with an infant sibling, apply the five rules as follows:

*1. Point out how you are handling your newborn, so that your older child can see how this is done.* Model appropriate holding, touching, and talking. Tell your child, "See how Mommy is carefully holding Megan's head while I move her" or "The baby likes it when you and I talk in a quiet voice when she is trying to fall asleep."

2. *Find opportunities for your older child to interact appropriately with your younger child.* An older child will most likely try to interact with a younger child whether or not you set up opportunities for him to do so. For example, the 5-year-old who comes into the kitchen half carrying and half dragging his baby sister is not being mean to his sister. He has simply seen his mother and father pick up the baby under her arms and is trying to do the same thing, but he is not tall enough or strong enough to do it. Thus, it is important to use such events as opportunities to model for the 5-year-old how he can carry the baby or have him practice coming to you when he wants to move her or interact with her. You can set up structured interaction times by involving the older child in routine caregiving activities such as changing diapers or playing with the infant. Make sure that such opportunities occur when your older child will have the most success, such as when the baby is awake, fed, and content. Set limits on when or how the infant can be carried, and allow the older child to practice this new skill under your supervision only.

3. *Provide lots of praise and feedback when your child handles a younger child appropriately.* Although you may get tired of doing so, the praise is essential to your child's learning the appropriate way to interact with a younger sibling or friend. When providing praise, focus on the specific behaviors your child is demonstrating, such as "Look at how carefully you are holding onto Andy's hand while he tries to walk." This type of praise will be much more helpful in teaching interaction skills than simply saying, "You are such a great big sister to Andy!"

4. *Instruct your child how to interact with the younger child.* Take your older child's hand and show her how much pressure to use when touching her baby sister. You can also verbally rehearse how you want your child to behave before he is actually interacting with a friend's toddler. Point out that you are going over to Jeffrey's house and that he needs to try to be really gentle with him. By

providing instruction, you can avoid the common mistake of wait-ing until your child interacts inappropriately with a younger child before you give him attention.

5. *Provide appropriate consequences for not being gentle with a young sibling or friend.* Again, you may have to set up "practice sessions" for your daughter. Tell her before the session that you agreed to babysit for your friend's son and that you expect her to be gentle with him. When he arrives, remind her again that you expect her to be very gentle. If she is a little too rough, im-mediately use a brief time-out as a way of giving her feedback that she needs to be gentle. We prefer the contrast between praise for appropriate behavior and time-outs (see chapter 4) for inappro-priate behavior as a teaching tool. The combination of praise for being gentle and a couple of brief time-outs for not being gentle will go a long way toward teaching your child how you expect her to behave.

These principles for developing and encouraging appropriate touch and interaction also apply to the family pet. Model for your child how and where to pet the family dog. Allow your child to repeatedly pet the animal, and praise him for strokes that are gentle and appropriate for your pet's temperament. Be careful of model-ing roughhousing with the dog, as your child may do the same and get bitten.

### Teaching Social Skills to Older Children

If your child, at any age, is not good at sharing and isn't particu-larly polite, you need to take a calculated, timely approach to try-ing to get these habits established. It is very important that you do not try to start working on such skills when you are angry with your child for embarrassing you with her rudeness toward a family friend. Important skills, like sharing and good manners, should not and cannot be taught in reaction to misbehavior. Rather, these skills require a fair amount of advance planning.

Begin by sitting down at a peaceful time (probably either before anyone's up in the morning or after everyone is in bed at night) and, with pen and paper, take stock of both your own and your child's strengths and weaknesses. Try to be as objective as possible. Even if this exercise takes you a week or so to complete, it's worth the effort. Include as many objective, verifiable attributes as possible. For your child, look over teachers' comments on report cards, your notes from parent–teacher conferences, and any comments you have received from coaches, tutors, and other adults involved in your child's life. You may also want to ask your child what she thinks she is good at and what could use a little work. This will help you know how insightful your child is into her own behaviors. For yourself, list your own strengths and weaknesses that directly or indirectly affect your child. If you always have dinner as a family and you regularly help with homework, write them down. If the behavior mainly affects work or aspects other than home life, disregard it.

The point of this exercise is to put your child's behavior in perspective to get at the bigger picture. If you are already an effective parent and teacher, and you can honestly say that you usually model good social skills, then you are ready to look at your child's behavior. If, on the other hand, you have not placed much of a priority on sharing and good manners, then you need to decide whether you intend to rearrange your priorities. There's only so much time in any given day, and you can set only so many goals for yourself and for your children.

If you decide that you want to encourage your child to share better, then you'll need to follow the five steps for teaching skills outlined earlier. Keep in mind that learning a complex skill such as sharing takes time and practice. Thus, try to arrange for multiple opportunities for your child to interact with both children and adults. If you are focusing on child-to-child interactions, at least one play date a week would be the minimum, and two play dates a week would be more optimal to help teach the social skills needed for successful interactions.

You should also talk with your child about small rewards that you would make available each time that he exhibits good manners. Our preferred reward is usually additional time with a parent, preferably time spent in an activity with the child. This might involve an additional bedtime story, running an errand together, watching a TV show together, or playing a game together. One of the most common misconceptions that parents have is that they can teach children new skills by disciplining or punishing them for not engaging in that new skill. Although we will devote an entire chapter to the topic of discipline later on in this book, suffice it to say here that children do not learn new skills from discipline. Rather, they learn new skills from parents' demonstrating and rewarding a new behavior.

## TEACHING LANGUAGE SKILLS

As with social behaviors, parents can use modeling and opportunity to enhance language skills and eventually verbal problem-solving skills as their child gets older. Children learn a great deal of language simply from their parents talking to them during routine situations such as mealtime, bathing and dressing, routine housework, and reading stories. For example, during each part of the meal, including its preparation, you can describe to your child what you are doing. "I am pouring your cereal into the bowl." "Now I am going to pour on the milk." "Now Mommy is drinking her milk." "Time to put the cereal back into the cabinet."

Similarly, while dressing your child, you can describe what you are doing, beginning with very simple descriptions, such as "I am putting your shirt on." You can gradually make the sentences a little more descriptive and complicated by adding adjectives and adverbs. "Mommy's putting on Michael's red shirt." "I'm putting on your shirt really fast because we're in a hurry." These expressions inform your child without requiring any response or even any indication that he is listening to you. The learning on your child's part is incidental to the activity that he is engaged in.

Over time, you can expect your child to begin to repeat what she hears you saying—not because you asked her to, or because you engaged her in a conversation, but because she is beginning to associate certain kinds of speech with certain kinds of activities. Try to refrain from correcting her—it's initially more important to stimulate speech than it is to stimulate correct speech. Your child will begin to use more proper speech in time because of what you have been saying and doing with her, not because you corrected her. Initially, you want to demonstrate a lot of speech. In time, you want to encourage speech in your child. And, in time, the speech will become more correct.

Your daily interactions with your child can also teach nonverbal language skills such as smiling, laughing, frowning, or gesturing. By modeling emotions that you are reading about or talking about, you will find that your child begins to imitate the emotions that she sees you modeling. Saying "The girl in the story was so sad" with a sad look on your face will begin to teach your child the emotional concept of "sad" without your having to directly discuss or define the emotion. The experience of hearing you tell jokes, seeing you and others laugh at jokes, and actually laughing at the jokes herself teaches a child about one more method or way of interacting both verbally and nonverbally—through humor. None of these examples requires or demands cooperation or compliance on your child's part. Rather, they are all very neutral interactions between speech and the environment that don't require either cooperation or the lack thereof. But such interactions do need to occur, and for most families they occur very naturally. It can be reassuring to know, however, that even during your most routine interaction with your child, you are teaching her worthwhile and lifelong skills.

## TEACHING PROBLEM-SOLVING SKILLS

By preschool, children's language development is usually advanced enough for parents to begin verbal modeling of problem-solving skills and to encourage their children to participate in the process. The modeling of these thinking tasks can include academic problem solving as well as social problem solving. For example, hold up two jars and exaggerate your efforts to figure out which jar is the heavier of the two. Encourage your child to feel the weight of both jars and try to decide which is heavier. Or, when pouring the contents of one container into another, encourage your child to watch. Ask him if he thinks all the liquid will fit into the new container (without really expecting an answer—it's conversation more to maintain his attention and stimulate intellectual development than a quiz!).

You can also model problem-solving skills by pointing out the natural comparisons you make every day. When picking up two objects, simply state, "These are both round" or "These are both fruit." Here are some simple comparisons you can use:

- "The orange and the apple are *both round.*"
- "The orange and the apple are *both fruit.*"
- "The bottle of water is much *heavier* than the bottle of ketchup."
- "I have *two pieces* of gum in my hand."
- Point to the blue block, to the red block, to the yellow block. Then say, "These are all different *colors.*"

Over time, with many, many repetitions, your child will begin to learn how to group objects without ever knowing that she is doing so. And, given the relaxed manner in which you are teaching her, she'll learn faster and retain it longer than she would if you taught it any other way.

The TV program *Sesame Street* provides excellent models for developing children's language. Parents should occasionally take the time to watch this program with their children, making an effort to practice what they see on the show. You can, for example, count houses, streetlights, or people. You don't have to count very high. The value comes just from counting with your child, over and over and over again. Show him you are interested in what he is learning. And, if you aren't able to watch *Sesame Street* because you are at work when it is shown, videotape it or rent a video of it and watch it with your child when you are at home.

You can also assist your child in developing problem-solving skills in social situations or when answering questions that she is curious about. The key to developing such skills in children may be more in what you do not say than in how you respond to their questions. Parents are often tempted to try to answer every one of their children's many questions with long, complicated answers to stimulate their children's thinking skills. It is much more challenging, for your child and for you, to allow your child to speculate on the possible answers to some of their questions.

For example, a number of years ago, a child we saw in the office had asked his mother how Spider-Man was able to climb up the side of buildings. Because his mother wasn't really sure how this was done, and she was aware of children's natural fascination with such things, she simply stated, "I'm not sure how. How do you think he does it?" Over the next several weeks, her son would periodically suggest how Spider-Man was able to climb up big buildings. One time he said that Spider-Man probably used big suction cups. When his mom pointed out that Spider-Man didn't have any pockets or a backpack to carry his suction cups, her son said that he didn't think they would work anyway because Spider-Man wouldn't have a way to get the suction cups off the side of the building. Later he said that he thought Spider-Man used glue. But when his mom questioned him for more details, he admitted that glue probably wouldn't work either.

Then one day he brought a copy of *TV Guide* to his mom and pointed to a picture of Spider-Man climbing up a tall building. On the same page was a picture of several stunt men pulling a clear cable that had been attached to Spider-Man's back. As Spider-Man climbed up the building, the stunt men kept tightening the cable, helping him to make his way up. It is clear to see how a quick answer by this child's mother in response to his initial question would have resulted in missed problem-solving opportunities for the child.

The opportunity to carry on such a dialogue with your child in response to a similar type of question is bound to happen hundreds of times over the years. When it does, instead of trying to answer the question, see if you can get your child to think aloud about the possible solutions to the scenario. In doing so, you will be using a naturally occurring opportunity to elicit possible answers or solutions about a matter of interest to your child. Use those opportunities to encourage your child to use problem-solving on her own, with or without your prompting.

## ESTABLISHING ROUTINES

Establishing a daily routine for completing tasks is another life skill that can be effectively taught through modeling and through planned involvement of your child. All families have routine activities that need to be completed on a regular basis, such as doing laundry and picking up toys. You can teach your young child to assist you with these tasks by modeling these behaviors consistently and gradually increasing your child's involvement. If a toddler sees you picking up his toys each day to straighten up the family room, and if you are relatively pleasant while doing it, he will learn by imitation to pick up his toys. You can speed up his learning process by giving him positive touches and encouragement when he makes even the slightest attempt to help.

Similarly, you can encourage your toddler to help every time you make beds. First, make your bed and encourage her to help you. Then go into her room to make her bed and encourage her to help you. Make sure there are no distractions while you're making the beds—no TV, no video games. You want to be the only game in town. Modeling and systematic involvement of your child can be applied to other daily activities as well, such as hanging up your coat, brushing your teeth, and sending thank you cards after receiving gifts.

If your child is 7 or 8 years old and has never learned to pick up his room or to make his bed, you may have to take a very different approach. And although you may be tempted to just insist that he do these chores "or else," you are unlikely to accomplish your purpose with the simple addition of negative consequences when the chores aren't completed on time. Getting into a power struggle with a school-age child over simple household chores is not going to get the chores done. The following five steps may help you accomplish your goal of teaching your older child how to participate in household routines:

*1. Plan ahead.* If you are going to make any significant or major changes in the way your household operates, plan your approach ahead of time. Find a time when you can sit down and outline the household responsibilities and whom you would like to do each of them. The other caregivers in your home should also participate in the assignment of these responsibilities, and caregivers should fully support each other once the decision has been made to add more routine and structure to your family life.

*2. Assign chores.* Assign chores to each child using a list of chores and the days of the week (see sample chore list).

| Chore | Monday | Tuesday | Wednesday | Thursday | Friday |
|-------|--------|---------|-----------|----------|--------|
| Dishwasher | Glenda | Glenda | Glenda | Glenda | Glenda |
| Backyard | George | George | George | George | George |

*3. Break each chore into components and write out exactly what each chore entails on cards.* "Emptying the dishwasher" probably includes opening the dishwasher, pulling out the top rack, drying off the bottoms of the glasses and putting them away in the kitchen cabinet with the other glasses, pulling out the bottom rack, removing the utensil bucket and sorting the utensils, and putting the large plates in one kitchen cabinet and the small plates in another cabinet. Initially, you should practice each component with your child to make sure she knows how to do it. Do not assume that because your child is a certain age she "should" know how to do it. Write out all the steps of each chore on the cards and practice each component to make sure the instructions are clear. This will also help avoid the common excuses of ignorance children use, such as "Oh, you didn't tell me you wanted me to empty the *whole* dishwasher."

*4. Be certain that your child can perform each of the task components independently.* The best way to do this is to perform the chore together at first. Inform your son in the morning, after breakfast but before he leaves for school, that tonight you are going to empty the dishwasher together after dinner. Do this for at least one week. Try to be as positive as possible during this time. If your son refuses to help you empty the dishwasher, he should at least be grounded from all privileges for the duration of the evening, with no recourse and no bargaining.

5. *Sit down with your child ahead of time and agree on rewards that she can earn by getting her chores completed on time.* Again, the rewards that seem to work best for children are added time with their parents. When rewarding your child, try to reward for a process rather than an outcome. Typically, you have a reasonable amount of control over the process she uses, but often you have little control over the outcome. A number of research studies on getting children to do chores have shown that children learn best when they are taught to break large responsibilities into several small ones and to complete longer term projects a little bit at a time. Withholding the reward until the child has finished learning a new skill or until a large, complex task is completed can actually be discouraging to a child. Providing rewards for smaller accomplishments works much better and makes the process more fun for both parent and child.

## ESTABLISHING LIFELONG INTERESTS

Parents also can use modeling to help children establish lifelong interests and hobbies. When parents read for pleasure at home, for example, they are modeling a behavior for their children that will help them do better in school. Even very young children will climb into a chair with a book and sit and turn the pages. If a child never sees Mom or Dad reading at home, he is less likely to develop an interest in reading. Do not be put off if your child does not seem interested in being read to or in reading. Simply find a quiet time to begin reading to your child, almost regardless of what he is doing. Sit down or walk around with a book that is age appropriate for at least 10 minutes each day, and read. Initially, your child may act out when you read out loud—running around, asking you to stop, or generally being a nuisance. Shortly, however, you may find that your child seems to enjoy being read to on a daily basis. He may start to bring you books, help with turning the pages, or even request that you read to him at other times outside of your "designated" reading time.

Taking the time to develop your child's interest in reading can also pay off when you are in public. One of the best ways to keep children quiet—while waiting in a doctor's office, in line at the store, and in the car—is to read a book to them. It's preferable to chasing them around and constantly scolding them. But if you haven't been reading to your child all along, you cannot expect to be able to pick up a book in a moment of need and magically transform her into one who loves to listen while you read.

Spending time completing your own quiet tasks, such as paying bills, can also help your child learn to manage his "quiet time" for tasks such as homework. Take time to sit with your child while he does homework and work on your own paper tasks such as reading, writing letters, or making the grocery list. The TV should not be on, and if possible, phone calls should be avoided. Homework time will run more smoothly for your child, and he will see that you value quiet time to complete important tasks.

If you would like to use TV as part of your quiet time, plan your child's TV time. Sit down with your child and a TV programming guide, briefly discuss what programs are on, and ask your child which show she wants to watch. State, matter-of-factly, what you're going to do (for example, balance your checkbook) while she finishes her homework. Then, you'll have a little time to watch TV together. When the show is over, turn off the TV. In that way, your child will learn to watch specific TV shows instead of just turning the set on and watching whatever show happens to come on.

Again, the key is modeling the importance of taking daily time for you to complete routine tasks or pleasurable activities.

This can help teach your children to balance the time they spend on chores and homework with the time they spend on recreational activities. As your children become busier with the demands of school and eventually their own families, they'll need these skills.

## CONCLUSION

Children learn by what they see and hear you do. Whether you plan it or not. Whether you intend it or not. And whether you like it or not. Your children are likely to behave the way they see you behave when you are around them. For this reason, it is vital that you be conscious of the influence that your behavior has on the behavior of your children. This doesn't mean that you have to be perfect. It does mean that you cannot behave one way and expect your children to behave another way. In other words, it is very doubtful that you will be able to correct your children's behavior without changing your own behavior.

Fortunately, you have control over what you teach your children. Modeling is a very powerful tool that is constantly available to you in influencing the way your children behave. By planning what you want your children to learn through modeling, you are being proactive instead of reactive. This is a very important parenting skill! Parents are often so busy with run-of-the-mill activities that they only react to their children instead of being proactive.

The other important part of modeling is providing your children with opportunities to perform the behaviors you are trying to model for them. Children do much better when they are frequently exposed to situations in which they can practice their skills—over and over again. Brief conversations about sharing, in the context of setting up situations that encourage sharing, may be useful, but they are not a substitute for sharing. Your behavior is your key resource in communicating what is important.

# CHAPTER 2

# PROVIDING POSITIVE FEEDBACK

In addition to modeling the behavior that you want your children to demonstrate and giving them opportunities to practice desired behaviors, another parenting tool to encourage positive behavior is providing your children with positive feedback about their behavior. The more effort you spend recognizing your child's neutral and acceptable behavior, the less effort you will have to spend on punishment. Throughout this book, we will refer to "catching your child being good." We use this phrase to remind you to pay attention to your child's positive, as well as neutral, behaviors—when he is just being a child. Thus, the word "good" is not meant to apply only to successful or perfect behavior; rather, you have to pay attention to your child when he is not misbehaving.

Children thrive on being recognized for their best efforts, just as adults do. There are certainly many examples of when we, as adults, do our best to help someone but are not recognized for our efforts. For example, you might have raked the lawn or cleaned the basement without any acknowledgement from your spouse. When adults put forth special effort and it is not noticed, they are disappointed. But what about children? Not only are they disappointed when effort goes unacknowledged, but often they may doubt whether you valued the behavior. Every time you miss a chance to catch your child being good, you miss a chance to teach her how you would like her to behave. If you miss opportunities often, don't be surprised when your child doesn't know what you want her to do. It is up to you to teach her. So how do you give your child positive feedback about behaviors that you would like to see? The remainder of this chapter is devoted to discussing ways to encourage your child to behave appropriately.

## THE IMPORTANCE OF TOUCH

Many researchers have elaborated on the importance of touch for children. Parents sometimes forget that an affectionate touch and the love that is silently communicated are very important to children. One of the most effective positive feedback skills that you can develop is that of providing frequent brief, nonverbal physical contact to your child when her behavior is acceptable or even neutral. Your child has many moments throughout his day when his behavior deserves positive feedback through brief physical contact, including when he watches TV while you finish your chores or allows you to finish a conversation with a friend while he stands by you at the store.

Physical contact can take the form of a hand squeeze, a shoulder pat, or a hair tousle. By using touch to communicate to your child when she is simply "being," you send the message that what is important to you is her, for being your child. Some children, especially adolescents, may be uncomfortable with extensive touch as a form of positive feedback. Thus, monitor your child's preferences for touch and adjust your efforts accordingly.

## THE POWER OF WORDS

In addition to the powerful tool of your touch, you can also use words to provide positive feedback. Your comments can help your child internalize your values and develop positive feelings about himself. One useful time to use verbal praise with your child is during naturally occurring breaks in activity or when he specifically brings an accomplishment to your attention. For example, if your daughter is working on a Girl Scout project and comes over to show you how she's doing, you have a perfect opportunity to make positive comments. Ideally, a balance between gentle touches, when your child is focused on a task, and verbal praise when she takes a break in the task will provide her with consistent, positive feedback.

### Guidelines for Praising Children

The following are some guidelines for providing effective praise. These guidelines and examples will help you offer positive comments to your child that not only show your approval, but also lead to your child's positive self-evaluation of her own efforts. In other words, she will be proud of herself, along with being proud that she pleased you!

- Use brief, descriptive terms. "Look at all of the colors on your painting!" "Wow, you really got dressed quickly this morning." "You have really been helpful with the babies this afternoon."
- Balance statements of your approval with comments on how your child might feel about himself. "I am proud of you." "You must be proud of yourself for getting that done." "I am so happy you got chosen for the team!" "You must be so excited to be able to play on the A team this year!"
- Avoid the overuse of words that are absolute or judgmental or that compare your child to others. Avoid the following: "You always get the right answers." "You are such a good

**3 3**

boy!" "You are the best artist in the class." "I wish everyone could listen like Johnny does."

- Focus your praise on the process of your child's efforts, and not the product. "You really studied hard for that test in math." "Your practicing really paid off in the game today." "You worked a long time on getting your room organized this morning."
- Avoid praise that is followed by a "zinger" designed to make your child feel guilty about a past wrong, such as the following: "You did a good job cleaning up your room. I wish you would do that every time I ask you to do so." "See how happy I am when you are a good boy. Please try to be good for the rest of the day." "You hit a home run! Now if we could only get you to care about your schoolwork as much as your baseball."

Here is another caution about praising accomplishments: Be careful that you are not using praise to push your child into participating in activities she doesn't enjoy. Some children enjoy sports, but they don't get nearly as wrapped up in the games as their parents do. Monitor your child's true enthusiasm for her activities, and discuss her continued involvement at the beginning of each season or session. It is perfectly reasonable to expect your child to finish a commitment to a team or activity once he has signed up for it, but be careful of putting too much pressure to continue or succeed in activities that are meant to be a source of enjoyment and not stress. Be sure your child knows you're proud, but don't use him to fulfill your own wishes.

### Other Types of Praise

Another way to use words to teach your child about the behaviors you value and instill good feelings is to engage in "second-hand" praise in front of the child. An example of second-hand praise would be telling her grandmother over the telephone about how helpful she has been with her baby sister, when you know that she can overhear you. Similarly, while the child is present in the room, one parent could tell the other parent how quiet the child was at a church event.

Another form of verbal feedback that can make your child feel proud is what might be called a "third-hand compliment." If Mom tells Dad, over the phone, what a nice job Scott did on a school project or how well he behaved at the Little League game, Dad can mention it to Scott when he gets home: "Scott, your mother told me how well you did on your book report. She seemed really pleased." These types of praise statements should be delivered honestly and without any added zingers. Such praise becomes less than effective if the positive comment is followed by a "but I wish you would have" type of statement.

Finally, in addition to touch and words, there are other ways to show children that they are loved and valued. For example, show your child you are proud of her efforts by displaying schoolwork on the refrigerator or using the key chain she made in art class.

You can also simply spend time in pleasant interactions with your child by combining activities of interest to you with those of interest to your child. Take your child to the library, read with him at home, or go to the local science center and ask him about the world he sees there. You could also cook with your child or play a game of cards. Each of these activities not only tells your child that you think spending time with him is important, but also provides opportunities for you to engage your child in discussions about experiences, both positive and negative, that may be influencing how he is coping with the world.

We call all of these ways of providing positive feedback through touch, words, and interactions "time-in." Your child is experiencing time-in with your attention as opposed to its counterpart of "time-out." In fact, in the purest sense, time-out is really the temporary stopping of time-in, or your positive attention. (See chapter 4 for more on time-out.) Time-in is very beneficial for parent–child relationships and has been shown to decrease the need for more negative types of discipline (see Appendix A at the end of the chapter for a summary of time-in).

Now that you have some ideas of how touch, words, and thoughtful interactions can be powerful parenting tools for encouraging positive behavior, the following sections discuss how to incorporate positive feedback into your parenting strategies in an age-appropriate way.

## CATCHING INFANTS AT BEING GOOD

One of the first behaviors that you can assist your infant (birth to 12–15 months) with is that of excessive crying when she is not in distress. New parents learn quickly that infants cry a lot, more than they ever dreamed a child would cry. When you first bring the baby home from the hospital, it doesn't take long to notice that she seems to go spontaneously from a sound sleep to loud crying. After she's about 3 months old, however, you'll notice that she may wake up and just look around her crib, making babbling or cooing noises before she starts crying.

This is a perfect time to start to catch her being good. If you go to her after she awakes but before she starts to cry, you can catch her lying or playing contently in her crib. In this way, you can teach your baby that when she wakes up, if she'll just play a little while, you'll be there soon to feed her and change her diaper. If you do this, you'll quickly discover that your baby cries less when she wakes up. In fact, she will quickly learn that if she plays quietly in her crib, you come in and pick her up.

What happens if you slip up several days in a row? If you start waiting again until your baby cries before you go in to get him, you're back to teaching him that if he wants you to come in to get him, he'd better start crying, because otherwise you won't come.

The point of this example is certainly not that it is bad for babies to cry. Crying serves useful purposes—such as letting moms and dads know that babies are uncomfortable, hurt, or hungry. But excessive amounts of crying when your baby is not in distress can quickly dampen the joys of early parenthood. This can make it more difficult to feel like you are being an effective parent. Thus, teaching your infant how to get her needs met and how to get your attention without crying can help make taking care of her a truly delightful and pleasurable experience. Furthermore, by building this skill so early in life, you will be providing your children a foundation of trust that you will respond to her needs as she grows, without her having to become overly distressed to get your attention.

As your infant begins to engage in more and more independent behaviors, make sure that you give him a lot of attention while he is playing. For example, if your son is playing with one of his stuffed animals, make sure that you regularly stop to pay attention to him with a hair tousle or pat on the head. Verbal attention, if it can be provided without interrupting his play, is also appropriate. Over time, you will find that your infant will be able to naturally play for longer and longer periods of time as his attention span increases and his interests expand. By providing positive feedback, you are helping your child to stay with activities for longer and longer periods of time. It is only through such perseverance that he will ever learn to complete the activities he starts. (Chapter 10 discusses independent play skills in more detail.)

## CATCHING TODDLERS AT BEING GOOD

Toddlers (12–15 months to 36 months) present a new challenge to parents. They move around the house and get into almost everything, but they have little knowledge of how to use the things they get into. Toddlers have a tremendous motivation to learn, but they usually aren't willing to wait until one of their parents is ready to teach them. Many parents say, "If I didn't have anything else to do, I'd be able to keep up with my toddler." Mom tries to go ahead with her work, ignoring her toddler as much as possible in an effort to get her tasks done for the day. The toddler, in turn, roams around, pushing and pulling on things, trying to see what makes everything work—which is all very appropriate for toddlers to do. Mom and Dad monitor their toddler and keep working on their tasks as long as the child doesn't do anything wrong or get into something she's not supposed to get into.

What are her parents teaching the toddler? As long as she behaves herself, Mom and Dad will ignore her. If she wants their attention, she'd better create an unusual noise, like something breaking, dropping, or falling over. Then they'll be right there. Rarely do parents intentionally ignore a child until she does something wrong—it just works out that way. So how do you make sure you are not ignoring the behaviors you want to see your child display? By changing your responses just slightly, you can teach your toddler what you want her to do and also find time to finish your chores, talk on the phone, and read the paper. Here's how.

Let's say you are cooking dinner and your toddler is at the kitchen cabinet where you store most of your pots and pans and he's taking them out one at a time, looking at them, and setting them on the floor. What should you do? Give him a quick kiss and positive statements to let him know that you know he is near and that that what he's doing is all right. He's better off playing with pots and pans than putting his hands on the hot oven. If he gets too close to the oven, move him away. This way, the toddler learns both what you want him to do and what you do not want him to do. He learns that it is fun to be in the kitchen with you when you're preparing dinner and that he gets the most attention when he is playing appropriately.

As another example, suppose Annie comes over to Dad's chair carrying a magazine in her hand. Every parent knows that magazines aren't sacred to toddlers and that you can't hide every magazine that comes into the home. So why not use this situation to begin teaching Annie what magazines are all about? If she sits down on the floor near you and puts the magazine in her lap (it doesn't matter if it's upside down and backwards), lean down for two seconds and pat her on the head or back. The point is that Annie has been caught being good and is getting attention for doing something appropriate for her age.

This example of paying attention to age-appropriate behavior can also have implications for developing other skills. For example, nobody expects a toddler to sit down and read aloud from an encyclopedia, yet when the child sits down and turns the pages of a book or a magazine, many parents don't see the connection between turning pages and learning to read. This is not to say that if children learn how to turn pages, they learn to like to read. The point is that children can be taught that sitting down for even 20 seconds with a magazine in their lap is enjoyable, not because there's some kind of kick from holding a magazine, but because Mom or Dad likes it and lets them know it. If on 100 different occasions, Annie sits with a magazine, turning the pages, and on many of those occasions Mom or Dad gives her a brief "love pat" or comment on the pretty pictures in the magazine, the toddler will learn to enjoy sitting and looking at a magazine. Mom and Dad are then well on their way to teaching their child about the basics, and possibly the pleasures, of reading.

You can also use positive touch and words to teach your child that you are pleased with her behavior toward others. If you see your toddler petting the dog gently, go to him and give him a kind word to let him know that he's doing something you like. He'll learn that you like for him to treat the dog kindly. The same thing is true if you find your toddler playing nicely with her brother. Let them both know, with a wink, kiss, or praise, that you noticed their positive interactions. By doing so, you are teaching them how you want them to interact with each other.

When using any type of positive reinforcement, it is important to be consistent to be sure you are sending the message you really want your child to receive. Let's say you're in the kitchen fixing dinner and your toddler gets too close to the stove, so you yell at him. Then you feel sorry because you lost your temper, so you pick him up and hug and kiss him. Particularly if you haven't been consistent about catching him being good, your son learns from such incidents that if he wants to get your attention, he has to do something wrong first, then get yelled at, and *then* you'll pick him up and love him. Why not start out by giving the boy lots of positive feedback to show him that you appreciate what he's doing when he's doing something right?

## CATCHING PRESCHOOLERS AT BEING GOOD

As children reach preschool age (36 months to 5 years), they may become more and more interested in activities that involve school-readiness skills such as prereading and fine motor control. You can teach your child that these skills are important by providing positive touch and praise and engaging in activities of interest to your child. Giving your daughter encouragement through a brief touch or words when she's working on a puzzle, coloring, or looking through a book is a beautiful way of supporting preacademic behavior.

Many of the prerequisite skills for successful academics are best taught to your child over an extended period of time, primarily by making certain that he knows you understand and appreciate his early attempts. Your child won't even know that what you're doing today is directed at encouraging him to enjoy studying and academic success later in his life. If you begin early to work on the skills that are later used in studying, you can be assured of a good start in making his entire educational process easier for both of you. By trying to use force or punishment to encourage studying once your child reaches school age, you not only will have missed many opportunities to let your child know that prestudying skills were important, but also will undoubtedly find yourself in unpleasant power struggles with your child.

Of course, by preschool age, you may become aware that your child might have learning difficulties. Sometimes children with learning problems may avoid activities associated with their particular limitation. For example, a child with poor fine motor skills may avoid coloring or cutting activities, while a child with hyperactivity may avoid quiet activities or resist sitting still for a story. Parents of preschoolers may also become aware that their child does not understand language or talk like other children in the same age group. Children with learning limitations can still benefit from frequent exposure to opportunities and positive feedback about preacademic or learning skills. Such children may take longer to learn what you are trying to teach them, which can be very frustrating for them and for their parents. Continue your efforts to the best of your ability, and seek the help of your child's preschool teacher, pediatrician, or mental health professional for support.

## CATCHING THE SCHOOL-AGE CHILD AT BEING GOOD

Much of what we have said about catching a child being good will become second nature to parents of school-age children (5 years to puberty) who used these strategies when their children were younger. It is never too late to start, however, and school-age children still have many lessons to learn about what behaviors you see as important. For example, if it is not too distracting for your child, have her work on her science project in the kitchen while you are making dinner so that you can provide brief comments about her progress. Or, gently rest your hand on your child's shoulder as he waits for his turn to perform at a recital to tell him that you are supportive of his interests and want to help calm his nervousness.

As children get older, they may seem more resistant to hugs, but you might be surprised to find that they are still receptive to other gestures such as squeezing their hand. Second- and third-hand praise and direct praise are usually still appreciated.

## CONCLUSION

Children like to do things that gain recognition from their parents. If a child earns lots of recognition from socially acceptable behavior, she is more likely to exhibit such behavior. Conversely, if most of a child's attention comes from inappropriate or obnoxious behavior, regardless of his age or the kind of attention he gets, that child's actions are more likely to be inappropriate or obnoxious.

Catching children being good is one of the best and most effective ways to teach them the behaviors their parents think are important. Parents enjoy being around their children when their children are behaving in ways the parents think are appropriate. It is reasonable, then, that parents make the extra effort to praise or encourage their children to exhibit the behaviors they enjoy. The brief amount of time and effort throughout the day that parents devote to positive feedback can help their children establish a lifetime of positive behavior and feel positive about themselves.

## APPENDIX A: THE IMPORTANCE OF TIME-IN

Parents can use time-in to let their children know that they are loved and valued. We use the term *time-in* to refer to a wide variety of pleasant interactions between parents and their children. Time-in activities include

- reading to your child and having him read to you
- talking with your child, letting her guide the conversation, and refraining from offering advice
- relaxing with your child, maybe just sitting in a park or on the shore of a stream or a river
- playing games with your child, anything from board games and card games in the house to baseball in the park
- cooking with your child
- helping your child with his homework
- helping your child prepare for a birthday party
- helping your child make a birthday present for her other parent
- holding your child's hand or putting your arm around his shoulder while enjoying a spectator event.

These interactions can be done repeatedly throughout the day, not because the child has earned it, but because the child is treasured. Time-in is used in addition to any rewards that parents already give their children for good behavior.

*Note.* Copyright 2001 by Edward R. Christophersen. Adapted with permission.

# CHAPTER 3

# COMMUNICATING WITH YOUR CHILD

Effective communication with your child involves being a good listener, working at understanding what your child is trying to tell you, and using words and concepts that he or she can understand. This chapter discusses how to listen and talk to your children in ways that will encourage their positive behavior and continued communication with you.

## LISTENING TO YOUR CHILD

Most people will tell you that their most satisfying communication occurs when a person whom they consider important listens to them and tries to understand what they are saying. Children feel no differently. Many parents incorrectly assume that communicating with children mainly means asking them questions or explaining things to them. Communication does include two-way conversations between you and your child. But one-way conversations, where you listen to your child, trying to understand what he is saying and feeling, are very important as well. You will find out more about how your child feels or the point he is trying to make by listening than by offering a judgment or opinion.

So how do you practice listening to your child? You can start by establishing what we call a "quiet time," which involves choosing one or two situations a week in which you don't initiate a conversation, such as when you are picking up your child from school or running errands. Do not use this quiet time to get any messages across to your child or interrogate him about an upcoming activity. Instead, simply stay quiet and wait for your child to talk.

This is hard, initially, for many parents to do. Most of us are accustomed to picking our children up at school or day care and immediately asking them what they did during the day. Instead, after an initial "Hello, it is good to see you this afternoon," keep quiet until your child has something to say. This way, if she has anything she wants to talk about, she has the opportunity to bring it up. Don't be surprised, however, if the first few times you try having quiet times, your child doesn't say a word. If she is tired from her day at school, she may not say anything. That is OK; you should still be quiet. You may have to have quiet trips home from day care or school several times in a row before she figures out that you are available to listen and not dominate the time with your questions.

Over time, your child may recognize that during these quiet times you are available to listen to his comments and concerns. He may then begin talking about issues that are important to him. True, much of these conversations will be about things that you don't think are important. But if your child thinks they're important, isn't that what counts? Too many times parents want to talk about what *they* think is important, regardless of what their children want to talk about. Then they wonder why their children don't enjoy talking to them! The point is to listen and not evaluate, redirect, or otherwise discourage your child from saying what is on his mind.

## Understanding Your Child

Now that you have set up opportunities for your child to talk when you are actively listening to her, it is important to use your listening and talking skills to try to understand what she is telling you. When children talk, they do not always say things in the same way as adults. If you take their words literally, you run the risk of misinterpreting what your child is saying. To avoid misinterpretation, restate in your own words what you think your child is saying. Refrain from saying anything judgmental or making any attempts to discipline her. That way, you'll make sure you understand the point she was trying to make. More importantly, your focus will be on understanding what your child is trying to say instead of debating with her or defending yourself.

For example, if your son says, "Sometimes I just hate my brother," there's a real temptation to reprimand him for talking like that and telling him that you won't accept such comments from him. What we're recommending is that you simply acknowledge what he said, and maybe restate it, but do not reprimand him for either what he said or how he said it. If you say something like, "You do?" or "You actually hate him?" and then be quiet, you leave him the opportunity to continue talking about how he feels, some of the time, about his brother. This response is very helpful to a child because it helps you avoid misinterpreting him and helps him feel free to explore what is on his mind. If he does not continue with the conversation, leave him alone. Resist the temptation to encourage him to say more, ask him questions about his feelings, or the like. You may find that if his behavior toward his brother had been less than desirable before such a discussion, such behavior may improve once he feels listened to, even if little brother's behavior does not change.

If your quiet time occurs on the way to soccer practice and your child says she doesn't ever want to go to soccer practice again, you may, like most parents, immediately begin to feel irritated and defend the need for soccer practice. You might start saying how much fun it is, how the child's best friend is on the team, or how good it is to get outside and get some fresh air. Instead of immediately defending soccer practice, just restate what your child said: "It sounds like you don't want to go to soccer practice today." Your child may say, "That's right, I don't want to go to soccer practice today," and, in many instances, the conversation may be over. Then, just continue on to soccer practice. There's a good chance that she'll go ahead with soccer practice even though she isn't thrilled about doing so. This is good preparation for being an adult someday!

Following up every comment that your child makes is simply not necessary. Just as we, as adults, sometimes vent our feelings by saying we had a long day or put in a hard week, children are not necessarily looking for their parents to address every statement they make either. Sharing their feelings with an adult who listens without judging or "jumping on them" gives children a chance to be heard. We all like to vent our feelings without being advised, questioned, judged, or even cheered up.

If your child says he doesn't ever want to play with his friend Mark again, you can say, "Really?" or "OK," or just rephrase what he said—"You don't want to go play with Mark anymore." If he drops the subject, you have to drop the subject. If you launch into a lecture about being a good friend or how much he liked Mark yesterday or observe that the situation probably isn't that bad, he may not be as willing to confide in you and share his frustrations in the future for fear of being evaluated and judged.

If during quiet time you can discipline yourself to listen to your child without responding every time, you'll be able to tell, by whether or not your child mentions the same thing several times or starts discussing it at greater depth, when it's a topic she is serious about and when it was just a comment made in passing. If your child seems serious about the topic, certainly take the time to respond to her concerns through further questions or by using the suggestions found later in this chapter in the sections on talking to your child.

Obviously, if your child starts talking about wanting to "kill his sister" or makes other such serious comments, you have to decide whether it is time to end quiet time. Use your judgment and the information you have gained from other talks with your child to guide you on when to use the time to discuss an issue more thoroughly.

## COPING WITH QUESTIONS

One of the greatest benefits of listening to and trying to understand your child is that you have a better chance of understanding and answering the real question she is asking you. Typically, toddlers and preschoolers will ask "easy" questions about these topics and thus often do not require the amount of detail that parents are hesitant to provide anyway. As an example, we are reminded of the story about the kindergartner who asked his mother where he came from. Figuring that he was old enough for an initial conversation about "the birds and the bees," his mother explained this life tale to him, including some details about a mother's "eggs" and such things. When she was finished, he stated that he was just wondering because there was a new girl at his school who said that she was from Cincinnati. So, if you aren't certain of the intent of his question, try asking some questions for clarification. Usually doing so will give you a much better idea of what he wants to know, as well as a moment to formulate your answer. It will also help your child feel more listened to and more confident about his or her ability to communicate with you and perhaps others. This becomes especially important when dealing with sensitive topics such as sexuality, alcohol or drugs, or other potentially uncomfortable topics.

If you're asked a question and you don't have the slightest idea what the answer is, exercise your child's problem-solving skills by answering her question with another question, such as, "I don't know what happens to it. What do you think?" The ensuing dialogue may help you come up with the correct answer, or you may end up concluding that neither of you knows the answer to the question, which will teach your child that it's OK not to be perfect and not to know the answer every time. It's also possible the conversation will stop right there. That's all right. Although it's not possible for parents always to know the answers to their children's questions, they can still encourage their children's questions by listening and remaining receptive, understanding, and nonjudgmental. (More information about how to use language to help your child problem solve can be found in chapter 1.)

The point of using quiet time in communication is not to discourage discussions of important issues with your child or that your child should be allowed to say anything he wants to without any restraints or limits. Rather, we're proposing that you find a quiet time when it's just the two of you and when you allow him to speak without the usual constraints on what he says or the way he says it. Because you will be having regular conversations the entire rest of the day, week, and month, you really don't have to worry that your child will learn that he can "get away" with anything or that he will feel ignored. If you begin this exercise when your child is a preschooler and continue until he is a teenager, you will find that you start out hearing about relatively minor things, and as you improve your listening skills, he will improve his ability to communicate with you about more serious issues.

## TALKING TO YOUR CHILD

Using your active listening and understanding skills will improve your chances of talking effectively with your child. When she is listened to and feels understood, your child may be more open to your comments or requests to complete tasks. There are important considerations in talking to your child, however, that involve differences in language skills, the difficulty of talking about sensitive issues, the need to encourage cooperation most effectively, and the limitations of talking in disciplining your child.

## Recognizing Differences in Language Skills

There are important differences between the language skills of children and those of adults. Common adult conversation skills include listening, understanding, being listened to, asking questions, and responding to the requests of others. These behaviors are reasonable to ask of adults. Many parents assume that such skills are also reasonable to ask of their young children. They believe that all they have to do is talk to a child and he will understand, or ask a child to do something and he will do it. And if the child does not do what he was asked to do, they feel, a brief conversation is all that is needed to clear up any misunderstanding.

For example, let's say a kindergartner is frequently late getting ready for school in the morning. Mom has a conversation with her about the importance of getting ready on time, pointing out how much less stress everyone would feel if she were just ready on time. Both the child and her mother feel good about the conversation. They have a connection because they have "communicated." Unfortunately, the very next morning the child is playing on the floor in her room at exactly the same moment she agreed she would be getting ready for school. Mom sees her "procrastinating" and reminds her child of their conversation the day before. They have the conversation again, and she agrees, again, to change her behavior. After a couple of these conversations, Mom starts to get really frustrated because her daughter is "refusing" to cooperate and perhaps even thinks her child is purposefully "lying" to her. Such frustration often leads to yet another conversation, more frustration on the part of the parent and child, and so on.

The problem is not that the kindergartner is refusing to cooperate or is lying, but that her mother is trying to use an adult strategy to change a child's behavior. Young children usually do not have the mental capacity to consistently carry out the agreements they make in a conversation, especially if any time passes between the agreement and their required response. In other words, children are not good at connecting their words with actions. They may agree to get ready earlier, to stay out of their sibling's room, or to stop using bad language, but that isn't the same as actually stopping the behaviors they discussed with their parents. Plus, what catches their attention at the moment, such as that new toy in the sibling's room, is much more important to them than some conversation they had the night before, and that is what will motivate their behavior. In short, children who have not learned to comply with parental requests typically don't change on the basis of one or two conversations with their parents. (In the "Talking to Encourage Cooperation" section of this chapter we will specifically address the issue of how to talk to children when trying to change their behavior.)

Another example of language differences between adults and children is children's limited understanding of cause–effect relationships and how other people feel. Parents frequently, and typically unsuccessfully, use these concepts to talk their children into behaving. For example, you might say, "It hurts my feelings when you don't clean up your toys" or "If we clean up now, we will have more time to talk with Grandma when she visits." Because of a child's cognitive immaturity, such reasoning typically does not consistently influence a child's behavior. Even when the child uses the same words you would use to discuss these concepts, his understanding of the words and concepts is different from yours. Thus, he may not respond to your explanations in the way you would expect.

Children thus require an approach to conversations that is appropriate for their age and ability. Limit yourself to brief, concrete statements or discussions with your child when she is younger. As she develops, she will have an increased understanding of more abstract concepts, leading to more complex conversations with you. For example, when the family dog dies, your comments to your preschooler might include statements such as, "Rover stopped breathing; he is dead." With your 13-year-old, you might discuss an afterlife or what physically happens to animals after they are buried. In the same way, when entering a grocery store with your young child, it will be much more productive to say, "Please stay with me and hold my hand" than the more traditional "I don't want you wandering all around the store and picking things up while I'm trying to shop." Young children are much more likely to follow positive instructions like "Hold my hand" than negative ones like "Don't wander around."

**Talking About Sensitive Issues**

Perhaps one of the most important but overlooked aspects of talking to children is that of actually allowing time to have day-to-day conversations, whether by establishing a quiet time, getting up 15 minutes earlier in the morning, or having some time before bed, to be together for some relaxed conversation. Children are typically not focused on "serious" topics, so most of their conversation will be about more mundane topics. As children get older, however, they may want to ask questions about or discuss more sensitive or personal topics.

It is always difficult to talk to your children about sensitive topics such as sexuality or alcohol or drug use. When your child brings up a sensitive topic, especially if it is one that catches you off guard, try asking a few follow-up questions to give you a little time to adjust to the topic and to ensure that you understand the question. It is also important for your child to know that you will listen without getting mad or yelling. Your negative or judgmental response to his question before you have all of the facts is the best way to ensure that he will not bring up a sensitive topic with you again! Thus, keep in mind the guidelines for listening to and trying to understand your child when addressing sensitive issues as well.

Fortunately for parents, the questions that young children ask are typically not extremely personal or intimate. Thus, a straightforward but simple answer is all that is required. As you deal with the relatively easy questions raised by a toddler and a preschooler, you should find that you grow more and more comfortable addressing more complicated issues as your child ages. If you are only starting to improve your communication with your school-age child or adolescent, you might expect your child to be more hesitant to confide in you, especially if you have been critical or quick to comment in the past. Time and experience with your more productive reactions may encourage your child to eventually open up to you. As you grow more and more comfortable, your child will also grow more and more comfortable.

It is important to know that you are not required to provide a specific answer to every question your child asks. In some cases, a specific answer to a very personal question is simply inappropriate. For example, if you and your daughter have spoken in the past about how mommies and daddies "love each other," and your daughter asks you how often you and Daddy "love each other," it's perfectly appropriate to give a general, nonpersonal answer. You might say, "Honey, that varies a great deal from one couple to another and from one week to another. It is different all the time." In this way, you have addressed your daughter's question without divulging personal information that you may never feel comfortable sharing with her. Most of the parents we know have said that, in this situation, their child accepted the general response rather than a specific and personal response.

If your child brings up an episode about his own behavior or a difficult situation he was in that upsets you, you may want to wait to discuss it until both of you are calm. Thus, one good rule of thumb to follow is to wait before discussing an event that either really upsets you or has the clear potential to really upset you. You can tell your child that you need some time to think about what she has told you before you respond, which will let her know that you are interested in what she has to say but need time to consider her situation. For example, if your child gets a poor grade or gets into trouble during a sporting event, it's probably more productive to tell him that you need to discuss the event later, at a calm time, than to immediately confront your child, especially in front of a friend or a sibling. When you tell him that you need to discuss the event later, you are modeling, for him, an appropriate way to deal with the situation. Over time, from seeing you model appropriate ways for dealing with frustrating or disappointing events, from hearing you describe what the options are, and from discussing the events later when calm, your child will be learning highly adaptive skills for dealing with many types of situations.

## Talking to Encourage Cooperation

How you tell your child to do something is at least 50% of the reason the task will or will not get done. Because children aren't necessarily responsive to the types of verbal instructions we use with other adults, we offer you some guidelines for encouraging them to follow simple instructions. These guidelines must be used in conjunction with your modeling of the types of behavior that you expect from your child. Teaching children to follow verbal instructions is not something that you can accomplish in a day or two—it may take you weeks of work before you see a definite improvement in your child. Here are our recommendations for effective instruction giving:

- Make sure you are close to your child when you give an instruction. Be within three feet of your child so you can make eye contact, and talk in a normal or calm voice.
- Give the instruction as a directive and not a question. For example, say, "Please get your coat on" instead of "Will you get your coat on now?"
- Be as specific and brief as possible when giving an instruction. For example, say, "Please put your two dolls in the toy box" instead of "Pick up all those toys."
- Try to keep your instructions positive. This will also help you tell your child what to do instead of what *not* to do. For example, tell your child, "Keep your hands to your side" instead of "Don't get into the cookie dough," or "please walk" instead of "don't run."
- Give your child time, at least 5 to 10 seconds, to respond to your instruction. Many parents give several instructions before they give their child a chance to respond to even one of them!
- Praise your child when she completes the task you have instructed her to do. Be specific. For example, say, "You did a great job putting your dolls away" instead of "You are such a good girl!"

## Talking and Discipline

Children typically do not change their behavior based on words alone. Most parents do use verbal warnings or explanations at some time to try to help their child change an unwanted behavior. Although you might be tempted at the time of your child's misbehavior to explain why you are so displeased with his behavior, doing so may have very little impact on his future behavior. It is best to keep your angry words and displeasure to a minimum and focus on your child's behavior and the resulting consequence. Angry or hurtful words from a parent can simply make a child feel more angry or hurt. Keeping your words to a minimum at the time of discipline will be easier to do if you follow other suggestions in this book, such as establishing positive behaviors and family rules that you want your child to follow. You then can refer to the rule such as "in our household we talk respectfully" and deliver the consequence without getting into a long discussion about how your child hurt your feelings. Discussions about respect or other social behaviors can be initiated when everyone is calm, but again will most likely do little to change your child's behavior at a time when he is acting out. If you use language during your discipline efforts, the following guidelines may help you use language more effectively. These are based on a study on verbal instructions and reasoning with young children.[1]

1. At the time the child misbehaves, any explanation or warning should be brief; approximately one word for each year of the child's age is a good guideline. For example, say, "No hitting, time-out," before placing a 3-year-old in time-out for hitting.

2. Long explanations of the reasons for a punishment should not occur at the time the child misbehaves. When long explanations are necessary, they should occur after the punishment is over and when both you and the child are calm.

3. Do not issue a command or warning unless it is very important that the child behaves differently and you are able to follow through with it. Before you give a command or warn-

ing, ask yourself, "Will I be willing to enforce the command or warning, even if my child strongly resists?" This will help you avoid the common phrase, "How many times do I have to tell you?" that parents often say when they have been unable to follow up on the command previously.

4. If the child does not respond to the first command or warning, another discipline strategy should be used. (See chapter 4 for more suggestions of how to get children to cooperate.) If, despite your best efforts, you cannot get these disciplinary techniques to work, you may want to discuss this with your pediatrician.

5. Do not rely on explanations or reasoning alone to change the child's behavior.

6. If your child does not follow your instructions, the use of consistent consequences for not following instructions will make your instructions more likely to affect the child's behavior in the future.

7. Verbal commands are generally more effective in initiating a behavior than in stopping a behavior.

These guidelines offer you ways to talk to your child in the context of discipline. Keep your explanations brief at the time you deliver the consequence. Then, after you have calmed down and your child has carried out whatever discipline strategy you enforced, you can discuss it with her if you feel it is necessary. You might feel that a lengthier discussion is necessary, including listening and talking, if the discipline occurred because your child broke a fairly new rule or because your child's behavior was dangerous and should be explored further.

A discussion may also help you understand a child's feelings about the situation that contributed to the misbehavior. For example, if an older child is feeling injustice because a younger child destroyed his property, you might be able to address this issue with simple rearrangements of the child's room. And by allowing your child to express her frustration and problem solve, the misbehavior may decrease. Negative feelings do not justify the behavior, however, and thus a consequence must still occur. Such a conversation alone most likely will not change your child's behavior for the long term.

## COMMON COMMUNICATION MISTAKES TO AVOID

### Relying on Lectures to Change Behavior

We remember the father of a 7-year-old who said he was furious that his son had fallen asleep the night before in the middle of a "good talk." The good talk, as you may have guessed, consisted of the father lecturing the child, who (to his credit) didn't fall asleep until after the lecture had lasted more than an hour. Or you may have seen a child place a hand over his mother's mouth whenever she starts trying to "reason" with him, whenever the real lecturing starts up again. In this case, the child knows he doesn't want to hear the negative feedback again, but he has been unsuccessful in changing his behavior after lectures, hard as he may try.

Just because you have repeatedly "talked" to your child about the same bad behavior doesn't mean he's going to change the way he's behaving. Although the constant talking will communicate to your child that you are unhappy with him, it most likely will have little effect on his behavior, which is really what you are trying to address.

### Coming in Under the Radar

Some parents have a habit of criticizing their children relentlessly while maintaining a façade of neutrality or "niceness." We refer to this as "coming in under the radar." Such parents give their children very negative feedback but manage to deliver the criticism without yelling or raising their voice and without using harsh words. Most children don't have the skills to defend themselves against such mixed messages, hence the terms "under the radar" or "beneath the child's defenses."

Such messages are confusing. Just because a parent says unpleasant things in a measured tone of voice doesn't mean that the child is going to feel any less hurt. As with adults, children would rather not hear many negative comments about their behavior from others. The way in which the criticism is voiced is secondary. For example, a parent might say "Thank you for embarrassing me" while smiling at the child who just misbehaved in public. Even parents can come in "under the radar" when they say angry words but use a neutral tone. For example, we remember interviewing an 8-year-old boy and his parents about the child's "unpredictable" angry behaviors. After the interview, we stepped outside the room to discuss our concerns and we overheard the child's mother say, in a very unemotional tone, "Do you know how embarrassed I was by the way you talked to the doctor?" The father then said, in an equally casual and calm tone, "I wanted to crawl under the table." When we returned to the office, we saw the boy visibly angry, with his jaw and fists clenched. He knew they were saying hurtful things, but their words did not match their tone or body language. He did not have the skills to interpret the situation or defend himself from his hurt feelings, confusion, and frustration. Thus, his defense was to predictably act out against the mixed messages being sent "under his radar."

How do you talk to your child when you are upset about his behavior without going in under his radar? Again, you need a plan if you are going to change your child's behavior. If your child embarrasses you in public, first give yourself some time. Don't "share" your feelings with him immediately, because you risk hurting his feelings without actually helping him. A good rule of thumb is to wait at least an hour or two; if the situation is really emotionally charged, wait until the next day. In this way, you substantially reduce any possibility that you will be unnecessarily harsh or critical with your son.

Second, think of a way to give him feedback in a constructive way. Working on and perhaps rehearsing how to give constructive feedback can be enormously productive. Review a situation that you encountered previously or that doesn't immediately affect anyone in the family and think of constructive responses.

Third, review the example you are setting. For example, if you are working at reducing interrupting, instead of immediately criticizing your child for interrupting, ask yourself if you have been modeling waiting instead of interrupting. Furthermore, ask yourself if you have pointed out when other adults have waited instead of interrupting, reminded your daughter about an upcoming situation where she needs to be careful about not interrupting, and praised her for not interrupting. On many of the occasions when you want to immediately resort to discipline, you may be able to think about the situation, however briefly, and identify a more positive strategy for encouraging the behavior you want to see.

Fourth, if your child embarrasses you by the way she talks to another adult, the problem is that your child doesn't know how to express herself in a constructive manner, and you need to come up with a strategy that will teach her to express herself better. You can start by modeling more appropriate ways of dealing with uncomfortable or frustrating situations, and when you do so, find a benign way to briefly point it out to your daughter. Plan on using this strategy over and over again. Over time, you will find that you are much more in command of your emotions and that your child is learning much more effective ways of expressing herself.

## Taking Immediate Offense

Children will be more inclined to converse with their parents about important issues when the parents can control their emotional responses to what their children are saying. Often when parents take offense at a question or comment, two very different interactions are blended together. First, your child needs to be able to talk to you about anything and know that you will listen to her and be accepting of her. But in addition, you have to teach your child that some topics or words are inappropriate. These two interactions must be separated if you are to deal with them effectively.

For example, if your son says that he doesn't like Uncle Jeff because "Uncle Jeff is a jerk," there are two conversations going on. One is that your son is trying to convey that he doesn't like something about Uncle Jeff's behavior. The other is that he is not saying it in an acceptable way. These two processes have to be separated.

When your son first musters up the courage to tell you that he doesn't think that Uncle Jeff is nice, you need to hear him out long enough to find out what it is about Uncle Jeff's behavior that he doesn't like. Only after hearing what it is that he doesn't like can you address the way that he said it. So your first reaction should be to say something that will encourage your son to continue expressing his thought about Uncle Jeff. Anything along the lines of "Why do you think that?" or "He hasn't been nice to you?" will do. You want to make sure, at least initially, that you understand what he is trying to say. He may continue on and say that Uncle Jeff always wants to show him dumb "magic tricks," which is pretty benign and relatively easy to deal with, or he may say that Uncle Jeff has always had a couple of beers before he comes over to your house, which makes him very uncomfortable. If you start out with a reprimand such as "Don't talk about your uncle that way!" you'll never give your child the opportunity to say what was on his mind about Uncle Jeff.

In the second part of the conversation address how to express negative feelings about someone more appropriately. For example, you might suggest that your child tell you, "I wish Uncle Jeff wouldn't come over when he's been drinking" instead of calling him a name like "jerk." As another example, let's say your daughter asks a question about a "dirty" poem she saw at school. If you immediately begin a sermon about how you will not have that kind of filth in your home, your daughter will never get the chance to discuss dirty poems with you, including why people write them, why people like them, and why you don't like them. You've left her no chance to discuss the topic with you and taught her that if she's going to ask anyone about dirty poems, it will have to be someone outside the home. Not only may that person have a different perspective than you on the topic, but you may have established yourself as a person your child cannot go to when she is faced with an uncomfortable situation. Once you have shown your daughter that you can talk about the subject without being negative toward her, you can have a discussion about how the language used in that poem is offensive and not what you prefer to be used around your home.

## CONCLUSION

Although the majority of parents are acutely aware of the importance of being able to carry on conversations with their children, some of the subtleties of these conversations aren't nearly as obvious. To be able to understand what your child is saying, you need to listen to what he has to say and to make some time or some occasions routinely available for your child to express himself.

Ultimately, unless you understand what your child is trying to communicate, you won't know what he's saying. Thus, the most important sections in this chapter are not about talking, but about listening and understanding, which often involve silence or non-judgmental questioning. If you are talking, however, be careful of the common mistakes parents make such as lecturing, "coming in under the radar," or taking offense that make it difficult for your child to trust you with her most sensitive topics.

Sometimes it's hard to believe that communicating with your child can be as difficult as it appears to be. If there is a single caveat in communicating with your child, it's that you have to be able to listen and understand what she has to say before trying to make your points. If you discipline yourself to listen to your child, you will find that she has a lot to say. You may also find that she is more willing to listen to what you have to say.

# CHAPTER 4

# DISCIPLINING YOUR CHILD EFFECTIVELY

A book with parenting suggestions would not be complete without some guidance on how to discipline your child. Discipline has been described many different ways, with an equal number of different ideas for when and how a child should be made accountable for his behavior. We believe that when discipline is used solely as a negative means of telling a child he has misbehaved, it typically will not be very successful. Discipline is more effectively used as a means of providing consequences for your child's behavior that will encourage her to behave more appropriately in the future.

The most important question in considering discipline is, "Is a disciplinary strategy the most effective strategy for accomplishing what you want to accomplish?" Obviously, if you want to teach your child how to read, you cannot discipline him for not reading, nor would you discipline a child for crying at bedtime when she doesn't have the skills for going to sleep on her own or for spitting out a new food when she has had no experience with that taste or that texture.

The strategies discussed in this chapter are most effective if you focus your efforts on teaching your child a skill or behavior instead of coming up with more and more severe consequences. If parents model appropriate behavior, establish daily routines, talk to their children about their behavior and how it influences others, encourage involvement in appropriate activities, and make sure their children get a lot of attention for good behavior, the need for discipline can often be minimal. Thus, it is important to have a clear understanding about what behaviors you want to see your child display, how those behaviors should be taught, and how to tell if your child's misbehavior is due to lack of skill or an intentional action. To do this, we suggest that you develop a "10-Year Plan" for your child.

## A 10-YEAR PLAN FOR YOUR CHILD

Parents need to have a 10-Year Plan for their children. In the business world, such a plan describes where its owners and managers want the business to be in 10 years—the size and type of business they want, the market share, and so on. We believe parents need to decide what they want their children to be like in 10 years and what behaviors they feel are important for their children. If you know what you want your child to be like in 10 years, then it's much easier to decide which behaviors you need to encourage or discourage now.

For example, if you want your child to develop a strong interest in learning and academic pursuits, then you can start figuring out how to set the steps into motion at an early age. You would, for example, begin reading to him in his infancy and try to make books an important part of his life. You'd be more likely to get him books for presents, and you'd be more likely to take him to the library to check out books. You would take him to science fairs and help him earn "academic" badges in Boy Scouts. You would also make sure that he saw you enjoying reading and learning on a frequent basis.

Similarly, if you want to encourage your child to pursue

sports, you would make every effort to get her involved in sports at an early age, and you'd make sure that her early exposure to sports was pleasant. You'd watch sports on TV with her, and you'd take her to sporting events. You'd subscribe to sports magazines, and you'd look up sports figures on the Internet. You'd try to get sports figures' autographs, and you'd collect sports paraphernalia. You'd read about sports in the newspaper. You'd be certain to be responsive to her questions about sports, and you would encourage her interest in sports. Certainly, you could also develop both types of skills, academic and sports, in your child. These are just examples of how such skills can be nurtured in your child.

It is interesting to note how little a role discipline plays in a 10-Year Plan. In fact, discipline almost seems foreign to such plans. But as you spend time with your child pursuing the activities in your plan, you will probably find that the need for discipline is just not very great. This is partly because you will be keeping your child busy, which reduces the chances of him getting into trouble. As you see your child making progress toward the goals you have set for her, you will feel much less of a sense of frustration when she engages in behavior that you find unacceptable.

Even children who are temperamentally more "difficult" respond to the guidelines we have outlined here, although parents will need to be more persistent and patient in following through. The strategies suggested in this book to encourage positive behavior, such as modeling, pointing out when others are displaying the desired behaviors, and praising a child for demonstrating the desired behavior, are less likely to be seen as confrontational by the "difficult" child. Thus, the child may be more receptive to learning about behavior in these ways than by being directly told what to do and what not to do as exclusive discipline strategies.

The 10-Year Plan also helps to place the focus on what skills you want your child to have and how to encourage the development of those skills. We obviously feel that independent play and self-quieting skills are very important, or we wouldn't have devoted entire chapters to them in this book, and we also believe that encouraging independent play and self-quieting skills will substantially reduce the need for discipline. That's the rationale for having a 10-Year Plan—to help you emphasize and encourage the development of the skills that you want your child to acquire. In so doing, the topic of discipline becomes much less important.

## CONSISTENCY IN EXPECTATIONS AND RULES

Before concentrating your efforts on disciplining your child for misbehaviors, you need to use effective strategies for teaching her how you want her to behave. In addition to modeling important behaviors and providing positive feedback, you must also model consistency and follow through. You can start by focusing on the family routines and rules you have established, as discussed in chapter 1. If you want your child to know and follow the routines and rules, you have to teach the routines and rules on a consistent basis.

For example, if you want your child to hang up his coat when he comes in the house, you must require that the coat be hung up *every* time he takes it off. If you require him to hang up his coat only twice a week, two things will happen. One, he will never get into the habit of hanging up his coat when he takes it off. Two, you will lose your temper more often when you do attempt to enforce the rule. You might find yourself saying to him, "How many times do I have to tell you to hang up your coat?" after finally noticing on the third day that he has not hung up his coat. If you want him to learn the rule or the behavior, you must check *every time* he takes his coat off and make sure *every time* that he hangs it up properly. You can provide positive feedback when he does and use the discipline strategies discussed later in this chapter when he does not.

Of course, be sure your child actually knows how to perform the behavior you are asking her to do. You can help her practice hanging up the coat or putting away the shoes and use reinforcement to encourage her cooperation in such practice. You can even make it a game or race if that helps your child to be cooperative. How many times will you have to tell her to hang up her coat? Until you, the teacher, teach her that you want the coat hung up every time. The only way you can teach this is by providing consequences every time she gets it right or wrong. In the long run, the more consistent and orderly you are in following the rules you make for your children, the better your children will behave, and the less you'll need to rely on discipline.

There are several areas of daily family life in which having a predictable routine can reduce arguments and encourage positive behavior: morning routines, bedtime routines, and chores.

### Morning Routines

A morning routine that includes eating breakfast and getting dressed for the day can be started when your child is a toddler. Try to establish a routine that you follow almost every morning. Perhaps you want to begin by gently stroking your child's hair to awaken him, followed by escorting him to the bathroom to begin his hygiene tasks.

If your child does not know how to perform a skill in the routine, be prepared to spend more time with her during that step, but still stick to your routine. For example, you will need to teach your toddler to get dressed as part of your morning routine. This skill doesn't happen overnight, but if you start on some of the basics early, you're much less likely to end up with a 4- or 5-year-old who can't dress himself. The secret is to teach each little step in getting dressed as if it were a skill all its own. Start by pulling the shirt over her head and eyes, and then gradually let your toddler do more of the pulling. Do the same thing when putting her arms through the shirtsleeves and her legs through the pants legs. She must learn each of these separate skills before she can dress herself.

## Bedtime Routines

Establish a reasonable bedtime for your child and stick to it. If you want to teach your child to go to bed when you tell him it's time to go to bed, you have to follow through *every time* you tell the child to get ready for bed. If you allow your child to change his bedtime by whining and fussing, you're teaching him to whine and fuss instead of teaching him to go to bed.

You can use the same type of routine you have in the morning for bedtime. Have your child use the bathroom, brush her teeth, get her pajamas on, and kiss everyone good night. Children also like snacks or stories before bedtime as a way of making going to bed a relaxing experience. It is also wise to lay out clothes for the next day during the bedtime routine and pack the backpack for school. Again, the most important part of establishing routines is to make sure *you* stick to them on a daily basis.

## Chores

As your child reaches toddler age and older, you can also establish family routines and rules regarding chores. Even a young toddler can be asked to help with picking up his toys. A preschooler can be asked to make her bed or bring her dishes to the sink when she is finished. Remember that you will have to teach each step first, of course, and that building these skills takes time. Also, remember to provide lots of positive feedback for even the smallest steps or efforts to make the bed or bring the dishes to the sink. When you show your child that you appreciate that he *started* making his bed, you're on your way to having him do it every morning. If you begin by waiting for him to make the bed completely, you may have a long, long wait.

When you first start on a chore like making the bed, it's probably best to require it seven days a week until your child is doing a good job of making it every day. No sense giving her days off before she's learned how to do the job correctly and has had lots of opportunities to practice her new skill.

One of the greatest accomplishments you can achieve is to teach your child the skills that he will need to be successful in life. If you spend much of your time doing jobs around the house while your child sits around watching you or the TV because "it's just easier to do it yourself," you are missing wonderful opportunities to teach your child and to communicate while doing jobs together. In addition, if your child helps with the routine jobs around the house, you will have more time to spend together on outside activities.

Carry on a dialogue while you are doing chores together. Most adults, when they share a task, end up talking about a lot of things. Sometimes they talk about the task itself, and sometimes they talk about things that are completely unrelated to the task. So, when doing the laundry, one day you might talk about "how soap works" by putting dirt into suspension. And you might talk about how good it feels to wear clean clothes. But you might also talk about an upcoming birthday party or a family outing. You can also use this time together to ask your child what is on her mind. In this way, your child will learn, from your modeling and from engaging in the task with you, that having a companion when you have a job to do can make the time pass much more quickly.

Children, like adults, thrive on predictability. If your child knows what is expected of her, and if your expectations remain fairly consistent from day to day and from week to week, it becomes much easier to meet those expectations. Because he can consistently meet your expectations and has the stability of a routine, the need for discipline often declines greatly.

## STEPS FOR DISCIPLINING A CHILD

Once you have provided your child with consistent messages about important life skills and routines, you can incorporate discipline to help with your teaching efforts. There is, of course, a role for discipline as a consequence for negative behavior when raising a child to behave appropriately. The following steps provide guidelines first for making sure you are attending to positive behaviors, then for determining when and how to deliver effective discipline.

### Step 1: Pay Attention to Good Behavior

Before worrying about what to do when your child does *not* behave, we recommend that you know what to do if your child *does* behave. We cannot emphasize enough that you must be able to identify the behaviors you want from your child, and encourage and reinforce those behaviors, before your child will be able to understand what behaviors you find inappropriate. Thus, step 1 in disciplining your child includes an emphasis on positive behavior. For a period of time, perhaps as long as a couple of days, you should begin using positive feedback before using any form of discipline.

For example, if your child has a long history of being disruptive when you are on the telephone, begin by concentrating on the behaviors you would prefer to see while you're on the phone. Discuss "telephone etiquette" with your child. Make sure he knows that the same rules apply to all members of the family; that is, when he is talking on the phone, you agree to refrain from interrupting him, just as you expect him to refrain from interrupting you. Tell your child that you will be watching for him to let you finish your phone call without interrupting you or fighting with his sister. Then, throughout the phone call, provide frequent positive feedback whenever he is *not* interrupting or annoying you, such as a thumbs-up or a wink.

It may also be helpful to establish a method for your child to tell you something important while you're on the phone, such as holding your hand or gently placing a hand on your forearm. Using this technique, you need only place a hand over your child's hand to acknowledge that an interruption is requested. You will then have a chance to interrupt your phone call politely if you choose to address your child's need. The same basic strategies could also be used for a child's behavior when you are trying to talk to another person or any other situation when you require acceptable behavior from your child. Only after you have gotten accustomed to providing positive feedback and proactive strategies should you begin to discipline misbehavior.

Finally, it is important to look at the circumstances surrounding the problem behavior to determine if issues other than the child's behavior need to be addressed. For example, if you spend excessive time on the telephone, you may be making it very difficult for your children to find a time when talking to you does not mean interrupting you. Try to come to an agreement about when calls can be made, as well as how long those calls will last, for all family members. Solicit your children's input on these issues so that they have some influence over the rules in your home.

In summary, if your discipline efforts are to be effective, your child must experience a contrast between being disciplined and the rest of her day. If the rest of her day, when she is behaving, is pleasant and filled with positive feedback, she will come to prefer those types of interactions with you to those she encounters when being disciplined. As with most situations, good times are preferable to bad, so whenever you are concerned that your discipline efforts are not working, start by making sure your child's world is rich enough with positive attention and feedback (discussed in chapter 2).

## Step 2: Decide When to Discipline

One of the questions we are asked most frequently about discipline is, "At what age should we start to discipline?" The answer is quite simple: When your child starts engaging in behaviors that you do not approve of and that they can reasonably be expected to refrain from. Sometimes you will have to differentiate between behavior that is developmentally appropriate for your child and behavior that is intentional and inappropriate. An infant's spitting out rice cereal the first time you feed it to him is developmentally appropriate. If he has never tasted cream of rice and has never had a texture like that of cream of rice in his mouth, spitting it out doesn't mean that he doesn't like cereal. Rather, it means that he has just been fed a food that is new in both taste and texture, and, not being familiar with the taste and texture, he's opting to spit it out. Similarly, when your daughter just learns that she can make bubbles with her saliva, it's a behavior that you should not, initially, think about disciplining.

A second and equally important question is, "Is there an alternative way of encouraging my child to engage in the behavior that I feel is important?" If, for example, you are having difficulty getting your son to eat a balanced meal, instead of coming up with innovative methods to punish him for not eating his vegetables, you should try to figure out innovative ways to encourage him to try vegetables. With such an approach, you would be much more likely to get him to eat a tiny little piece of a vegetable, knowing that if you can get him to eat a tiny piece, you can probably get him to eat a bigger piece. You may have to offer any given taste or texture numerous times before he will eat it. Be prepared to offer the same one 10, 20, or 30 times over a period of weeks. The important thing is that he becomes accustomed to the taste and texture—not that he takes more or less time to do so.

### Step 3: Decide What Behaviors to Discipline

In addition to asking yourself if a particular behavior should be part of your child's 10-Year Plan, you must also decide whether the behavior is compatible with the way the members of your family behave. For example, it's rare to see children exhibiting aggressive behavior in a home where the parents are not aggressive and where exposure to aggressive behavior through sports, movies, or playing with peers is strongly curtailed or nonexistent (see chapter 13). Thus, if the behavior you decide to discipline is aggression, be sure that it is not being encouraged by your own behavior or that of other family members.

Once you have decided on the behaviors that you feel deserve a negative consequence, it is often a good idea to discuss your list with your child, providing, of course, that he has the verbal skills to carry on such a conversation, beginning at about 5 years of age. Children's input is valuable because they often have really good insights into the inner workings of their families and because they are much more likely to cooperate with the rules you establish with their input. This discussion may also lead to alternative solutions to problems that will reduce the need for discipline. For example, if you have listed "yelling at your little brother for going in your room" as a behavior to discipline, you may learn from your child that she simply wants some time alone with her friends without her little brother tagging along. You could make up a house rule about private or special times with friends without the intrusion of siblings. Such consideration of the other child's feelings may reduce the need for discipline about yelling because it may not occur as often with the new rule in place.

Discuss the list of negative behaviors and consequences at a time when no misbehavior has occurred and when you are not upset with the child. During this conversation, it's good to point out that you are talking about behaviors that are unacceptable for everyone in your house—not just for the child. So, behaviors such as interrupting and forgetting or neglecting to say "please" and "thank you" are just as important for you as they are for your daughter. You may even be surprised by what she has to say to you. It's not unusual during such a conversation to have your child say, "Well, you use bad language, why can't I?" Once the rules are established, posting them for everyone to see can be a useful reminder for all family members. Even children who cannot read will know what the list says if you refer to it regularly.

When establishing the behaviors to be disciplined, you should talk with your partner, family members, and babysitters or day care providers who spend time with your children to make sure that you all agree on what behaviors you are not going to tolerate. Identifying which behaviors you are not going to allow will help you take a proactive approach to discipline, rather than just waiting until your child does something and then immediately punishing him for it. If the other adults who care for your child are allowing or even encouraging him to engage in behavior that you find displeasing, your attempts at punishment will most likely fail, in addition to confusing your child.

Specific plans for managing whining and aggression, which many parents choose to manage with discipline, are in chapters 13 and 14. The format we set forth for dealing with those problems can usefully be applied to most behaviors that you decide to address with discipline. That format consists of a five-step process:

1. Discuss, with all members of the family, the problem behavior and the more positive behaviors you would like to see.
2. Model the positive behaviors.
3. Point out when you see others exhibiting those positive behaviors.
4. Prompt your child to engage in those behaviors.
5. Praise or reward your child when she engages in those behaviors.

Using this process, you can encourage the development of appropriate behaviors in both parents and child.

## Step 4: Decide How to Discipline

The more unpleasant the discipline is to the parent, the less likely it is that the parent will use it. That's just human nature. So don't pick a form of discipline that you won't want to use.

Yelling and spanking are problematic as discipline techniques. Some research has concluded that yelling at children might actually encourage violent behavior.[1] Research conducted in our office showed that children who were spanked at home were more likely to exhibit aggressive behaviors at day care.[2]

As with deciding what behaviors to punish, you need to come to an agreement with your child's other caregivers about *how* to discipline your children. Ideally, this would include not only parents and grandparents, but also stepparents and other adults living in your home. If your discipline is going to be effective, it is important that as many caregivers as possible agree on how your child will be disciplined.

It's quite common to have family members who think that spanking, for example, works much better than alternatives such as time-out. If a caregiver disagrees strongly with your opinion, especially if he or she prefers spanking or yelling, you may have to limit or eliminate the time your child spends in the care of that person to reduce conflict and the risk of confusing your child.

## Step 5: Deliver Effective Discipline

One of your most important jobs when delivering discipline is to remain as unemotional as possible. The enforcement of discipline should be as unemotional, low key, and matter-of-fact as possible. Remember, you are modeling for your child how to deal with frustration when you deal with their misbehavior. If you model yelling, name calling, or belittling as you state the consequence, you may be teaching your child to do the same thing when he is frustrated or mad.[3] For example, telling your child, "Well, if you are going to have a fit like a big baby, you don't deserve to have a friend over tonight" models belittling as a response to anger. Furthermore, when you get angry, *you* are the one who is paying for your child's rule violation, sometimes more than the child herself does! In other words, when you get angry, you often expend more energy and feel more lingering stress and frustration about the situation than your child does.

One way to avoid getting overly upset with your child when he misbehaves is simply not to wait too long before you deliver the consequence. If there's a single mistake parents make with discipline, it's that they wait too long to do it. The longer they wait, the more likely they are to get upset, and the less the child learns from the discipline. Thus, if you find yourself in an escalating argument with your child over a rule violation or yelling "If I have to tell you one more time!" it is time to start delivering the consequence, and next time try to deliver it well before you reach those levels of emotionality. Dr. Tom Phelan's book *1-2-3 Magic* offers good examples of the counterproductive discussions parents get into with their children.[4] The essence of his "1-2-3" system is that parents need to refrain from getting into arguments with their children over the rules. Such arguments only teach children that such strategies as badgering, martyrdom, intimidation, and buttering up are viable alternatives to doing what they are asked to do.

Another guideline for delivering consequences to your child for misbehavior is to allow your child a "clean slate" once her consequences are over. Your child will most likely break the rule again, giving you another chance to state your displeasure and deliver a consequence. Children learn most effectively by doing things and getting feedback on what they've done. This usually has to occur many times before children learn what their parents want them to learn. Typically, the long discussions that parents often want to have after their children have broken a rule may not have a direct impact on the children's behavior. Thus, do not become too frustrated if your child misbehaves again, even after you've had a "good talk" about it. (More ideas on how to talk to your child are found in chapter 3.)


## DISCIPLINE STRATEGIES TO USE WITH CHILDREN

The following are some strategies that you can consider adding to the strategies you already use that are effective with your child. We'll begin with a discussion of time-out, followed by the use of logical consequences and removal of privileges.

## Time-Out

One of the most frequently discussed and used form of discipline is the "time-out," or removing the child from pleasurable interactions and experiences. Time-out is truly effective only when it removes a child from an enriched environment filled with positive feedback that the child enjoys and doesn't want to leave. The range of ages for which time-out is now recommended goes from about 7 months to at least 8 or 9 years of age. Unfortunately, there have been so many variations of what constitutes time-out that many parents are mistakenly encouraging their child to misbehave through the improper use of time-out. Thus, this section discusses the time-out technique in detail and provides guidelines for its proper use.

Children learn several things from time-out. They learn that their misbehavior results in a negative consequence, that they would rather be having a good time than sitting in time-out, and that they don't get to enjoy positive interactions with others when in time-out. Time-out can also help children build their self-quieting skills. If time-out is done correctly, as explained below, and a child is required to be quiet and calm before ending the time-out, he can develop good self-quieting skills. If a child is timed-out many times a day or week, he will have many opportunities to learn these important skills.

If you asked three parents about how to use time-out, you would probably get three different answers. The same might be true if you asked three "experts" or read three different parenting books. There are many different opinions on when, where, and how time-out should be handled. The age-specific guidelines that follow are those that we know work the best based on our experience with thousands of children.

TIME-OUT FOR TODDLERS. For young toddlers, time-out can simply mean removing your child from whatever she is doing wrong and placing her elsewhere. You may accompany this by a short statement such as, "Time-out, hitting." If she hits again, then give her another time-out. She'll soon learn that when she misbehaves, she is removed from the area of fun and required to miss out on the interactions and activities of the household.

You may also place your toddler in his playpen for time-out, then walk away. As soon as he is quiet for five seconds, go back, pick him up, and take him back to where the action is. With a young toddler, five seconds of quiet is all that is necessary to get across the idea that you won't pick him up while he's still crying. It's unrealistic to expect an unhappy toddler to go to his playpen and be quiet for three minutes, so simply wait until your child is quiet only briefly before picking him up. Although experts disagree, we could find no evidence that children learn to "fear" their playpen or associate it with negative experiences. If your child is always relaxed before she leaves the playpen, she'll come to associate going there with relaxing and will actually get better at calming herself down. Certainly if you aggressively place your child in her playpen or ignore her when she is quiet, she will not associate her playpen with relaxing and may want to avoid being placed there to play in the future. When used correctly, however, there is no evidence that children fear or avoid places where the time-outs occur.

Many parents of toddlers try to use strategies such as taking away their privileges, sending them to their rooms to "think about what they did," or offering to purchase special toys if they stop engaging in particular behaviors (bribery). Although these strategies have immediate appeal, they are notoriously ineffective with toddler-age children. Toddlers do not have the cognitive ability to associate losing privileges with the performance of particular behaviors, although they often have the verbal skills to carry on a conversation about consequences. For example, you might explain to your son that you won't buy a certain toy for him until he picks up all of the rest of his toys in his room. He might even be able to repeat your rule back to you. But, then, he doesn't pick up his toys. You repeat your threat to him and he acknowledges what you say, but he still doesn't pick up his toys. Then, when he wants the new toy, he gets upset because you won't purchase it for him. You can certainly take away a toy as a form of "losing a privilege" or simply put the toy in time-out, but return it within a short amount of time so your child can make the connection between misbehaving and losing a toy.

TIME-OUT FOR PRESCHOOLERS AND SCHOOL-AGE CHILDREN. If your child is of preschool age or older, you can teach your child about time-out by practicing it first. If you begin by practicing the rules of time-out when your child is not upset, you will be less tempted to excessively explain or repeat the rules when your child is actually in time-out. Start by telling your child that when in time-out, she must sit in the time-out spot of your choice (chair, step, or couch) until she is quiet. Have her practice sitting quietly for a few seconds, then tell her time-out is over. Try this several times so she begins to learn that being quiet is one of the most important requirements for getting out of time-out.

After a few practice sessions, start using very brief time-outs for the first week or two, beginning with a few seconds and gradually requiring longer amounts of time he is to be quiet before ending time-out. It is far more important that your child learn to calm down in time-out then to worry about how many minutes time-out lasted.

It is crucial that you always wait for your child to be quiet before allowing her to get up from time-out. Never let a crying child out of time-out. Explain once (if the child is at least 3 years old and of normal intelligence), briefly, that if she gets up, you will help her back to time-out. With practice, children learn to sit in the chair and do their time, making disciplining them much easier. It often becomes matter-of-fact, reducing your temptation to try less effective strategies such as yelling, spanking, or trying to reason with the child. The chair becomes a quiet time for both parent and child.

While the child is in the chair, no one should be allowed to speak to him or interact with him in any way, not even to remind him about the rules for getting out of the chair. This can be difficult for parents if the child engages in negative behaviors during time-out. For example, if your child says he hates you while in time-out, it is tempting to respond with a comment such as, "We don't say such mean things; that's three more minutes to your time-out." What you have actually taught your child is that such a comment on his part gets your full attention, rather than teaching him not to say hurtful things. Thus, do your best to ignore behaviors that occur during time-out, understanding that this does not mean you approve of them but simply are following the rules of time-out.

WHAT TO DO WHEN TIME-OUT IS OVER. Once your child is quiet and relaxed, go over to her, place your hand gently on her back, and tell her it's all right to get up now. If she says, "No!" cries again, or looks at the floor angrily, the time-out starts over again. You can tell her that it has started over, but you don't necessarily have to make any announcement to that effect, just start the time-out over again. The reason for this is simple: If the child gets up while she's still angry or in a bad mood, she'll just end up in the time-out chair again, and the parent runs the risk of getting angry with her in the process.

Some children will try very hard to make you think that going to time-out doesn't bother them a bit. That is fine; the procedure wasn't developed with torture in mind! Just let them sit there looking as if they enjoy it. Take our word for it—they don't like being in time-out. But if children can convince their parents that it doesn't bother them, perhaps they think they can get their parents to switch to something that isn't nearly as effective.

Once the time-out is over, many parents are tempted to tell the child they "never want to see that type of behavior again." This type of comment sets up the child to fail. Besides, children learn much faster if they are given many opportunities to practice whatever it is their parents want them to learn. Thus, a child who is put in time-out five, six, or seven times in a row for the same misbehavior will learn the rules much faster than he would if he broke the rule but had inconsistent consequences or only verbal reprimands about his behavior.

If you would like to discuss why your child was in time-out, wait until you are both calm before doing so. The focus of the discussion, which should be brief with your preschooler, should be on the house rule that was broken. Most children will not be able to say why they broke a rule or why they keep breaking the rules when they "know better." Such questions directed to your child will only make her and you frustrated, as no answer is forthcoming.

WHERE TO DO TIME-OUT. So where should time-out take place? It's best to select a time-out place where the child can see you and see that you are not mad but calmly going on about your business. You also want him to be able to see what he's missing, so select a place where he is not a part of what is going on in the house but can hear or see the rest of the family engaging in pleasurable activities. Be sure your child cannot see the TV and does not have access to hand-held video games, books, or other enjoyable activities. We do not recommend placing your child facing a corner or in a bathroom or closet. These places can be scary for children.

Can you use the child's room for time-out? Sure, but just

make sure that you have prepared her bedroom first. Remove any-thing that can be broken or harmful (lamps, knick-knacks, base-balls and baseball bats, hockey sticks) long before the tantrum starts. It is also important that there is no TV, phone, or computer in her room. To send your child to her room for a time-out and expect her to not turn on the TV or play with the computer will probably just cause you more frustration. If your child's room has these things, you may need to remove and store them until she has developed better anger management skills and can cope with your requests for time-out quickly. Some professionals say that you should lock the bedroom door. Others say that you should hold the door shut.

Whichever option you choose, do not wait to respond to your child's tantrum until it has escalated to the point of a meltdown—this will only encourage more meltdowns. Such episodes should help to convince you of the fruitlessness of confrontation and the need for better self-quieting skills for your child—or perhaps pro-fessional help for your family.

WHEN YOUR CHILD WON'T GO INTO TIME-OUT. When a parent and child have a heated, emotional confrontation, it's often more pro-ductive for the parent to exit the situation as quickly as possible, perhaps by going into the bathroom and closing the door. The parent should state that he or she is going to take a few minutes alone to calm down. If you do need the solitude of the bathroom, there should be no communication with your child, who almost certainly will be on the other side of the door, doing everything he can to get you to answer him, such as hitting or kicking the door. If you respond to him out of anger, you are only perpetuating his tantrum and giving him cause to have another one the next time you have an angry confrontation. If you do excuse yourself to the solitude of your bathroom, you should come out as soon as your child has clearly regained control of himself. Again, both you and your child may need more work on self-quieting and anger management skills, with the help of a professional, if indicated.

You shouldn't need to be concerned for your child's safety while you wait in the bathroom, because you should be able to hear her on the other side of the door. If you open the door shortly after you can tell that she has calmed down, there shouldn't be much opportunity for her to get into additional trouble. And you can expect a child who is having a tantrum to get upset when the door closes. We've had parents say that they couldn't go into the bathroom when their child was having a meltdown because the child "didn't like it." The fact that the child doesn't like it is precisely the reason you go into the room. Of course, if your child is at risk for leaving the house or other dangerous behavior if you go to your room or bathroom, this strategy may not be the best choice. Your situation may require the help of a mental health professional.

WHEN TIME-OUT DOESN'T WORK. When time-out doesn't work—your child refuses to go to the time-out location or will not quiet down—there are a few things you can do:

- Be sure you are not warning your child one or more times before sending him to time-out. Warnings only teach your child that he can misbehave at least once (or more) before you'll use time-out. Warnings make children's behavior worse, not better.
- All adults who are responsible for disciplining your child at home should be using time-out. You should agree when and for what behaviors you send your child to time-out. You should also provide other caregivers the time-out guidelines (see Appendix B) and ask them to follow the guidelines for certain behaviors.

- To maximize the effectiveness of time-out, you must make the rest of the day pleasant for your child. Remember to let your child know when she is well behaved—don't take good behavior for granted. Most children prefer to be in time-out than to be ignored completely.

- Your child may say, "Going to time-out doesn't bother me," or "I like time-out." Don't fall for this trick. Many children try to convince their parents that time-out is fun and therefore not working. You should notice over time that the problem behaviors for which you use time-out occur less often.

- When you first begin using time-out, your child may act as though time-out is a game. He may put himself in time-out or ask to go there. If this happens, give your child what he wants—send him to time-out and require that he be quiet before the time-out is over. He will soon learn that time-out is not a game. He will learn this not from discussing it but by experiencing it. Your child may laugh or giggle when told to go to time-out or while in time-out. Although this may aggravate you, it is important for you to ignore him completely when he is in time-out.

- You may feel the need to punish your child for doing something inappropriate during the time-out (for example, cursing or spitting). However, it is very important to ignore your child when she behaves badly during a time-out. This will teach her that attention-getting strategies do not work. If your child curses when the time-out is over, be sure to put her back in time-out. Remember that it is this repetition that helps to teach your child to calm down during a time-out.

- Leaving the TV or radio on can make time-out more tolerable, but it will prolong the length of time your child needs to calm down. Try to minimize such distractions.

- You must use time-out for major, as well as minor, behavior problems. Parents have a tendency to feel that time-out is not enough of a punishment for big things. Consistency is most important for time-out to work—for big *and* small problems.

- Be certain that your child is aware of the rules that, if broken, result in a time-out. Frequently, parents will establish a new rule ("Don't touch the new stereo") without telling the children even once (and only once). When their children unwittingly break the new rule, they don't understand why they are being given a time-out.

- Make sure that time-outs are occurring in the context of teaching your child the appropriate behavior that you would prefer he exhibit. You need to be modeling the appropriate behavior, pointing out when you see another person exhibiting the appropriate behavior, encouraging your child to engage in the appropriate behavior, reading stories to your child about the appropriate behavior, and praising or rewarding him when he engages in the appropriate behavior.

- If you find that you are using time-out for the same behavior over and over again, find a peaceful time, perhaps during a family meeting, to discuss both the appropriate and the inappropriate behavior with your child. Family meetings are an excellent time for this, because they give everyone in the family an opportunity to share their feelings about the behaviors in question.

- Review these time-out guidelines to make certain you are following the recommendations. During a difficult time-out, read these guidelines aloud to yourself. Doing so will help to take your focus off of what your child is doing as well as remind you how time-out is supposed to be done.

When assessing whether time-out is effective with your child, look for a decrease in the behaviors for which she is being sent to time-out, not whether she expresses dissatisfaction at being in time-out. If you give your daughter a time-out when she sasses you and you see a decrease in the amount of sassing, then time-out is working. If there's no decrease in sassing, then either time-out isn't working or you may not be doing time-out correctly. That is why it is important to regularly review the rules for how to do a time-out.

### Logical Consequences as a Form of Discipline

Logical consequences for inappropriate behavior can also be effective in disciplining children of all ages, especially older children. Logical consequences are those that follow as a result of a child's poor choice of behavior. For example, if your child breaks the rule of not wearing his expensive tennis shoes to the swimming pool, where they might get stolen, the logical consequence would be that the child does not get new, expensive tennis shoes to replace them, but must wear his old sneakers. Similarly, eating all of the snacks when told not to should result in the logical consequence of no more snacks until the next trip to the grocery store.

It's important that you do not express any displeasure at your child when following through on the consequence. Rather, carry on with your own activities in a neutral way and simply let her experience the consequence for herself. If she asks you about it —wanting new sneakers or more snacks, for example—you can say matter-of-factly that there won't be any more snacks until the next time you go to the store. Don't get involved in long discussions.

You can often determine the logical consequence for a given situation if you ask yourself what would happen if you stepped back and didn't intervene. Logical consequences are very effective in most situations, although you will need to use your discretion. For example, you obviously would not want your child to experience the logical consequence of dangerous situations, such as running out into the road without looking to retrieve a ball.

It is important when using this discipline option, as with others, to make sure that all caregivers agree with and uphold your decision. If Mom decides to take Sam to the store to get a few more snacks to tide her over until grocery day, Dad's efforts at using a logical consequence will be undermined. Thus, it is important to communicate to all caregivers which consequences are in place on any given day.

## REMOVAL OF PRIVILEGES AS A FORM OF DISCIPLINE

You can also use the removal of privileges as a form of discipline for your child. A privilege is anything your child favors or desires beyond the basic needs that you provide. Privileges can be playing with toys, with video games, or with friends; receiving a special treat; watching TV; or attending a social event. If you want the removal of privileges to work for you and your child as a discipline strategy, the following six guidelines will increase its effectiveness:

1. Be careful about what you remove. Make certain that whatever privilege you choose to remove can actually be removed. If you remove a beloved toy that the child needs to get to sleep, you both may be exhausted the next morning. If you pick TV viewing, then the entire family will have to be restricted from watching TV in order to carry through with removing privileges. If you remove the privilege of going to a movie, you must get a babysitter for that child if the rest of the family is going. Thus, be sure you choose a privilege you can stick to!

2. If your rule is that the privilege is lost if your son swears,

then the first swear word should result in the loss of his privilege. Warning him that he will lose the privilege, instead of actually removing the privilege, can actually result in an increase in the misbehavior, because he knows that you aren't going to follow through with your threat.

3. Limit the length of time that the privilege is withheld. A time limit is much easier to enforce if it is stated as part of the loss of privileges. If your daughter uses a swear word at dinner, she loses her computer time after dinner. This should not affect whether she gets the computer the next night. The longer you take something away, the more likely you are to forget, give it back, or allow your child to bargain with you to get it back.

4. Be prepared to vary the privileges you remove. If your child does not seem too upset about the privilege you remove, try removing a different privilege for the next misbehavior. Just as a child's interest in rewards can change, what they find to be a "privilege" can also change.

5. If your child is socially isolated or has poor social skills, you may not want to remove privileges involving social activities as a discipline strategy. These children typically need any social interaction they can find to develop their social skills and ensure social interaction. Thus, choose watching TV or video game time as privileges to remove.

6. If your child does not seem to have many favored activities or things, removal of privileges may not be effective, and you may want to try a different discipline strategy. Such a child may be depressed or have some other mental health problem; thus, you should seek the help of your pediatrician or a mental health professional if your child seems difficult to motivate and does not have many interests.

## DISCIPLINE MISTAKES TO AVOID

The following are some common discipline mistakes to avoid with your child:

- Waiting too long to use discipline. Every time parents allow a child to get away with a behavior that they find objectionable, they are encouraging their child to engage in that behavior again.
- Using too many warnings instead of discipline. Every time parents warn their child about a behavior without actually disciplining him, they are encouraging the child to engage in that behavior again.
- Making too many excuses. Every time parents make excuses for why their child engaged in a certain behavior, they are encouraging her to engage in that behavior again. Excuses include the fact that your child is tired or not feeling well. If she's well enough to break the rules, then she's well enough for time-out.
- Giving too many commands. Parents should not give a child a command unless they intend to follow through with it all the way—up to and including time-out.
- Giving commands without expecting action. If parents allow their child to wait until the TV commercials before getting ready for bed, they should wait until the commercial is on before asking him to begin getting ready for bed. That way, you don't get caught by the child trying to stall. By waiting until the commercial is on, you avoid teaching your child to try to negotiate or ignore you when you give an instruction.
- Talking too much when your child misbehaves. Long-winded discussions or lectures about misbehavior are rarely effective

in improving your child's behavior. They result in increased frustration on your part and often hurt the self-esteem of your child. See chapter 3 for guidelines on how to talk to your child about misbehavior.

The most important consideration regarding discipline is that much of what we, as parents, want our children to learn cannot be learned if the children aren't at least reasonably well behaved. By beginning to teach your children to follow simple verbal commands at a young age and continuing to expect a respectable level of compliance through childhood, you are actually doing a lot to prepare your children for a world where they must follow the directions and rules of others. The child who is reasonably, fairly, and unemotionally disciplined by her parents learns to accept discipline as a part of life—which is the way life is for most adults.

## SPANKING: AN INEFFECTIVE FORM OF DISCIPLINE

Even though both the American Psychological Association and the American Academy of Pediatrics have taken positions against spanking children, some surveys show that as many as 80% of parents spank their children at one time or another. The following are some of the reasons that both groups of professionals discourage spanking:

- Children's behavior typically does not change just because they have been spanked. Although there might be a temporary decrease in the behavior that you spank for, without teaching your child some alternative behaviors, he will probably resume the behavior that you spanked him for.
- Spanking children teaches them that hitting is an acceptable form of trying to get your way or expressing anger. It models

aggression and conveys that such behavior is appropriate for them to display as well.

- Spanking may lead to negative feelings in children. They most certainly may feel scared, intimidated, and threatened, and spanking in anger can create anxiety. Older children may recognize the injustice of the punishment and may retaliate in anger.

- Spanking can and has led to serious injuries and even death in children, despite the intention of the parent simply to "teach" their children a lesson.

Clearly, spanking can have many negative consequences and is not an effective way to teach your child appropriate behavior. Any time you find yourself getting frustrated by your child's behavior, concentrate your efforts on teaching him what you want him to do, not what you want him to stop doing. Make sure that you really are concentrating your efforts on positive feedback (see chapter 2). Also, familiarize yourself with the strategies we discuss in chapter 5, and use them on a daily basis.

## CONCLUSION

Discipline, by itself, is notoriously ineffective in teaching children how to behave. All you can hope to accomplish with discipline is to teach a child what you *don't* want him to do. Unless you teach him what you *do* want him to do through positive feedback and direct instruction, discipline alone will not get the results you want. Parents who feel they are spending an inordinate amount of time disciplining their children are usually neglecting to notice their children's positive behaviors, and overuse of discipline tends to result in more inappropriate behavior, which is what the parents are trying to avoid! As a rule of thumb, you should strive to provide positive feedback 10 times for every 1 time you have to discipline. Obviously, on some days this might seem impossible, but it's a good goal.

Our main rationale in recommending that you develop a 10-Year Plan is to give you perspective on the child rearing you are doing now. If you seriously think about the skills that you want your child to have 10 years from now, you will probably find that you have a fair amount of work to do, but that discipline will play a relatively small role in your plan.

Perhaps the biggest mistake that parents make with reference to discipline is that they are in a hurry for their efforts to pay off. That hurry can be your downfall. Children won't learn important skills like sharing, taking turns, and self-quieting overnight. If you allow yourself to get upset because they aren't learning as fast as you would like, you will sabotage your own efforts. Age-appropriate discipline, however, along with the other skills and activities discussed in this book, provides parents with an effective approach to parenting.

## APPENDIX B: TALKING TO YOUNG CHILDREN WHEN THEY MISBEHAVE

The following guidelines may help you use language more effectively when disciplining your young child:

- At the time the child misbehaves, any explanation or warning should be brief; approximately one word for each year of the child's age is a good guideline. Say, "No hitting, time-out," before placing a 3-year-old in time-out for hitting.
- Long explanations of the reasons for a punishment should not occur at the time the child misbehaves. When long explanations are necessary, they should occur after the punishment is over and when both you and the child are calm.
- Do not issue a command or warning unless it is very important that the child behave differently. Before you give a command or warning, ask yourself, "Will I be willing to enforce the command or warning, even if my child strongly resists?"
- If the child does not respond to the first warning, another discipline strategy should be used. If you do not know another strategy or cannot get other disciplinary techniques to work, you should discuss this with your pediatrician.
- Do not rely on explanations or reasoning alone to change the child's behavior.
- If your child does not follow your instructions, the use of consistent consequences for not following instructions will make your instructions more likely to affect his behavior in the future.
- Verbal commands are generally more effective in initiating a behavior than in stopping a behavior.

- Find a time to discuss your child's behaviors, both appropriate and inappropriate, with her when both of you are calm. Keep in mind that her negative behavior may be her way of reacting to a change in her life, such as the birth of a sibling, rather than willful misbehavior.

# CHAPTER 5

# BUILDING PARENT COPING SKILLS

To have an enjoyable and productive relationship with their children, parents need coping skills. Parents need to have the skills to deal with the everyday emotions, including frustration, disappointment, anger, anxiety, and irritation, that are part of being a parent. The term *coping skills* refers to your ability to maintain your composure and avoid anger or any of the other negative emotions when your child is unpleasant, noncompliant, or confrontational.

Many challenges to your coping skills occur when your child is in apparent distress related to frustration over an undesirable situation. For example, when your baby is fussing in her crib at bedtime or your teenager is arguing with you about curfew, it takes a great deal of your effort to leave your baby alone to quiet down or to stop arguing with your teenager and stand by your rule.

Situations like these test a parent's coping skills because a child's "distress" provides a great temptation to do whatever is necessary to relieve that distress as soon as possible, such as pick up the baby or change the curfew. If parents help their children quiet down and relax, it makes them feel better immediately because it temporarily relieves their distress, but it also keeps them from learning important skills. Parents may tell themselves, "This time I'm going to give in, but tomorrow, when I have more patience, I'll be able to follow through properly." Unfortunately, that tomorrow often never comes.

So how do you, as a parent, learn to cope with stressful situations and emotions and make the best choices for your child? One strategy to help you through these hard times has to do with what you say or think to yourself—your self-talk. Self-talking can take two distinctly different paths. One is hurtful thoughts, and the other is helpful thoughts. A description of each type of self-talk follows, along with some strategies for making sure your self-talk is helping you cope with the demands of parenthood.

## SELF-TALK: HELPFUL AND HURTFUL THOUGHTS

"Helpful thoughts" are things we say or think to ourselves that "help" rather than "hurt" our ability to cope with the situation. For example, the first time you took your infant in for an immunization, you probably reminded yourself that, although getting an immunization may be distressing for you and for your baby, he will be permanently protected from getting a serious illness. Thinking such a thought helps you to get through the situation and constitutes a helpful thought.

"Hurtful thoughts," on the other hand, refer to things we say or think to ourselves that not only do not make coping with the situation any easier, but frequently make it more difficult. Hurtful thoughts are often a distortion or misreading of the situation. An example of a hurtful thought would be your thinking "My child hates me" if he cries because you told him "no." This thought is unrealistic because it bases an erroneous generalization—"my child must hate me"—on a limited, temporary situation—"my child is crying." Likewise, if after playing with, feeding, and changing your baby you place her in her crib for a nap and she starts fussing, you may think thoughts such as, "I can't just let her cry," "She thinks I have abandoned her," or "She is going to hate bedtime if I don't help her calm down." Such hurtful thoughts make us doubt our competence as parents!

Hurtful thoughts are perfectly normal parental reactions to uncomfortable situations, but they can and do interfere with parents doing what they know, intellectually, is the right thing. The problem with hurtful thoughts is that they more or less give you, as a parent, permission to allow your child to do something that you know is not in your child's best interest. Parents quickly learn that acting on a hurtful thought can often bring immediate, but temporary, relief. For example, the tense parent who is attempting to get a child to do something that the child doesn't want to do might be thinking, "I can't get him to do anything for me." That parent is likely to feel a tremendous sense of relief when he gives up on getting the child to do it and does it himself. Over time, these episodes of giving up and feeling immediate relief end up reinforcing the parents' conviction that their hurtful thoughts are correct.

Another type of hurtful thought is exemplified by parents confronting the school-age or adolescent child who frequently doesn't get her homework done. When asking whether she has done her homework, the parents think and may even say that their child is "lying" if she says her homework is completed. This hurtful thought (and comment) about "lying" is often emotionally charged and makes the situation more difficult to handle.

Parents who experience hurtful thoughts in situations like those we've described must first be able to identify their own hurtful thoughts before they can do anything to improve the situation. To assist you in identifying some of your hurtful thoughts, here are some typical child-related situations that might result in hurtful thoughts.

| What Happened | Hurtful Thoughts |
|---|---|
| Baby is fussing for no obvious reason | "I am such a bad parent." "This baby is never happy." |
| Children are fighting over a toy | "I can't stand it when they fight!" "They hate each other!" |
| Child lied about grade on test | "He is always lying to me." "His teacher must think I never help him with homework." |
| Something gets broken at Grandma's house | "She probably thinks I can't raise my kids to behave right." "He always acts up over here to make me look bad." |
| Child misses curfew by an hour | "She is always so irresponsible." "When I was her age, I never would have been so disrespectful to my parents." |

## HOW TO IMPROVE YOUR SELF-TALK

Several strategies are often necessary to improve your self-talk by reducing hurtful thoughts and increasing helpful thoughts. Parents need to learn how to *stop* the hurtful thoughts, *challenge* them with at least one or two alternative thoughts that are possible and less hurtful, and *act* on the helpful thoughts.

### Stop

The first step in dealing with unpleasant feelings and hurtful thoughts is to recognize when they are occurring and stop them as soon as possible. Usually this is easier if you begin by practicing stopping your thought processes in less intense or less emotional situations. For example, although it may simply be too difficult to stop yourself in a confrontation with your child, you may be able to find a situation at work or in traffic where you can practice. If you stop at the dry cleaners to pick up your jacket and the person at the counter tells you that it is not back yet, you may feel yourself getting angry, and you may start to engage in hurtful thoughts. The hurtful thought may be that you cannot possibly attend the dinner tonight if you don't have this jacket. The first thing to do in this situation, that many people already know how to do, is to catch yourself at the very beginning of the hurtful thought and force yourself to stop.

*Thought stopping* refers to the practice of stopping a hurtful thought the instant you recognize that you are thinking it. In the example above, the instant you are aware that you are having a hurtful thought—when you start thinking to yourself that you simply cannot go to the dinner without the jacket—ask the clerk to go ahead and wait on the next person or simply leave the store. Some people count to themselves slowly or force themselves to take a deep breath. Doing so gives you one or two minutes when you do not have to interact with the clerk, briefly postponing the interaction and giving you time to stop your hurtful thoughts.

The earlier you begin to recognize your own thought pattern, the more quickly you can stop hurtful thoughts, and the better your chances are for regaining control of your behavior. If you become aware of your own behavior, you can often spot specific signals that warn you of approaching anger. Thoughts such as, "Oh no!" "Darn it!" "This is all I need!" or "How could you?" are all signs that you are starting to get angry. Once you are able to recognize your hurtful thoughts and stop them, you are ready to challenge these thoughts with some more realistic and positive ones.

### Challenge

Once you force yourself to stop thinking hurtful thoughts, you should challenge them with more helpful and less distressing thoughts. Examples of challenges from the dry cleaning scenario might be, "I have certainly attended lots of functions without this jacket," "No one even knows I was planning to wear this jacket," and "If I wear something else will it really ruin my evening? Of course not!"

As with thought stopping, you may want to practice the challenge step with less emotional situations than those provoked by your child. For example, in a long checkout line you might stop the hurtful thought, "Why do I always get the slowest cashier?"

| What Happened | Hurtful Thoughts | Challenging Thoughts |
|---|---|---|
| Baby is fussing for no obvious reason | "I am such a bad parent." "This baby is never happy." | "I take good care of him. All babies fuss sometimes, even when nothing is wrong." <br> "He is happy most of the time, just a little fussy at bedtime I have noticed." |
| Children are fighting over a toy | "I can't stand it when they fight!" "They hate each other!" | "I don't like it when they fight, but I can stand it and will see if they can work it out in the next few minutes." "I fought with my brother too, but I didn't hate him." |

*continues on next page*

continued

| | | |
|---|---|---|
| Child lied about grade on test | "He is always lying to me." "His teacher must think I never help him with homework." | "He tells me the truth most of the time. I wonder why this class is so hard for him?" "His teacher has not called or seemed concerned during our conferences." |
| Something gets broken at Grandma's house | "She probably thinks I can't raise my kids to behave right." "He always acts up over here to make me look bad." | "I know that my kids behave well most of the time, I guess I should have reminded them about grandma's fragile things." "I doubt he is thinking revengeful thoughts about me when he is playing, he just gets carried away." |
| Child misses curfew by an hour | "She is always so irresponsible." "When I was her age, I never would have been so disrespectful to my parents." | "She does follow most of the rules I have set." "I stayed out late a few times too when I was her age." |

and challenge it with a more helpful one, such as, "This long line will give me time to write out my errand list."

By exercising these cognitive coping skills in less emotional situations, we can begin to identify exactly when we are engaging in hurtful thoughts so that we can challenge them. Virtually all of us engage in hurtful thoughts some of the time, so the exercise is useful for almost everyone. It may take a fair amount of soul searching and time, however, before you can identify when you are engaging in hurtful thoughts about interactions with your child. Starting with less emotional situations can give you practice until you are ready to apply this strategy to your parenting situations. The third column (of chart beginning on p. 104) lists challenges to hurtful thoughts.

When you first begin to challenge your hurtful thoughts, you might come up with nice, slick reasons for why they're true, because that's the nature of hurtful thoughts—they have to be difficult to challenge, or we wouldn't believe them. But hurtful thoughts interfere with a parent's problem-solving abilities and lead to responses that may not be in the best interest of the child. Some parents have learned to carry a note card with them that lists helpful thoughts, especially those that challenge their typical hurtful thoughts. Each time they begin to experience an emotion that may interfere with their ability to handle a situation to the child's benefit, all they have to do is read the helpful thoughts to remind them how best to challenge their hurtful thoughts.

As you practice stopping and challenging hurtful thoughts, you should notice that nothing "disastrous" happens during the 10 to 15 seconds it takes you to challenge them. The situation will wait the seconds that it takes you to think about what you are doing, and the mere fact that you are able to take the extra time should help to convince you that you do have the ability to control your thinking.

## Act

When you get proficient at identifying, stopping, and challenging hurtful thoughts, you can then act on the helpful thoughts that you have generated as alternatives. For example, when your child is crying and not wanting to go to sleep, you may think, "I can't stand it when he cries at night." Your challenge to this thought might be, "He really needs to learn how to go to bed on his own, so me staying with him will not help him." Then you can act on this more helpful thought by kissing your child on the head, saying, "I will see you in the morning," and allowing him to get to sleep on his own. The fourth column (of chart on p. 108) lists actions that correspond with the helpful thoughts.

In addition to using the "stop-challenge-act" strategies yourself, you can also teach them to your child who is school-aged and older. Initially, perhaps the best way to introduce your child to helpful and hurtful thoughts is to share both with her. If your blazer isn't ready at the dry cleaners, tell your daughter what you are thinking. Let her know that you have the option of engaging in either helpful or hurtful thoughts. So, you can tell her that you were initially very disappointed that your blazer wasn't ready, but that you know you can just pick out another outfit to wear. You might even ask her to help you pick one out when you get home.

Then, when your school-age daughter says, "I can't stand it when Jennifer comes into my room," you can help her identify such a statement as a hurtful thought. You can tell her that getting upset at Jennifer would be like you getting mad at the lady who works at the dry cleaners. What you had to do with your blazer was substitute a more positive thought, which is what she has to do with the situation of Jennifer coming into her room. You might model for her the "Act" part of the strategy by saying, "You could say to yourself, 'I can stand it if Jennifer comes into my room even if I don't like it. I know she comes in because she wants to play with me. I will help her find something to do in her room or with Mom instead, then go back to my room.'" The combination of her observing you modeling stopping, challenging, and acting with difficult situations and you prompting her to stop, challenge, and act on difficult situations, will set the occasion for her to use these strategies. As with all learning, however, expect the mastery of such coping skills to take a long time for your child, and perhaps even for yourself.

| What Happened | Hurtful Thoughts | Challenging Thoughts | Action |
|---|---|---|---|
| Baby is fussing for no obvious reason | "I am such a bad parent." "This baby is never happy." | "I take good care of him. All babies fuss sometimes, even when nothing is wrong." "He is happy most of the time, just a little fussy at bedtime I have noticed." | Let him fuss until he falls asleep. Put some toys in his playpen to see if that helps with the fussing. |
| Children are fighting over a toy | "I can't stand it when they fight!" "They hate each other!" | "I don't like it when they fight, but I can stand it and will see if they can work it out in the next few minutes." "I fought with my brother too, but I didn't hate him." | Put the toy in time-out. Send each child to his room. Listen for fighting to stop so you can go in and "catch them being good". |
| Child lied about grade on test | "He is always lying to me." "His teacher must think I never help him with homework." | "He tells me the truth most of the time. I wonder why this class is so hard for him?" "His teacher has not called or seemed concerned during our conferences." | Make a note to call the teacher about his progress in the class. Take away a privilege for lying. Provide extra assistance on the next assignment to watch for problem areas. |

| Something gets broken at Grandma's house | "She probably thinks I can't raise my kids to behave right." "He always acts up over here to make me look bad." | "I know that my kids behave well most of the time, I guess I should have reminded them about grandma's fragile things." "I doubt he is thinking revengeful thoughts about me when he is playing, he just gets carried away." | Replace it. Replace it and ask the kids to pay me back out of their allowance. Bring outside toys next time you go to grandma's house. |
| Child misses curfew by an hour | "She is always so irresponsible." "When I was her age, I never would have been so disrespectful to my parents." | "She does follow most of the rules I have set." "I stayed out late a few times too when I was her age." | Take away a privilege for breaking a house rule. Ask her to come home 30 minutes before curfew next time as a consequence for being late. |

## HOW TO USE YOUR PARENT COPING SKILLS

Now that you are familiar with the basic steps for improving your self-talk and coping with common childhood issues, following are some age-specific examples of how these strategies can be applied.

### Stop-Challenge-Act With Infants

If you put your infant to bed awake but drowsy and let her cry for one or two minutes until she self-quiets, you will probably have hurtful thoughts initially, such as, "She's afraid of the dark" or "I'm afraid that she thinks that I have abandoned her." If you stop to think about it, though, it will probably occur to you that she's too little to know what "abandon" means. Rather, she's probably just grown accustomed to having you help her go to sleep at night, and she misses that help. The challenging and helpful thoughts that you can substitute would be something like, "I know that she may be unhappy for a couple of nights, but I can stand it. Once she learns self-quieting skills, she can use them the rest of her life." After you have put your baby to bed for naps for many days and your baby has been successful at settling down and falling to sleep on her own, then you will be better able to think even more self-thoughts that are helpful.

You have to discipline yourself to be able to put up with your own discomfort so that your child can learn important survival skills. Another example might involve your baby fussing because he can't reach a ball that's on the floor immediately in front of his hand. Your hurtful thought might be, "I had better help him reach that ball, or he will get too frustrated." Your helpful thought might be, "It won't hurt him to get frustrated. He has to learn that if he wants the ball, he's going to have to stretch forward enough to get to it." This thought should, of course, be followed up by the action of you not helping your child reach the ball.

## Stop-Challenge-Act With Toddlers

It's common for toddlers to be quite insistent on getting their own way and to get quite unpleasant when they don't. One context that can make you think hurtful thoughts is mealtimes. Your toddler may have a picky appetite, leading to hurtful thoughts such as, "She always eats junk. I can never get her to eat enough." More helpful thoughts might include, "Well, she did eat a good breakfast, and she typically has a good bedtime snack." Appropriate actions might include having only healthy snacks available to your child and trying to fix at least one of your child's preferred foods at every meal.

Toddlers also seem to have a talent for acting out in public. For example, when your toddler wants something at the checkout counter, and he begins to complain and fuss the instant you say no, you may have some hurtful thoughts such as, "I can't stand it when he acts up in public. I'll bet everyone in this store thinks that I can't control my child's behavior." Some challenging and more helpful thoughts might be, "I am not going to let him get the best of me today. Every toddler cries when he doesn't get his way." The appropriate action to take is simply to leave the counter without giving in to your child. (Chapter 6 discusses managing your child's behavior in public in more detail.)

Many parents have found that it is easier to work on identifying, challenging, and changing the way they react to their children when they are at home than when they are in public. So if you find it difficult to challenge these thoughts in the middle of a grocery store, you might resolve to work on your child's inability to accept the word "no" when you are at home and you don't feel nearly as much social pressure. Only after you have mastered numerous situations at home should you expect yourself to be able to successfully challenge your hurtful thoughts in a public place like the grocery store.

## Stop-Challenge-Act With School-Age Children

With school-age children, you may find that many social and academic situations provoke hurtful thoughts. When preparing to depart home for an event, for example, parents often let their children poke around and stall until the last second and then get angry. Hurtful self-thoughts at that time might be something like, "She knows that she's got to be out of here in two minutes, and she's intentionally stalling." Most children don't have the same concept of time that their parents do, though, nor do they place the same importance on being on time. A more helpful self-thought could be, "If I'm ever going to expect her to get ready in time, I'm going to have to teach her how to do things in a timely fashion." Then —and this is the hard part—you need to take action by finding times during the week when you can have your child practice getting something done on time. If your child has a hard time getting ready in the morning, work on it after school and on weekends when the stalling won't interfere with the few precious minutes you have in the morning.

It may also be useful to work on stalling in general by making attendance at a desired activity contingent on the completion of a less-desirable activity, such as chores or homework. For example, if your son has had trouble getting his chores done, require that they be done before soccer practice, and make up a plan for doing both. Figure out how much time he has available before soccer practice and how long it takes him to do his chores. Sit down with your son and come to a verbal or written agreement on when he will do each chore, and make your expectation clear: You will not leave for soccer practice, or for a soccer game, until his chores are completed.

There are numerous ways to remind your child to complete her chores, so both of you should also agree on the means of reminding, as well as the timing. Decide together how many warnings, if any, you are to give her about getting her chores done. Some children will want almost hourly reminders, and others would rather you stay out of it. She may want you to post her chores on the refrigerator door, or she may want to add her chores to the notebook where she writes down her daily school assignments.

Your child needs to be an integral part of this decision-making process. He needs to have input at every step of the way. Notice that we said reminders about chores, not reminders about when soccer practice starts. When the chores are completed, take him to soccer practice, even if he gets there halfway through the practice. It's not your responsibility to get him to practice on time, nor is it your responsibility to protect him from whatever the coach might have to say. Be sure that you do not give in to the temptation to skip the practice or the game because he will be late. It's better to go to the practice field and let him sit in the car because he doesn't want to get to practice late than to allow him to miss it completely. And if he doesn't get to practice at all, you need to have a prior agreement as to how the rest of the day or evening should proceed. For example, if his chores aren't completed on time and he doesn't get to soccer practice, it might be reasonable to add that he will not be allowed to watch TV or talk on the phone until his chores are completed.

If you feel yourself starting to engage in hurtful or angry thoughts, stop those thoughts, challenge them, and deal with the situation immediately. Seeing how well you deal with an uncomfortable situation will serve as an excellent model for your daughter. You may need to write out your helpful thought on a note card, such as "She may take a long time to learn these things now, but once learned she can use them for the rest of her life." Each time you feel yourself starting to get upset because "she knows I want her to get her chores done faster," you can take out your card and remind yourself that this is a teaching process, not something that happens in a couple of minutes. After your daughter has had 30 or 40 opportunities to get ready in time and has stalled long enough to sit out a fun activity instead of participate in it, she will probably "learn" how to move faster when you ask her to do so.

Finally, another helpful strategy to use with your school-age child or preschooler is to verbally rehearse difficult situations with your child before you actually get to them. For example, when you are parking at the grocery store, tell your child that you are not going to purchase any candy for him. Then, ask him to repeat the rule to you. After he has repeated it, then remind him, again, that you aren't going to purchase any candy for him. Then—and this is a really important component—make certain that you do not purchase any candy for him. You might even want to stop at the grocery store on the way to his favorite fast food restaurant for lunch. Tell your child that you intend to go to the restaurant after you are done at the grocery store, but if he begs for candy at the store, you will go straight home and make lunch there instead. If you make such a statement, be prepared to follow through with it.

## Stop-Challenge-Act With Adolescents

Adolescents often use situations involving social pressure to provoke hurtful thoughts in their parents. For example, a fairly common comment for a teenager to make is that if you do not allow her to attend a particular social function, she will be the only one at her school who doesn't get to go. This may set you up for hurtful thoughts such as, "Do I want my daughter to be the odd one— the only one who doesn't get to go?" "What right do I have to be so severe with my daughter?" Teenagers know how to make their parents doubt their motives—they know exactly how to provoke hurtful thoughts in their parents. A helpful thought to challenge the hurtful thought might be, "I know that she would like to go, but I also know that there won't be adequate supervision" or "I know that her feelings will be hurt if she doesn't get to go, but she'll get over it." A more general helpful thought might be, "I know that I have to make some decisions that my daughter doesn't like, and decisions that might make me feel uncomfortable, but that's my responsibility as her parent." The action to take would be to stand by your decision and perhaps encourage her to invite over another child who is not allowed to attend the function.

It is important, especially with adolescents, to have enough control over your own emotions and responses that you give yourself the necessary time to think about and weigh your options before you have to commit yourself to one plan of action. You and your adolescent may need to write out the situation and possible options. Plan what kind of hurtful thinking you might get in to, and what helpful thoughts you will use to challenge the hurtful ones. Also plan on what kind of hurtful thinking she might get into and what helpful thoughts she can use. The point of these exercises is that you address potentially troublesome situations together and proactively. And if the first couple of times you try this you or your child doesn't handle the situation very well, stick to your new strategy. The role modeling that you do for your child is invaluable. And the feeling that you experience when the strategies begin to be successful more than they are unsuccessful will reward you for all of your efforts.

## THE IMPORTANCE OF PRACTICE

Learning coping skills takes practice, just as learning almost any other skill takes practice. Although most people cannot improve their coping skills overnight, they can, with practice, learn how to recognize when they are not coping well with a situation and how to cope better. The rationale for starting out with situations that are easier for you than ones that involve your children is based on one very important fact—you will be much better able to teach your child coping skills if you have some ability to cope yourself.

Parents may be the only people we expect to be really good at a skill before they have had enough time and practice to learn it. We would never expect a child to be able to play baseball like an adult, nor would we expect a beginning photographer to be able to take the same kind of pictures as a professional. Yet when it comes to dealing with emotional situations, we, as parents, often expect ourselves to be able to handle almost anything.

The authors of a book called *Managing and Understanding Parental Anger*[1] suggest the use of worksheets to help parents identify their hurtful self-thoughts and learn more helpful self-thoughts. On these sheets, parents are to list answers to the following six questions:

1. What happened? (i.e., the situation that occurred)
2. What did you think to yourself that didn't help?
3. What did your behavior look like?
4. What could you have thought to yourself?
5. What could your behavior have looked like?
6. How could your child have handled the situation differently?

We would add a seventh question to their list: Is there an easier situation where I could begin teaching my child the same lesson? So, if you have an infant who isn't able to fall asleep alone at night, the final question might be, "Is there a less emotional situation where I could apply these same questions and help my daughter learn the skills she needs?" The answer might be, "Yes, I can teach her self-quieting skills during the day." Then, during the daytime situation, you can go through the list of questions and develop an effective action plan.

The following list is an example of how to apply the seven

questions using the situation of your adolescent who wanted to go to the social function, and in this case you gave in to her pleas:

1. What happened? *She wanted to go to a party at someone's house.*
2. What did you think to yourself that didn't help? *"Do I want my daughter to be the odd one—the only one who doesn't get to go?" "What right do I have to be so severe with my daughter?"*
3. What did your behavior look like? *I gave in and looked like a pushover. It looks like I don't think my own rules are important to follow.*
4. What could you have thought to yourself? *"I know that she would like to go, but I also know that there won't be adequate supervision." "I know that her feelings will be hurt if she doesn't get to go, but she'll get over it."*
5. What could your behavior have looked like? *I could have stood by my decision and stayed calm while she begged me to change my mind.*
6. How could your child have handled the situation differently? *By accepting "no" for an answer and finding another event to attend or having a friend over instead.*
7. Is there an easier situation where I could begin teaching my child the same lesson? *I could teach her to accept "no" for an answer more readily by saying no to situations that don't involve her social life or situations that tend to make me feel guilty. For example, I could tell say no to staying up late or watching an "R" rated movie.*

## CONCLUSION

As a parent, you will experience many negative feelings about your child as you try to manage his daily behavior as well as your own expectations about parenthood. Although it may take time and effort to learn coping skills that are useful to you when you are dealing with your child, the effort you put into it will be well worth it. The need for good coping skills starts when your child is an infant, and it is helpful to develop effective coping skills then, because you will definitely need them when your child gets older and more challenging.

If you know before you have a child or when your child is very young that you tend to have a bad temper, get started on learning coping skills before you need them—learn how to use them in situations at work or with other family members. Usually, if you can discipline yourself to use helpful thoughts instead of hurtful thoughts, you can transfer this learning to situations that involve your child. Consider taking a class or reading a book on stress management or on relaxation strategies. Begin learning how to keep your emotions in check before you have the added responsibility of dealing with the behavior of your child. You will never regret the effort that you put into learning these skills. If you find out that it is much more difficult to keep your emotions in check than you thought it would be, you may need to seek professional help.

If your child is already 8 or 10 years old, the effort on your part to learn coping skills is still vital. You will have to work together with your child before a difficult situation, during it, and after it to practice using helpful thoughts as a basis for your actions. By doing so, your child will see that you are now able to approach a situation without losing your temper or getting angry, and you will be an excellent role model for him. By experiencing and mastering difficult situations, your child will also start to build up his own confidence in his ability to deal with difficulties.

The power of your behavior during difficult situations with your child should not be underestimated. Over the years there will be many opportunities to model hurtful thoughts and ineffective ways of handling unpleasant or unfair situations. For that reason, it may not be adequate just to model helpful thoughts occasionally. Rather, you need to make a concerted effort to detail a plan for teaching your child helpful thoughts. For example, before your child participates in a sporting event, church activity, or academic project where there is even a remote possibility that she could benefit from the stop-challenge-act strategies, you should discuss and rehearse the process with her.

If you begin encouraging your child now to be more thoughtful about how he approaches potentially difficult situations, he will be much more likely to appreciate the fact that he has some control over how he reacts. As adults, most of us have had to learn how to deal with difficult situations with no assistance from our parents. If you are able to encourage your child to be more thoughtful about the difficulties she encounters, she will be much more likely to almost "automatically" use helpful thoughts instead of hurtful thoughts. You will have, in effect, taught her an adaptive way to deal with life stresses—a way that she will not have to "unlearn" later.

# Part II

## SPECIAL PARENTING TOPICS

# CHAPTER 6

# MANAGING YOUR CHILD'S BEHAVIOR AWAY FROM HOME

Taking a child out in public can create problems for parents when it comes to managing their child's behavior. One reason public settings can be trouble is that parents are easily distracted from their role as teachers, and they frequently demand a level of behavior that the children are not used to performing at home. Taking your child along with you can offer many opportunities to teach your child a variety of concepts, as well as a chance to enjoy his company as you engage in pleasurable outings or routine community activities. The grocery store offers literally hundreds of opportunities for children to learn about numbers, shapes, textures, weights, and sizes. This chapter provides guidelines for managing your child's behavior in public places such as stores, restaurants, and churches.

## USE YOUR PARENTING SKILLS

To effectively manage your child's behavior in public, you must use the parenting skills discussed in this book to teach your child what behavior you expect of her when away from home. Going public can test your knowledge of the strategies discussed so far and your ability to put them into practice.

For example, you should model good manners at restaurants and while interacting with store clerks, and you should provide positive feedback when your child is behaving the way you want him to behave. Scolding your children for fighting over who gets to ride in the cart and ignoring them as they walk quietly next to you will only reinforce the fighting. Similarly, ignoring your child as she colors contently while you talk with your spouse at the restaurant table but yelling at her when she whines about being hungry will only encourage more whining.

It is also important for you to communicate your expectations to your child and to be careful not to relax them or your discipline efforts simply because you are distracted by the activities at hand. It is very common for a toddler to reach out and grasp a candy bar while you are unloading the shopping cart at the checkout counter. You can take the candy bar away and say, in a neutral voice, something like, "No, Robert. You are not allowed to take candy from there." Do not give in to the resulting tantrum, no matter how embarrassed you are, and you will teach your child that he cannot take candy bars while in the checkout line. However, if you let him keep it or give it back to him when he starts screaming, then you are teaching him to do the same thing next time he has the opportunity.

If your child is older, take a moment to explain the rules before entering a public place. Tell her, for example, that you are going into the store to purchase some food for dinner tonight and that you will not be purchasing anything for her. You can tell her that you understand how much she may want something during this shopping trip, but that she will have to wait for another time. Tell her to please stay with you and to keep her hands off of items in the store. Then, when you are shopping, talk with her frequently and ask her to help. Repeatedly thank her for staying with you and for keeping her hands to herself.

If you are faced with having to discipline your child while in a store or other public place, you can tell your child who misbehaves to sit quietly in a particular spot for a minute or two. In the store, for example, put your toddler into the cart or choose a tile on the floor by your cart and have your child sit there. In the park, have him sit on the park bench next to where the entire family is eating. At the pool, have him sit on a chair or bench away from the water, but where he can still see the other children having a good time. The length of time is not really as important as the fact that your child knows you are going to enforce the rules when you're away from home. There are times when you may have no choice but to take him out to the car for a couple of minutes until he gets calmed down.

Don't worry about what the other people are thinking—just concentrate on getting your child's behavior under control while she's still young enough to handle. If you think it's embarrassing to have a 2-year-old act up in a restaurant, think what it's like to get the same behavior from a 10- or 12-year-old. Once the consequence is served and you are both calm, you may discuss the rule and allow your child to express her displeasure if you wish. It will then be important to both acknowledge her feelings and repeat why you have the rules you do about being in public. For example, you might say "I know that you love candy, and I do too, but that does not mean you can take it without paying for it. The rule is no stealing. You cannot do things that can get you in trouble with the store or with the police."

With an older child, you might offer a reward based on his conduct in the store. For example, you might tell him that if he stays with you and doesn't put anything extra in the shopping cart, you will allow him to stay up later that evening. The actual reward is not as important as the agreement between you and your child on the way he behaves in the store. Allow your child to help you decide the reward so that he will be more invested in following the rule.

## PROVIDE OPPORTUNITIES FOR PRACTICE

For your child to become "good" at behaving in public, she must have the chance to practice the behavior you want her to display. You should take your infant along with you to grocery stores and restaurants on occasion. At first she just rides along in her infant seat, but even this gives you an opportunity to make the trip a pleasant experience by talking to her. These trips also help the infant adjust to being around crowds, noise, and motion. As your infant sits next to you in her carrier or on your lap, you can periodically lean over and touch her gently and talk to her in a soothing voice. You will be wise to start your infant off knowing that trips to stores and restaurants are fun because Mom and Dad pay a lot of attention to her.

Your toddler can also enjoy going out in public if you set him up to succeed. First, place your child in the shopping cart or high chair so you can monitor him and keep him close enough to provide lots of positive feedback. Such monitoring and feedback are important, because many public places purposely put tempting displays where you wait in line to pay, often resulting in your child testing your reaction when he grabs the candy or toys. Do not allow your child to have the item if you want to teach him that he must ask first or that he will not always get a treat when you go to the store. If you allow him to have it to avoid a tantrum, you will be giving him lots of practice in taking things and throwing tantrums, but not in behaving in a store or restaurant.

You may be able to avoid such scenes by encouraging your child to help you shop throughout the store and unload the cart at the end. Hand the items to her one at a time and she can drop them into the cart, and describe them to stimulate her language skills. You can hand her the "bottle of ketchup," the "box of cereal," and the "bag of potato chips." Over time, your toddler will begin to identify the various items and to have positive, pleasant shopping trips.

Older children also benefit from being involved in the activities of public outings, such as the grocery shopping. Ask your preschooler to help you drop the groceries in the cart or choose between two cereals. Your school-age child may be able to go further down the row and retrieve the items on your list. If you take your young child with you to a restaurant, start with a child-friendly place with quick service. You can eventually build up to fancier restaurants that require your child to sit attentively for longer periods of time. Success in such settings, however, may require additional training.

## Training Sessions

One strategy for teaching your children appropriate behavior in public is to conduct "training sessions." For example, during a training session your children can practice appropriate restaurant behavior at home. It isn't necessary at every meal, but you should have some meals at home, perhaps once each week, when your children dress nicely, comb their hair, and practice their best manners. For many families, this is an enjoyable and festive occasion. During these special meals, parents should concentrate on exactly how each child is behaving and give feedback. Parents must model what they consider to be appropriate behavior, and they should praise positive behavior in their children. During these special meals you will concentrate on how the children are behaving for the sole purpose of teaching them how you want them to behave in a restaurant. Once you've taught your children how to behave during dinner at home, you will also feel much better about inviting guests to your house for dinner.

Training sessions can also be used any time your child has to sit for a long time in public, such as during a religious service. First, you may want to "practice" the children's part of the religious service in your home. The family can sit on the floor in the living room, just like they would be asked to do at the religious service, and you can pretend that you are the minister or rabbi. Although your child may find the pretend service quite humorous the first couple of times you practice it, he will start to take it seriously when it is obvious to him that you are taking it seriously.

Once at church, you can hold training sessions by having your child sit with you briefly, providing her with lots of positive feedback, and then allowing her to go to children's church or the day care services provided at the church. In many situations, like church services or ceremonies, it is unrealistic to expect a small child to remain attentive the whole time. That's why many public gathering places now have a nursery, so parents can participate in the activity that's drawn them there without worrying about noise from their children.

Of course, it is unreasonable to expect your child to suddenly be able to behave in church at 7 years of age if he has never had any practice sitting quietly in church. Thus, whenever you decide to teach your child how to behave in church, you should start with brief training sessions. Over a period of weeks and months, gradually lengthen the amount of time you spend in church. The way you know you've lengthened the time too soon is if your child starts acting up every time. At that point you should go back to shorter trips so that your child learns that you leave church while she's still behaving. Whatever you do, don't wait for her to misbehave each time before you leave. Also, it's unfair to others to stay through an entire service while you're nagging your child to "be quiet" or "stop that" or "sit still."

**Training Trips**

A variation of the training session is the training trip. The training trip involves taking your child out in public to a frequent destination. For example, start with a two-minute trip to a convenience store to teach your child to stay with you. When you arrive at the store, briefly state the rule—"Stay with me. I know there are so many interesting things to see here, but you need to stay with me. Don't touch things we aren't going to buy." Then lead your child into the store and down a few aisles. Be sure to provide your child with positive touches and praise for staying with you. This positive feedback should occur every 15 to 20 feet at first and then gradually be reduced to just at the end of each aisle. You should also offer your child praise and attention for not handling items on the store shelves. Then exit the store and thank him for following the rule and staying with you. You can also acknowledge how much he wanted to buy or touch something and that he did a very good job following the rules.

It does not matter whether you buy anything on these initial trips, because the purpose of the trip is to teach your child how to behave in a store. The focus of the trips should be on positive feedback and not on warnings or threats, such as "Now, if you don't stay with me here, you will get a spanking." Gradually extend the amount of time you stay in the store, and purchase something to teach your child how to wait in line appropriately. As with the training sessions, extend the training trips only to the point when you can leave before your child misbehaves, regardless of how many trips it takes your child to master the shorter trips.

## CONCLUSION

Public outings with your child can be pleasant experiences if you keep in mind that your child is learning the whole time she's there, and you are the one most responsible for what she learns. You have the tools available to teach your child not only about the types of fruit at the grocery store, but also how to be polite, follow directions, and enjoy your time together. It's impossible, of course, to include examples that are relevant to each and every parent, and the examples we offer are taken from the situations we encounter most frequently in our practice. If a certain behavior that is not covered here is important to you, try using a training session or trip to teach your child how you want her to behave. This book recommends and describes procedures that will work for you, but the decision about what behavior you want to develop in your child is yours.

If you are having significant problems taking your child out in public and these strategies do not help, you should talk with your pediatrician about a referral to a mental health professional. You may need to work on behavior at home first, such as compliance or minding, before you will be successful in getting your child to behave in public. Alternatively, you could try shopping with your child early in the morning or late in the evening, when stores are less crowded. In the meantime, you may have to structure your day so that you do your shopping and other public outings when your child is at school or with a babysitter or relative.

# CHAPTER 7

# GETTING THE MOST OUT OF TOYS, GAMES, AND SPORTS

Children and their parents spend a lot of time on recreational activities such as toys, games, and sports. These activities provide excellent opportunities to teach children language skills and social skills such as taking turns, following rules, sharing, and being a good sport. If you take a proactive approach to recreation and plan your activities and your approach to those activities in such a way that you teach your children important skills, you and your children can benefit substantially from them.

When you play with your child, one of the most important goals is that your child has fun interacting with you! Make the experience as pleasant as possible. That statement might sound obvious, as we are talking about play. But sometimes a parent will get carried away with playing the "right way" or with being so competitive that the child does not have a good time playing with his parents or participating in sporting activities. Furthermore, if the child learns from such a parent to be very competitive, she risks hurting the feelings of other children who do not appreciate her competitive nature.

This chapter discusses the importance of play and the skills it can build and provides information about age-appropriate play activities for your child. We will also give you some guidelines on your child's use of the computer and Internet for play and how best to use sporting activities to develop your child's physical and social skills and interests. Finally, we will discuss how to help the child who is not a "good sport."

## THE IMPORTANCE OF PLAY

The toys and activities parents select, and the ways children use them, can serve both immediate and long-term goals in child development. With your help, toys, games, and physical activities can assist children in learning some very important concepts such as taking turns, following directions, sharing, dealing with winning and losing, and respecting others' abilities. For example, board games are a great way to teach children the value of turn taking. You can emphasize this concept by pointing out whose turn it is and that you are all taking turns: "Now it's Kenny's turn" or "John, your turn will be after Kenny moves his piece." It is often necessary to ask the other children playing to wait until it's their turn to move.

You can also point out instances of turn taking in everyday situations. For instance, at a stop sign, you can say, "It will be our turn to go next" or "The car in front of us gets to go next." At meals, you can say, "It's Daddy's turn to use the salt and pepper" or "It's Mommy's turn to pour the drinks." You can start pointing out turn taking when your child is very young, but don't be in a big hurry for her to master this concept. If your child shows frustration at waiting, you can say, "Sometimes it's hard to be patient and take your turn, but other people wait for you when it's your turn. That's how we play together." If you praise your child when he waits and make the experience of taking turns rewarding, he will naturally want to play the game like the others. Even if it takes him many games and several months to learn how to take turns without interrupting others or getting upset when it is not his turn, once learned, this skill will be useful in many other life situations.

You can teach your child to share by regularly sharing toys with her and asking her to share her toys with you. If you are the one pouring the blocks on the floor, give half to your child and say that you are happy to "share" the blocks with her. Once you both start stacking the blocks, there will undoubtedly be times when you need another small block or another big block to complete the structure that you are working on. Ask your child, "will you please share a small block of yours with me?" Similarly, your child will find that she may not be able to build what she wants with the blocks she has, and she will have to ask you for some. You can then willingly share them as well.

Praise your child each time he shares something with you, and point out times when you are sharing with him as well. You can also encourage sharing by purchasing one toy for your children to share instead of one for each. Then, tell your children that they are to share that toy, and assist as needed with a sharing "schedule" if they choose to play separately with the toy when it is their turn.

Your child will certainly become upset if she is asked to share something that she would rather keep to herself. You can acknowledge her feelings by stating, "I know it is hard to share sometimes," but make sure you do not give in to such fussing or you will undo your work of teaching sharing skills. If parents make the sharing of toys an expectation from the beginning, their children will be much more successful with sharing when they are asked to share with other children in their home and at school.

Finally, activities can also be useful in teaching children to follow directions. For example, when you are playing basketball, point out to your child where he should stand to shoot a basket. Or instruct your child that only two cards at a time can be turned over when playing a game of Memory.

As with teaching turn taking and sharing, pointing out times during the day when you follow directions reinforces this concept. If the sign at the checkout counter says "Express Lane: Up to 10 Items," read that sign to your child and then have him help you count the items in your shopping cart. You can then tell your child that you are going to follow directions and go to a different lane because you have more than 10 items. Or, if a sign says "No Parking," point out the sign to your daughter and tell her that you will have to park in another space because that space says "No Parking."

Play can also teach children how to handle competition and how to win and lose respectably—in other words, how to be a "good sport." Children aren't necessarily born with the need to beat others at games or to pout when they do not win. Rather, it is their experience with playing games that teaches them what is important and how to act. Thus, it is important to start by playing with toys and games with your child that do not encourage competition and that do not require a winner or loser. For example, if you start with activities like puzzles, where there isn't a winner or a loser, and you do them many, many times, your child will come to enjoy engaging in the activity with you, with virtually no concern for winning or losing.

As your child's ability to play games improves, you can begin to introduce the concepts of winning and losing. Play Old Maid with your child, and after playing a number of games, begin to label the one who got the Old Maid as the "loser" and the one who did not get the Old Maid as the "winner." If your child's previous experience has been that is was fun to play Old Maid with Mom or Dad, this new labeling shouldn't make much difference, if any. A toddler playing Old Maid with a parent learns to take turns, and learns, by parental modeling, how to respond when he gets the Old Maid. If you draw the Old Maid and laugh about how you're the Old Maid now, your child learns that it's fun to get the Old Maid. If you act upset when you draw the Old Maid, then your child learns that the Old Maid should be avoided at all costs. We believe that it's only when you get exuberant about winning and losing, like giving high fives to the winner and verbal scorn to the loser, that your child will start to associate winning and losing as good and bad.

Are we being a little idealistic about game playing with children? Yes, we are. We are because we don't believe that children have to place nearly as much importance on winning or nearly as much disdain on losing as they do. Over time, practically no one will keep playing a game if she consistently loses and is subject to verbal scorn for losing. Rather, we take the position that children enjoy playing games because of the social interaction involved in the play.

Play provides a means for parents to socialize their children. From the elementary concept of taking turns to helping each other plan strategies, your child will learn, from experience, how to play the game and how to interact while playing a game. Play is a valuable tool for teaching your child the behaviors that are important to you, and these behaviors will serve him well as he plays with other children and adults.

## HOW TO CHOOSE TOYS AND GAMES FOR YOUR CHILD

Given how important play is for children, parents often wonder what kinds of toys are best to provide for their children. Parents must select from an unrelenting barrage of toys and advertising claims that every toy is not only irresistible but educational too! You need to live with a child only a short time to find out that many toys are not irresistible and that few toys, by themselves, are really educational.

Children learn through exploring, manipulating, seeing things move, and hearing things make different noises. If a child is to be kept occupied for reasonable lengths of time, and if she is to learn anything from this activity, then she needs toys that hold her attention. Thus, one of the most important considerations in selecting a toy is whether or not your child will play with it more than once, and whether or not he will play with it for more than one or two minutes at a time. Every parent has brought home a seemingly appealing toy only to find that the child does not care to play with it. It would be helpful if toy manufacturers and consumer testing groups tested toys to see which toys maintain attention. Unfortunately, there are few if any published reports saying which toys attract and hold a child's attention. Of course reports are available about the safety of toys, often based on information provided by the Consumer Product Safety Commission. Reports indicating how much children like particular toys, however, are often sponsored by the toy manufacturers rather than generated from objective research.

What, then, can parents use as a basis for decision, at least until such evaluations of toys are available? You can guess what toys your child will play with consistently by noting what toys your child has played with in the past. (We say "guess" to leave room for that fickleness of children that we've all come to appreciate over the years.) If your child plays with the same toy each time you go to a friend's house, then chances are he'll play with the same toy at home. If your daughter loves to ride on a neighbor's Big Wheel®, then buying one for her would probably be a good investment.

Some toys are used only when several kids are playing together, and some are usually played with only when a child is alone. Thus, when choosing a toy, keep in mind the play circumstances you expect for your child. If you have an only child and you find that he loves to play catch with his friends, buying him a ball will occupy his time only when he is with his friends. Parents can sometimes prompt a child to play alone with a toy by first playing with it together. This doesn't always work, but it is a good way to tell whether you can expect your child to learn to play with the toy herself. Try demonstrating the toy, but don't concern yourself with how it should "best" be used. Children frequently use toys in ways parents never dreamed of.

A good example would be giving a Monopoly® game to a younger child. Chances are he'll line up the pieces in a row or throw around the "Chance" cards. You can be sure that he isn't going to set out all the play money and begin a correct game of Monopoly, particularly if he's by himself. Independent play is an important skill to have, so do not be afraid to let your child be creative with games. You can establish the rules of the game at a different time. In fact, you can have a silly version of the game and say you are playing "Ryan's way," and then play again following the directions.

Another general guideline regarding toys is to try to limit the number your child has to select from on any given occasion. In some homes you can barely walk through the sea of toys. Children don't have time to play even momentarily with dozens of toys in a typical period of play. Parents should limit the number of toys available at one time by storing extra toys in some inaccessible place. You can then rotate them, keeping the ones your child plays with handy and storing those he doesn't play with regularly. Eventually you'll have a small collection of toys your child favors. You can find many other ideas about toys and play for children of all ages at www.kidsource.com in their handout entitled the "Toy Manufacturers of America Guide to Toys and Play," provided by the U.S. Consumer Product Safety Commission and the American Toy Institute.

Perhaps the most important concern when choosing toys is safety. The most obvious safety precaution is to require your child to use a helmet and safety pads for elbows and knees when riding a bicycle, skateboard, roller blades, or foot scooter. Bicycle accidents alone cause about 600 deaths and over 30,000 hospital admissions in the United States each year.[1] Most of the serious injuries could have been prevented with the use of safety equipment.

Whether their parents use safety equipment is probably the biggest factor in whether a child uses safety equipment. Many parents who appreciate the need for their children to use safety equipment don't use safety equipment themselves; this is tantamount to telling their children that safety equipment isn't necessary. Other safety guidelines are found in the following sections on how to pick toys and games specific to your child's age.

## PLAYING WITH YOUR INFANT

The play you engage in with your infant typically involves modeling behaviors over and over. Eventually, your infant will begin to imitate your actions and, in time, respond to your words. For example, when you pretend to hide behind a blanket or diaper pail and say "Where's Mommy?" before showing your face and saying "Peekaboo," you are playing. After doing this a couple of times, your infant will become familiar with the game and smile or laugh when you say "Peekaboo." When you play peekaboo or patty-cake with your infant and establish a rhythm that alternates your modeling a behavior with your child imitating your behavior, you are using one of the strongest teaching tools available—modeling and imitation. Each time you cover your infant's face with a cloth and say, "Where's Jennifer?" and she responds by giggling, she is in the very early stages of learning the give and take of a game. As she gets used to the game, you will notice that she begins to anticipate her part and your part. She'll probably start laughing earlier in the game in anticipation of what you are about to do. Games with infants are fun. This fun starts to set the stage for later participation in games.

You can make sure that your infant has plenty of opportunities to play by making such routine tasks as diaper changes and baths into experiences enjoyed by both parent and infant. Singing, talking about what you are doing or about nothing important, or playing peekaboo during daily tasks all count as play to your infant. Perhaps most important, you don't have to explain to an infant that you are about to play a game called peekaboo and that you expect to take turns playing the game. Rather, you begin the game, and after several repetitions, your baby knows what the game involves and willingly takes part in it. Keep in mind that the more opportunities your infant has to play, the more he will learn.

Intensity doesn't normally matter, but if too intense, the play could discourage your infant. It is best to follow your infant's cues, such as crying or reducing eye contact with you, to know when your child may need a break from play. If your child seems unhappy or restless with your attempts to interact, try some other type of interaction or simply let your child relax.

There are two considerations in selecting a toy for an infant: Will she play with it, and is it safe to play with? Many toys are available that will stimulate your infant's senses, including rattles, overhead "gyms" with various toys, and objects of different colors, textures, and sounds. Until your infant can sit up on her own, these types of toys are usually very visually stimulating without much effort from your infant or can be easily grasped and explored with her mouth.

Once your infant can sit up, sturdy cardboard picture books, stacking rings, cups, or blocks can provide stimulation and help with fine motor development. These are just some ideas of the toys infants typically enjoy playing with. You can also experiment by providing your child with other types of toys, but remember to consider safety.

There are many obvious dangers that you should be aware of for all toys. Stay away from toys with lead paint on them, those with sharp points or small pieces that might be swallowed or inhaled (such as the cute eyes on some dolls or stuffed animals), or those that have plastic beads inside them. Damaged beanbags should be either repaired or discarded immediately, because infants and children can easily inhale the small beans.

Many experts recommend the use of a "choke tube," which is simply a cylindrical piece of plastic; if a toy or a part of a toy will fit inside the choke tube, then it presumably will fit in a child's throat. A good substitute for a choke tube is the cardboard center from a roll of toilet paper, which is almost identical in size to a choke tube. Another consideration is the flammability of a toy, although it's almost impossible for a parent to tell whether the composite materials of a toy are flammable. For that reason, sources of combustion or flame must be controlled in homes with children.

The most important safety tip for infants and playing is to provide them with constant supervision. The toys of older children are often within reach of their infant siblings, presenting frequent dangers that require your vigilance.

## PLAYING WITH YOUR TODDLER OR PRESCHOOLER

As with an infant, you can use routine activities with your toddler or preschooler as times for play. You can engage a young child who has his shirt pulled halfway over his head in a playful interaction by commenting, "Where's John, where's John?" Similarly, you can "race" your preschooler as a means of getting him to help you pick up his toys, or you can sing a toy-picking-up song.

In addition to using routine activities as play times, you can also engage your young child in simple interactive games such as hide-and-seek or tag. It is important to keep the game simple enough that your toddler can play it, yet difficult enough that there's some challenge to it. Your child should be able to find you or catch you easily until her skill at the game increases. If you make the game too difficult, you're likely to discourage her, and she will not learn to enjoy playing games.

If you find that your toddler is really competitive, you can change games a little to remove the competition. For example, when playing a board game such as Candy Land®, you can help each other with every move so that you both win instead of one of you winning and one of you losing. You can explain to your child that it's important to play the game "together" first until you both know all of the rules and strategies. It's also fun to be able to talk about the game after it's over, both between yourselves and when Dad or Grandma and Grandpa get home. Often you'll find that your child enjoys talking about the game later as much as participating in it.

By the time your child is a preschooler, he can start to play more physical games like baseball as well as games that require more skill, such as checkers. Choose games that encourage turn taking and perhaps a small amount of strategy. For example, preschoolers can typically learn how to play Go Fish and use the "strategy" of asking for different cards when it is their turn. A younger child, on the other hand, may keep asking, "Do you have any kings?" over and over simply because she has three of them and wants the fourth. Playing games that require good social skills like sharing and turn taking and some strategy will build the basic skills required to play the more advanced board games like Monopoly and Sorry!®.

## Playing to Win

Again, it is important that you emphasize how much fun it is to play the game and avoid emphasizing winning or losing. Thus, do not worry about whether to let your child win or whether it's wrong always to beat your child if you can. Simply agree to play for a certain period of time, and then either put the game away or save it for later when the amount of time you agreed to play has passed. In this manner, your child will learn to place much less emphasis on who wins and will be more likely to simply enjoy playing the game. Playing until a specified time has lapsed is also beneficial when you are playing a game and your child's bedtime arrives. Instead of pleading his case to finish the game (to stay up later), your child will have learned to just set the game aside and finish it later.

If children's early years are spent enjoying games without concern for who is the winner, most children can then accept both playing to win and playing until a certain amount of time has passed. As your child matures, you will need to introduce the "rules" of a game, which may then result in a "winner." When it comes to whether or not you play by the rules, it's probably more important that you agree to the rules before you start each game. In this way, you can experiment with many different sets of rules, rather than one set. Once you begin playing a game by a given set of rules, however, it's preferable to continue with those rules rather than to allow your child to change the rules on a whim.

If your child becomes upset because she's not doing well in a game, it is a wonderful opportunity for her to practice some of the coping skills that we have discussed throughout this book. For examples of coping skills related to how a child uses helpful or hurtful thoughts, see chapter 5. Chapter 9 covers skills on self-quieting. Games are an excellent example of a naturally occurring activity that parents can use to help their children learn coping skills. You can tell her that you see how upset she is about losing, prompt her to use coping strategies when it's her turn, and praise her for her efforts at trying to use her coping skills.

The use of discipline while playing a game is appropriate for behavior that involves blatant rule violations or not being a good sport. But any time you feel the need to discipline your child while playing a game, make sure that it's because he will not follow your established ground rules and not because he isn't doing well in the game. Once again, ideas for helping a child who does not cope well with games are discussed later in this chapter.

### Playing to Teach Language Skills

Playing with your toddler or preschooler gives you an opportunity to encourage language development through the liberal use of simple verbal descriptions of what you and your child are doing. You can describe how the train is going "around the corner" and "under the bridge" and "stopping to let the other train go." In this way, you are pairing appropriate speech with the activity your child is engaging in. If you are playing with a doll, you can describe the color of her clothing, as well as what she is doing.

Similarly, if your child is stacking blocks, describe each of the moves your child makes in stacking the blocks. For example, "You placed the white block on the floor. Now, you're putting the green block on top of the white block. Now, the blue block next to the white block, and the black block on top of the green block. All of the blocks just fell over. Now, you're back to the green and black blocks to stack." Your child will be hearing about colors, shapes, sizes, spatial concepts, and sequencing as a natural part of the play. Over time and with repeated playing, your child will begin to spontaneously describe what she is doing based on the descriptions she has heard you using.

It is best to concentrate your narration on the actual physical moves, rather than strategies, and to leave out any details about whether your child is playing the game "properly." The key to this type of play is to discipline yourself to use simple declarative statements about what you and your child are doing, instead of commands that your child can then either follow or not follow. Using simple declarative statements and keeping demands, interrogations, and instructions to a minimum will almost eliminate the possibility of your child failing to comply with your requests.

## Toys for Toddlers and Preschoolers

The toys that toddlers and preschoolers are most likely to play with are construction toys, such as blocks; creative–artistic toys, such as crayons, Play-Doh®, soap bubbles, and watercolors; and mobile toys that can be ridden or pulled. Children of this age like to use their creativity and begin to engage in lots of imaginary play. Thus, having a wide variety of toys available for them to create their own play scenarios can help them to develop their skills. Young children also like to be active, so providing toys such as balls, wagons, and tricycles can help to develop gross motor skills. In selecting toys, consider some findings we identified in our research[2]:

- There was no relationship between cost and use; low-cost items such as crayons and bubbles fared very well.
- Age recommendations given by the manufacturers were unreliable; toys marked for older children were found to be popular with younger children and vice versa. Most age estimates are just guesses.
- The sex of a child is as important as age in toy appeal; girls preferred artistic toys and boys preferred construction toys, but both kinds of toys were popular with the other sex as well.
- Some toys quickly attracted children but did not hold their attention for long. Watch for this when you're in the store,

because toys that are cleverly packaged to attract children's attention are not necessarily toys they will play with.

- Some toys look safe on the outside but when broken expose a variety of hazards.
- Some toys and games naturally encourage social play; examples were playing cards and finger paints.
- Some toys naturally encourage solo play; some noted were Tinkertoys®, crayons, Play-Doh, and toys that make a sound or speak when a string is pulled.

These findings suggest that children like a variety of toys for a variety of reasons. It is not important to spend lots of money on toys or to make sure your child has the latest, greatest toy being advertised on TV. With your modeling and reinforcement, children can learn to use any type of object as a toy and to use their creativity to supply the fun. There's an old expression that children will play with the box that a toy comes in as much as they will with the actual toy. This can be as true today as it was many years ago, as long as children are having fun with the toys they are given. Once again, part of that fun is the opportunity to play with them with you.

## PLAYING WITH YOUR SCHOOL-AGE CHILD

By the time your child reaches school age, he should have hundreds of hours of time spent playing with you. He should look forward to playing games with you—not because he wins or loses, but because he simply enjoys the activity. Many of the games school-age children play require strategies. Whether it's chess, Life®, or Monopoly, children have to learn both the rules of the game and the strategies necessary to progress in the game. To build these skills in your child, initially play the game as partners. If you are playing something like checkers or Monopoly, instead of making it competitive, start out by playing the game with your child, not against her. When you are making a move in checkers, talk out the ramifications with your son, and when it's his turn, do the same thing. If you are playing Monopoly, help each other make decisions about how to proceed. You can discuss whether or not to purchase a particular piece of property and, if purchased, what you or your child will do with it.

You can also draw verbal references between games played across time. If you have all three of the "red" properties (Illinois, Indiana, and Kentucky), remind your daughter that she had all three of them the last time you played. Discuss with her, once you have all three red properties, how much you will have to mortgage to build hotels on them. Talk about how perhaps it's more realistic to put just one or two houses on them and wait for someone to land on the properties who can, by paying rent, help you purchase more houses. This will give you the opportunity to discuss strategies and take the pressure off of winning. Games can quickly become something that you literally play "*together*."

Try to convey that games are games and that as soon as one is finished, you can play another. Also, try to put off competitive play as long as possible. Once you start truly competitive play, it's often hard to go back to the simple play that you and your child enjoyed so much. If you are throwing basketballs, you can start by playing "horse" together. Each time either one of you makes a basket, you add a letter to the word. It's only after you have played horse many times that you would even consider competing with your child to finish spelling "horse" before he does. Children will have lots of exposure to competition outside the home. Allow them to safely build their noncompetitive skills in your home to help them succeed once they begin to feel the pressure to win.

The likes and dislikes of school-age children vary greatly when it comes to "toys." Some children enjoy recorded music or instruments, books, and board games. Those who enjoy sports may prefer football, basketball, or soccer equipment. Many school-age children begin to develop lifelong hobbies or even career interests as they explore with science sets, crafts, and electronic toys. This is also a good age to encourage physical play using bicycles, skates, and scooters, with the appropriate safety gear in place, of course. The interests of school-age children often follow popular themes on TV or those of their friends. They may enjoy a series of books by an author or a games based on a popular TV show.

You can also contact your child's teachers to see what they are talking about in class and try to build play activities around these topics. For example, one of the teachers in our area gave her class an assignment to identify numerous trees by both their common name and their scientific names. Parents then took their children to the local nursery and made a game out of finding the names on the trees and collecting sample leaves for their project scrapbooks. Similarly, if your child learns about an activity through scouting or through a church group, follow up on that activity at home. Almost any time that your child is engaged in an activity that is supported by both her teacher and her parents, she will find the activity more interesting.

In addition to providing toys and sporting goods, it's a good idea to encourage your child to sample new activities. For example, you might go to a local recreation area and rent a small boat for an hour on several occasions. You may find that after enough time has passed, your child develops a preference for a new activity that you can also enjoy. Depending on where you live, the line of activities is almost limitless, from trips to the library to spectator and participation sports.

## GUIDELINES FOR PLAY WITH COMPUTERS, VIDEO GAMES, AND TV

### Computers

We've seen children who would play on the computer, with games, and on the Internet, for much of their waking day if they were able to. This is unacceptable and potentially damaging. There is adequate research now to demonstrate that the more time children spend on computers, the less time that they spend socializing with other people. Because the use of the computer can be so addictive and time consuming, you must establish rules before purchasing one. Your child is most likely to be willing to agree to limits if you make this agreement a condition for the purchase of the computer.

The use of an actual written contract for the terms of the use of the computer is an excellent idea for children 8 to 10 years of age or older. Such a contract should specify the number of hours per day and per week the child can use the computer and what types of sites he can access, and it should stipulate that you, as the parent and the owner of the computer, have the right to monitor the programs and Web sites your child can access. You can ask for your child's thoughts about how much time is acceptable and allow him to show you the Web sites he enjoys. The other aspects of the contract such as the monitoring and off-limit Web sites, however, should be nonnegotiable.

Most professionals also recommend putting your computer with Internet access in a very public area like the kitchen or the family room, preferably out in plain sight and not hidden in a corner. Most ISPs (Internet service providers, the companies that provide Internet access) have "filters" that can automatically block access to undesirable sites including pornography, gambling sites, and hate and violence sites. If your child objects to the use of such filters, then sell her computer or find a way to use a password for the family computer. The Internet offers such ready access to undesirable sites that you can't compromise on the use of filters.

Even with these rules in place, children may still have access to sites that seem innocent but can be cause for concern, such as chat rooms or sites that have found ways around the filters. *Chat rooms* are sites that can be accessed via the Internet where computer users can write messages back and forth in real time. In other words, when one child types, another child can read what is being typed and then answer back. Some of the problems encountered with chat rooms have included adults with suspicious purposes pretending they are children; other children, such as potential runaways, looking for mischievous activities; exposure to sites that carry pornographic images of adults and children; and exposure to hate groups and violence. With over 350 million Web sites already in use as of early 2001, there are virtually no limits to what can be accessed over the Internet. If your child does come across undesirable Web sites, encourage her to come to you. Take the time to discuss her feelings about what she saw, as well as your objections to the site and the dangers that lurk there. The best strategy is to use filters and monitor your child's computer time.

Many parents have arranged for their children to have access to the Internet, only to be disappointed that their children either accessed undesirable sites or ran up expensive long-distance phone bills. For these reasons, it's better to be proactive than reactive. Be careful to frequently monitor your child's use of the computer. It is also important to limit the amount of time you allow your child to spend on the computer to be sure he is not using it in place of social interactions. The amount of time you allow should depend on how your child is functioning in school, at home, and socially. If the computer can be used only after all homework is completed, your child continues to be active in school activities, organized sports, or church groups, and the use is carefully monitored, a few hours each day should be the absolute maximum.

### Video Games and TV

Similar guidelines and restrictions should be considered for video games and TV viewing. These activities, done in excess, also create problems for children and should thus be monitored and reduced if necessary. One recent study showed that when children's TV and video game use was decreased from 15 hours per week to 7 hours per week, there was a significant decrease in their aggressive behaviors at school.[3] In addition to TV and video game restrictions, the children in the study were instructed in alternative ways to spend the time that they were not using to watch TV or play video games. Until more such studies are done, the only viable conclusion parents can draw is that they need to monitor their children's activities and help them participate in a variety of activities besides excessive media viewing.

In addition to keeping your child's involvement with TV and video games at a reasonable length, you should also monitor what your child is watching or playing. Research any rating systems being used by your TV company or the video game company to determine which shows are appropriate for your child. Watch the TV programs and video games with your child. Also, decide ahead of time how much TV you are going to allow your child to watch and then, on a nightly or weekly basis, sit down with your child and review either the TV section from the Sunday newspaper or *TV Guide*. Decide what show she can watch at what time. If she, with your approval, selects a cartoon on the Disney channel, turn the TV on just in time for the show. At the end of the show, turn the TV off. This is a good way for your child to learn how to ration the amount of TV she watches. If you choose to use the TV to entertain your child for an extended period of time while you complete tasks, it is best to have him watch movies on videotape or DVD that are appropriate for his age instead of allowing him unsupervised access to all available TV stations. Of course, a better choice may be to have your child play outside or engage in quiet, independent activities such as coloring or puzzles. If your child does not have good independent play skills (other than watching TV), chapter 10 has suggestions for building these skills.

## GUIDELINES FOR SPORTING ACTIVITIES

Parents typically have many questions when they consider enrolling their children in a sporting activity. This section provides you with some guidelines on when to start your child in a sporting activity, the risks involved with physical sports, and ways to make sure your child benefits from participation in sporting activities.

### Starting Children in Organized Sports

The American Academy of Pediatrics recommends waiting until children are 6 years old before beginning team sports because they do not understand the concept of teamwork until this age.[4] They advise free play until then. "Free play" refers to, for example, throwing a ball or shooting baskets without division into teams or competition. Children's physical build also determines their ability to perform in certain sports. In puberty, boys gain more muscle mass and, therefore, more strength. This means that the less physically mature boy is at a disadvantage and may have an increased risk of injury and discouragement. Parents should encourage late-developing teens to compete in individual sports such as swimming and martial arts until their bodies have caught up with those of their peers.

Age, weight, and size should not be the only measures when deciding whether to compete in a sport at any given level. A child's emotional maturity is also important. Although no child should be pushed into a sport that he is not physically or emotionally able to handle, if he has a strong interest in a sport, then it might be proper to allow participation.

In recent years, sports participation for girls has been encouraged as strongly as sports for boys. By participating in sports, girls can gain self-confidence and a healthy respect for physical fitness. Until puberty, boys and girls often compete together because they are about the same weight and size. Girls generally enter puberty between 10 and 12 years of age, although recent studies suggest that the onset of puberty for girls is occurring earlier. After puberty, boys have an advantage in both strength and size. Therefore, after puberty, boys and girls may no longer compete against each other in most sports. However, if there are no teams for girls in a certain sport, some state laws allow girls to compete for a position on boys' team.

These suggestions are not meant to limit boys or girls and the athletic ability they aspire to achieve. You will most likely have to use your knowledge of your child's strengths and weaknesses to determine which sport to encourage. Be careful not to use your child to fulfill your own needs, however, and listen to her requests and ideas for activities to pursue.

## When Your Child Wants to Quit a Sports Program

A child has the right to share in the decision to end his involvement in a sport. If your child talks to you about his desire to quit a sports program, gather as many facts as possible. Talk with your child, and ask why he wants to quit. There may be a blunt and simple reason, such as not getting along with the coach or the frustration of never playing in competitive games. Sometimes a child doesn't really want to quit as much as he would like to have a new coach or simply needs some verbal encouragement and validation from you that he should keep trying. Many times, a child will say that he doesn't want to play "that stupid game" more because he's sad about his dismal performance than because he really doesn't enjoy playing it.

As a parent, there are many times when you should just allow your child to vent without responding immediately. If you wait 30 minutes, you may very well find that she willingly admits that she was just discouraged by the outcome of the game but that she wants to keep playing it. Had you pushed her to discuss the game right after the conclusion, she may have felt much more obliged to ridicule the game, and then you would feel like you had to argue with her about it. Most interactions like this one can wait a half hour or more before being discussed, with the result that the discussion is much more productive.

If your child seems serious about wanting to quit, talk to other parents of team members to get more information. Observe your child while he plays the sport. Look for signs of stress related to participation, such as nausea, loss of appetite, or headache. Does your child seem to be depressed—sleeping more than usual or acting lethargic or withdrawn? These symptoms may suggest that the degree of stress is great enough to warrant withdrawing from the sport. If not, it may be best to encourage your child to stay with the activity until the end of the season to teach him the importance of commitment to others and to himself.

If your child wants to stop her involvement not only in organized sports but also in other organized activities, such as church groups and scouting, you need to explore whether your child might be depressed or at least emotionally vulnerable. An office visit with your pediatrician or the school counselor might be a good idea to see if more serious problems are present.

It is best to base your decision on what your child says and what you hear and observe. Remember that children have to learn how to decide when to quit as well as when to stick it out. Use this as an opportunity to assist your child in gathering facts before making a decision. Allow him to quit some activities and to stay with some until the end of the season. That way he can learn to trust his own judgment about when an activity is suited to his interests and abilities.

### Risks Related to Sporting Activities

INJURY. Despite safety measures such as protective padding and helmets, the risk of injury is present in all sports, and you and your child should be aware of the risks involved with the sports activity you choose. Some sports pose a greater risk than others, with football leading the list. The chance of injury increases with the degree of contact in each sport. Sports with a risk for significant injuries include football, wrestling, gymnastics, soccer, basketball, and running. Boxing involves a high risk of brain damage; therefore, children should not be allowed to participate in this sport. Horseback riding also has the potential for risk. About 20% of injuries to young riders are to the central nervous system, including cerebral contusions, concussions, or skull fractures.[5]

Most sports injuries involve the soft tissues of the body, not the bony skeleton. In fact, only about 5% of sports injuries involve fractures.[6] Two thirds of all injuries involve sprains and strains. Sprains are injuries to the ligaments, which connect one bone to another, and strains are injuries to the muscles. Knee injuries are the most common serious injury in major sports.

If your child wears protective equipment, she will minimize the potential for many sports injuries. Teach your child that wearing protective gear will increase his long-term enjoyment of the sport, and do not allow him to play without it.

OVERSCHEDULING. Children, like adults, can handle participation in only so many activities at one time. Research has shown that children benefit from participation in structured, adult-supervised activities, but as a parent, you need to continuously monitor the number and types of activities that your child is involved in and help her to see when she is overcommitted or overscheduled. We have always said that the first activity that a child should be involved in is her family. If the family is functioning well, with an equitable distribution of responsibilities and effort and with adequate time to do things together, then she can add a second activity.

It is also important to consider academic performance when deciding how many activities your child should be participating in. A child who is having trouble in the classroom still needs all the benefits of exercise, competition, and a sense of accomplishment. Sports may be the only avenue of success in a child's life, at that time, and it could be harmful to take it away. Thus, when considering limiting or ending your child's involvement in sporting activities, you should first look for the other causes of poor classroom performance. Conflicts with a job or other activities might be one problem; too much TV watching or video game playing might be another cause. In some cases, the family and school may decide that the child is not studying enough. In this situation it is reasonable to make sports involvement dependent on achieving better grades. If the school has rules that forbid your child from participating because of his academic performance, help him to achieve academically rather than complaining about the rules.

Only when family, school, and one activity are well balanced should you consider allowing your child to take on another activity. If your child seems stressed or irritable or is losing interest in activities at home or away from home, talk with her about her schedule and see if an alteration is needed to allow her to relax and have more free time. Remember, it is just as important for your child to learn independent play skills as it is for her to learn how to participate in group events like sports.

SPORTS-RELATED STRESS. The main source of stress in young athletes is the pressure to win. Sadly, many coaches and parents place winning above the values of learning and play. Measure your child's performance by the yardstick of effort; a young athlete should set goals and then strive to fulfill them. He will respond better to rewards for trying hard or for gaining skills than to punishment and criticism for losing.

Stress can also occur in sports, or in any competitive activity for that matter, when a child realizes she is not as good as her peers in the activity. Children can have a difficult time coming to terms with the fact that they are not as good as they want to be, or that others are better than they are no matter how hard they try. It can also be difficult for you as a parent to hear your child putting himself down in such situations. As with many of the issues in this book, your child will have to learn to cope with such feelings. You can be helpful, perhaps indirectly, by following the many strategies in this book that emphasize building your child's skills, taking time for positive interactions, and modeling appropriate coping skills yourself.

More directly, allow your child to talk about her frustrations and feelings of disappointment. See if she will allow you to problem solve with her about the best solution to the issue, such as trying a new sport, practicing more, or finding a different team. If she is not ready to take action, simply be there for her, encouraging her efforts and not focusing on her performance, until she succeeds or is willing to try something new.

Learning to cope with stress is an important part of growing up and an important part of participation in sports. To help your child to learn to cope with the stress of participation in a sport, make certain that you maintain an open line of communication with him. When you hear him making initial comments about his participation or the outcome, be alert for whether he is engaging in helpful thoughts or hurtful thoughts. From the very beginning, try to help him to use helpful self-statements. When you hear him talking about his participation, be mindful of what he is learning in the long run.

Participation in sports is one more opportunity for you to model helpful thoughts for your child. For example, if she is on a losing team, you can state, "It's hard to lose a game, but it's not the end of the world" or "I don't like to lose in competition, but I know that I can stand it." Children hear what their parents have to say and often pattern their own statements after the statements their parents have made. It's also helpful to emphasize the benefits of playing in and of itself, regardless of whether one wins or loses. For example, you could say to your child, "I know it can be hard to lose, but it's fun being with the other kids on the team anyway."

EXPOSURE TO AGGRESSION AND VIOLENCE. Participation in sports does not necessarily mean that your child will be exposed to aggression or violence. However, if the level of competition means that the children with whom your child is playing are trying to win at any cost, including unnecessary violence, it's probably time for you and your child to decide whether continued participation in that sport is in his best interest. Furthermore, sometimes it is the parents, along with the children, who are modeling aggression or violence related to sporting competition. In some communities parents have participated in extremely violent behavior toward coaches, referees, or other parents when they perceived that their children were not being treated "fairly." This is not a lesson that you want your child to learn from sports.

If you feel yourself getting too emotionally involved in your child's success or failure in sports, you need to step back from the situation for a moment to determine exactly why you want your child involved in the sport. If the answer is that the winning is very important to you, you may want to try to figure out why you are reacting so competitively. For example, as a child, did you experience a lot of pressure from your parents to win? Do you feel that your child's performance somehow reflects on you? Such reflection may help you set a better example for your child. You should consider not attending her events for a while to allow yourself some time to put the participation in its proper perspective. You may also want to re-evaluate with your child the appropriateness of the activity and the lessons it is teaching you and your child.

## HELPING THE CHILD WHO IS A "POOR SPORT"

Teaching children about winning and losing is a long process. Children (and adults) can be quite devastated by losing at activities that are important to them. When your child is calm, engage him in discussions about how it feels to win and lose. Ask for examples of times when he, as well as other people he knows, has won and lost to help him see that no one wins or loses all the time. School-age children and adolescents may even appreciate an example from your childhood when you were upset about losing, as long as you keep the story short.

Parents have frequently asked us what to do with children who can't stand to lose a game. These parents often felt it necessary to stop playing games with their children because the children got too upset when they weren't winning or quit games prematurely. This is probably exactly the wrong approach to take, because it's not possible to keep your child from playing games the rest of her childhood just because she is a sore loser. Rather, it's important for all children, but particularly children who are sore losers, to have many, many opportunities to play games under their parents' supervision. If children have a particularly difficult time losing, it's probably because they have seen too much attention focused on winning and losing and too little attention focused on the enjoyment that comes from playing games.

If your child can be considered a poor sport, you might want to start by limiting your game playing to games like puzzles and blocks that don't have any winners or losers. During these initial training games, make sure that the atmosphere is pleasant and conducive to both of you enjoying the game. Point out during the game how much fun it is, and at the end of the game, observe that a good time was had by all. Refrain from any comments that could be construed as praise or condemnation for winning or losing.

At the next level, try activities that you aren't particularly good at so that any chance of you unwittingly encouraging competition is eliminated. For example, you might try roller skating or ice skating, an activity that most parents are not particularly great at and that children often enjoy doing. If you find it a little humbling that you can't skate well, it means that you chose an appropriate activity to engage in with your child. While you are skating, refrain from any kind of competition like racing. If your child keeps asking you to race, point out that you enjoy skating, not racing. In time, your child should get the idea that you came to skate, not to race.

Later, you might want to introduce a game like Old Maid or Go Fish that is totally dependent on chance and that can be played fairly quickly. Because games are brief and depend on chance, the importance of winning and losing is minimized and a new game can be started immediately. While playing, refrain from any comments about how many games either of you have won or lost.

When you begin to introduce more competitive games, you need to prepare your child by pointing out, verbally, how well he did playing the card games and skating. Verbally rehearse with him that you are going to play, for example, five games of checkers and that you expect to start a new game as soon as the previous one is completed. Don't take unnecessarily long to make your moves

—doing so makes you appear more competitive. Provide lots of verbal encouragement and praise for the strategies that he implements, and explain each of your moves in terms of the strategy involved, not the winning or the losing.

Over time, and after playing many, many games, you should find that your child is beginning to enjoy playing games with you independent of whether she wins or loses. Make comments about the games at other times directed at how enjoyable the games were, and not at who won and who lost. Whenever she loses a game and handles it well, make sure that you provide her with a lot of praise, and then drop the topic and start another game.

Some children, particularly those who really lack self-quieting skills, will still find it difficult to lose a game. You need to prepare such a child before starting a game by helping him identify which strategies he intends to use if he finds that he is getting upset over losing the game. If he decides, for example, that he is going to practice "blowing his bubbles," then get the bubbles out before the start of the game, and both of you practice. Then, just before you start the game, ask him, again, what strategy he is going to use when he feels that he is starting to get uptight. Strategies such as the "blowing his bubbles" one used here are discussed in detail in chapter 9.

There's a good research study on a high school age student who got so mad during tennis matches that he would fling his racket, thereby getting himself disqualified.[7] In the research study, his parents were given an auditory "cue" that they could use to let him know when they noticed that he was starting to get mad—a loud clicking noise from a small metal "cricket." Interestingly, the first couple of times the parents made the clicking noise, the boy said that he didn't understand why they were doing it. It was only after numerous matches that he began to agree with his parents about when he was starting to get upset. The fact that he was able to identify the feeling that immediately preceded his getting mad made it much easier for him to use his anger management strategies. After he had some practice identifying the precursors, he was able to get his anger under control.

In addition to helping your child identify what to do when she is angry, take time to discuss with your child why she gets angry, especially if your child is school-age or older. You may find that she has some underlying anxiety about wanting to please you or other stressors such as school performance that are simply being expressed in anger about losing (or in bragging about winning). Younger children may not be able to express themselves and may be upset just because they have poor coping skills. Older children, however, may have additional reasons for their negative behaviors, which are worth exploring with a calm and timely discussion or two. Remember, the point of such discussions is for you to mainly listen to your child and ask what you can do to help. Unsolicited advice at these times is often not appreciated and can cut the conversation short. Focus on helping your child problem solve instead of being critical or trying to solve the problem yourself.

## CONCLUSION

If approached in a sensible, deliberate fashion, toys, games, and sports can go a long way toward promoting the goals that you have set for your children. You can use games and sports to teach your child to take turns, to share, and to follow directions. Games and sports can also be used to teach violence and competition, so be careful to assess what each activity truly teaches your child. If you are careful to assess what a particular sport is teaching your child, you can make sure that his involvement complements what you are teaching him at home. Check out the sport and the coach before you enroll your child. Be sure you are comfortable with the level of competition that is expected of your child. Sports and games that encourage fierce competition may not teach your child the value of personal strengths and weaknesses or humbleness. Verify the safety and age appropriateness of toys and allow your child to be creative in playing with them. Play games with your children before you allow them to play the games with each other and with their friends. In short, you can help to cultivate your child's interests in a way that also supports the goals you have set for your child as she enjoys herself and interacts with the world.

# CHAPTER 8

# DEALING WITH DIVORCE

One of the most devastating things that can happen to a couple with children is to get a divorce. Try as many couples will, some just cannot make their marriages succeed. When this happens, there are always questions about how the divorce is going to affect the children. In addition to the hurt and confusion caused by the divorce, sometimes a precipitating situation before the divorce, such as an addiction problem or abuse, compounds the negative impact on the children.

Obviously, children are hurt by the fact that their parents are no longer living together as a family. Once parents are divorced, the children will almost always have to be "shared" during holidays, birthdays, and other special events, spending separate time with their two parents. Such arrangements may take them away from their friends or familiar surroundings and routines. Children may also be exposed to negative exchanges between their parents that cause them to feel anxiety, fear, confusion, anger, or depression. Unfortunately, everything from daily events to the child's emotional state is typically affected by divorce. If both parents commit to conduct the divorce and ensuing interactions with the best interests of their children in mind, however, the negative impact can be decreased for most children.

Divorcing parents can address a number of issues to minimize the detrimental effects of their divorce on their children. These include taking steps to reduce conflict and avoiding inappropriate communication with the children, including any attempts to use them as spies or messengers. How parents handle the divorce and the issues surrounding it makes a big difference in how damaging the situation will be for their children.

## REDUCING CONFLICT

Children suffer the most when their parents are in constant conflict with one another, whether their parents stay together or get divorced. Because conflict is one of the main reasons couples get divorced, the risk is high for continued conflict after the divorce. Frequent areas of conflict include arguments about what time the child should be picked up and dropped off at the other parent's home, whether the child should be enrolled in a particular sport or another, and whether a child should receive elective medical care.

It is the conflict, rather than the parents' marital status, that produces adverse effects on children. Thus, although ideally parents who are divorcing would try to be amicable, talk about things peacefully, and never engage in negative behaviors around their ex-spouse, this situation frequently does not exist, especially in the beginning. The following suggestions are provided to help you protect your child from distress.

### Put It In Writing

One effective way to minimize conflict is for parents to arrive at a written agreement regarding custody, times of changes, places of changes, and such, and then stick to that agreement as much as humanly possible. For example, if Dad is supposed to pick the children up at 6:00 p.m. at Mom's house, then Dad (or his representative) should be there at 6:00 to pick them up, and they should be ready to be picked up. Generally, pickup and drop-off times should be kept as short as possible—literally, a minute or two. Certainly, some parents might be able to maintain a friendly exchange, but for many parents, such an exchange is much easier to achieve if the interactions are fairly short and to the point. We recommend that Dad not come into the house and socialize with Mom. Mom's social life and Dad's social life are no longer the other parent's business. Also, the less you know about what your ex-spouse is doing, the less judgmental you will be.

One viable alternative is to agree to change physical custody via the school. Dad can drop the children off at school on Monday mornings, following his weekend custody, and he can pick them up from school on Friday afternoons. In this way, there is less contact between the parents and less opportunity for negative interactions or violence. Or find a public place such as a fast food restaurant that is conveniently located between both households and simply have your child move from one car to the other. You may also need to send a representative in your place if you or your ex-spouse has difficulty keeping conflict to a minimum.

Written agreements are especially useful regarding holiday visitation schedules. Many parents have asked their attorneys to amend the written agreement to the divorce decree to include these arrangements so that it becomes a part of the permanent court record. Then, in the event of a substantive disagreement, the court has a written record of what the parents agreed to. You can write these agreements for an extended period of time so that there is a reduced need for renegotiations each year as the holidays approach. For example, the holiday season can be defined as the time from noon on December 23rd until noon on December 27th. On odd-numbered years the children will spend the holidays with their Dad, and on even-numbered years the children will spend the holidays with their Mom. In this way, parents can make plans for the holidays as much as an entire year in advance with the knowledge that there won't be any haggling over when the children spend time with each parent.

With such arrangements, the fact that the parents came to an agreement and are willing to abide by it is far more important than who sees the children when. In families where one parent must work during the major holidays, for example, if Mom is a physician, nurse, or emergency medical professional, written agreements are almost essential for minimizing or avoiding conflict or disagreements over when the children spend time with each parent. Should a discussion arise in your extended family about the holidays, it's important to remember when your child is going to be with you. Far too often, one parent will make arrangements with their siblings or parents that necessitate getting the ex-spouse to agree to substantial changes in the visitation schedule. Far less conflict will arise if you just keep the visitation schedule in mind before you agree to holiday plans with your family. This same principle can be used for deciding when the children spend time with each parent during the summer months.

Finally, if your ex-spouse has a history of not picking your child up for scheduled visitations, you have no choice but to make alternative arrangements for the times that he or she is supposed to be with the children. Although making such alternative arrangements may be time consuming and perhaps costly, doing so helps to protect the children from the disappointment and negative comments that are almost certain to occur if you don't have a backup plan.

### Be Responsible for Yourself

It is important that you do not count on your spouse to relay information to you about school or other topics involving your child. Although such communication may be necessary from time to time, a general rule is to be responsible for obtaining such information yourself. For example, ask the office at your child's school to provide two copies of any handout that is to be brought home by your child—one copy your child brings home, and the other copy gets mailed to the noncustodial parent. You may even want to give the school a stack of self-addressed, stamped envelopes to make sure that the notification gets done. In this way, the school becomes responsible for communicating with your ex-spouse, and not you or your child. If your relationship with your ex-spouse is conflict ridden, we also recommend that you schedule separate appointments for parent–teacher conferences. With separate appointments, you don't have to worry about saying the wrong thing or bringing up something that may cause an argument with your ex-spouse. However, if your relationship permits it, it will benefit your child to see the two of you working together in a cooperative way. It is also important to refrain from making any negative comments about your ex-spouse to the teacher. In addition, it is reassuring to your child if you are able to say something positive about the other parent when the opportunity presents itself. This can help relieve your child's anxiety about your family's situation.

When enrolling your child in a sporting activity or music lessons, try to make commitments for only those times when your child is with you. In that way, you will avoid committing your ex-spouse to an activity that he or she may not be enthusiastic about and prevent the unpleasantness that often stems from his or her feeling that you are telling them what to do.

The most important point to remember is that you must put your child's needs first. Your child needs to be protected from anger and conflict. At times you may feel like you are paying a high price for such considerations, but your child will pay an even greater price if you do not.

## REDUCING INAPPROPRIATE COMMUNICATION

### Avoid Making Negative Comments

As difficult as it may be, it is extremely important for parents to refrain from making negative comments about the other parent, either directly to the child or within hearing distance of the child. Comments about payment or nonpayment of child support, the parent's dating habits or new patterns of socialization, or even the other parent's refusal to pay a deductible for an office visit with a physician should not be made to the child. Your ex-spouse is and always will be your child's parent. Any negative comments you make about your ex-spouse have significant potential for damaging your child.

It is also important to avoid indirect but equally damaging comments about your ex-spouse. For example, it is harmful to tell your child that you would take her someplace like Disneyland but cannot because her dad or mom gets most of your paycheck or doesn't pay you enough to live on.

Some parents say that their child "needs to know what kind of person" his other parent is. If he lives with that parent at least a couple of days each week, he will learn, firsthand, what kind of a person that parent is. There isn't any need for the other parent to help with this process. As hard is it may be if your ex-spouse doesn't keep promises to your child, your best response is to simply be there for your child with a hug, a listening ear, or a distracting activity. Your child will give that parent many more chances to get it right and will need you many more times to be a source of comfort and not criticism. Let your child talk about her hurt feelings, but be careful not to add your own negative comments so your child knows she can trust you with her concerns about the situation.

**Avoid Using Your Child as a Messenger**

Along with protecting your child from conflict and negative comments, you should also refrain from using your child as a messenger. Any conversation about changes in routine, child support payments, or who is to show up for the Boy Scout pancake dinner should take place between the two parents. Asking your child to act as a messenger puts the child in a potentially awkward situation without any possible benefit to the child. The ease of communication, particularly with cell phones, simply does not justify using your child to carry messages back and forth.

Once again, be careful not to engage in heated exchanges about issues that involve your child over the phone when your child can overhear; typically, this means when your child is in the house with you. We are always surprised when a parent tells us that his or her child is completely unaware of issues with the ex-spouse and the child can tell us, almost word for word, about the latest fight over the telephone. Yes, some of these recommendations may seem like an inconvenience, but they are a small price to pay for limiting the negative impact of your divorce on your child.

**Avoid Using Your Child as a Spy**

Do not ask your child for information about what is going on at the other parent's house—not out of concern for your children, not out of idle curiosity, and not out of nosiness. After a separation and divorce, it is, to put it bluntly, none of your business what your ex-spouse is doing. You can say that you are just looking out for your children, but in reality most questions you could ask your child about your ex-spouse have little potential for any positive outcome and have the potential to harm your child.

If you do have a concern about your child's safety at your

ex-spouse's house, it usually will not do any good to threaten or nag your ex-spouse about his or her behavior when the children are at the house. Unfortunately, you may have to wait until something does happen to your child; then make sure that you document what happened as quickly and as accurately as possible. Most courts will not even view, much less consider, a videotape made by a parent, so making a videotape of your ex-spouse yelling or cursing will most likely never be seen by the court. And the message when you are making the tape is damaging to your child.

If you think your child has been traumatized at your ex-spouse's home, one option is to immediately transport her to the emergency room at a large teaching hospital where you know that they have pediatric staff on duty. Large teaching hospitals with a pediatric staff are usually the only hospitals that have physicians in the emergency department who are trained in interviewing and examining children who may have been the victim of some type of trauma. Probably the most important consideration is whether the physician who sees your child is experienced at representing the interests of children in court. The majority of the primary care practitioners we know are very reluctant to appear in court. Thus, merely taking your child to your family pediatrician can complicate the situation if he or she is not trained to perform the forensic evaluation you need for the court. A call to your pediatrician to request appropriate resources, however, would certainly be appropriate.

## Avoid Asking Your Child to Keep Secrets

Children should not be asked to keep secrets from their other parent. Whether the secret is about a new boyfriend or girlfriend, the purchase of a new house, a new job, or the like, you will put your child in a very difficult position if you ask him to keep a secret. If it's important to you that your ex-spouse not know something about your life, then don't tell your child. Conversely, if it's important to you that your ex-spouse know something that is changing in your life, it's your responsibility to tell him or her, not your child's. Children typically have a great loyalty to both of their parents, so do not ask your child to choose between wanting to please you and keep your secret and betraying his other parent. This conflict can cause many negative emotions for him and may affect his behavior in general or interactions with each parent specifically.

### Avoid Using Your Child as a Confidant

Typically discussions about the divorce benefit the parent, not the child. Find another adult or find a therapist, but don't use your own child as a sounding board. Sure, it's difficult after you've been hurt by a divorce, but you may cause harm by confiding in your child the worries or concerns that you have about the divorce. It is important for you to find ways to cope with your divorce without using your child as a source of emotional support. Review the recommendations in chapter 5 on parent coping skills, and practice using them as often as you can.

## OTHER WAYS TO HELP YOUR CHILD COPE WITH DIVORCE

It is important to maintain, as much as possible, the consistency and routine your family had before the divorce. If you and your ex-spouse always wanted your child to sleep in her own room, then keep that up after the divorce. Do not fall into the trap of changing the rules or expectations to "help" your child get through the divorce. Most of these "helpful" behaviors, such as letting a child sleep with you, are really more comforting to you and will result in negative interactions when you try to re-establish the rules.

Although it would be wonderful if you and your ex-spouse could live very similar lifestyles and keep very similar hours, it's far more important for you each to maintain consistency in your own schedules than to risk conflict by trying to get your ex-spouse to see things your way. Make every attempt to get your child up at the same time every day, get him to bed at the same time every night, keep him involved in extracurricular activities, and keep his meals at the same time. Such routines will provide your child with stability during the transition and uncertainty that almost always accompany a divorce. It is also important to maintain your routines and house rules, regardless of what your child says she does or does not do at the other parent's house. Children are quite adaptable and can easily learn what to expect at each house if the rules are kept consistent.

It is crucial that you remain as physically and emotionally available during and after the divorce as possible. Many children lose this access when their parents become preoccupied or depressed as a result of the breakup. How much your child may or may not want to talk about the divorce will vary by individual child and from time to time. Some children are comfortable with very little information about the situation and do not need to talk about it extensively. Other children may need more conversations and information, especially about how the divorce will affect the routine aspects of their daily lives.

One way to know what your child needs to know about the divorce is to listen to him when he initiates a conversation. In chapter 3, we made a case for setting aside specific quiet times when your child is allowed to bring up any topic he wants and, at least as important, is allowed to stop talking about any topic when he wants. If he is concerned about something, he will almost always bring it up, and if allowed, he will talk about it as long as he needs to.

If you think that your child has concerns but is not bringing them up despite your being available, use specific situations related to the divorce to initiate conversations. For example, choose a quiet time when you will not be interrupted to ask your child how not being with her dad on the holidays will feel this year. If your child does not want to open up to you, which is understandable given the fact that you are, in fact, part of the reason she is experiencing pain, try to find a supportive relative or mental health professional for your child to talk to about her concerns. If you don't get anywhere with this approach the first time, then try it again later. Your goal should be to learn more about how your child feels, not to get closure to the conversation in one sitting.

Finally, remember the power of the behavior that you model. If you handle your divorce and the custody changes matter-of-factly, your children are more likely to do the same. On the other hand, if you get kind of "crazy" and upset every time custody changes, your children are likely to follow your example. It is very important that you remain either neutral or positive about your child's other parent. Try hard never to put him or her down in front of your children or, for that matter, in front of other people. Regardless how you feel about your ex-spouse, your child needs to respect him or her. The only way to encourage that is to be respectful yourself. For more suggestions on how to help your child cope with divorce, *Helping Your Kids Cope With Divorce the Sandcastles Way*[1] is a great book on the topic.

In many areas of the United States, "divorce workshops" are offered for parents and children experiencing divorce. In fact, in several states, such workshops are required of couples with children going through a divorce. If you are considering attending one of these workshops, look for concrete suggestions about what you can do to minimize the negative impact of the divorce on your children. These workshops cannot and do not provide "therapy" in any detailed sense, but they can provide a review of the kinds of problems and situations that arise and offer suggestions about how to deal with them.

## SIGNS INDICATING THAT YOUR CHILD MAY BE HAVING DIFFICULTY COPING WITH YOUR DIVORCE

Most children will have some problems dealing with the changes brought by your divorce. So how do you know when your child is having excessive difficulty coping? One rule of thumb is to watch for major impairment in your child's academic, social, or home behavior or changes in mood. Thus, if your child merely complains that he doesn't enjoy the time he spends with the other parent, you really don't have much to go on. If, however, there is a decline in his academic performance, he chooses to drop out of sports or other activities, or he no longer spends time playing with friends, you have cause for concern.

When in doubt, a scheduled visit with your pediatrician is probably the safest step to take initially. Your pediatrician will refer you to a trained professional if he or she feels that your child may be exhibiting signs of emotional distress. Such referrals are often necessary because, as a parent, you might have difficulty being objective or really knowing when your child is being exposed to detrimental conditions. Again, it may require some effort to find a mental health professional who is trained in forensic evaluations that can provide custody and other divorce-related recommendations to you, the court, or both.

If you are convinced that your child is suffering irreparable harm from spending time with his other parent, we recommend having your attorney contact your ex-spouse's attorney about scheduling a forensic evaluation of both parents. The forensic evaluation should be scheduled only with a professional who is certified in the forensic evaluation of adults. If the evaluation is approved by the presiding judge before being scheduled, the results of that evaluation will become a part of your permanent divorce record. This is the only way that you are assured that the court will actually honor such an evaluation. Many parents schedule their children for evaluations with psychologists or psychiatrists only to be disappointed to find out, later, that the professional was not really qualified to conduct such an evaluation and the final report will not be honored by the court. Thus, protect yourself and your child by finding the appropriate resource for your concerns.

## CONCLUSION

Divorce, unfortunately, is a part of life for many people. Although divorce always has a negative impact, you can take a number of steps to minimize its effects on your child. By keeping your child just that—a child—and keeping him out of the middle of your divorce and the conflict it brings, you can keep the lines of communication open with your child and help him cope. If a reputable divorce workshop is available in your area, plan on attending it before your child develops problems. Even if your ex-spouse does not attend the workshop, you should be able to pick up pointers for helping your child cope. We usually recommend that attendance at the workshop be agreed on during the divorce proceedings and that a stipulation be included in the child custody agreement that both parents will attend. Some states mandate such workshops.

The skills we have addressed throughout this book, including how to model appropriate behavior, give positive feedback, communicate with your child, and cope with your own emotions, can help you minimize the detrimental effects of the divorce on both you and your children. Although divorce clearly has a negative impact on children, vigilance on your part regarding all aspects of the divorce can go a long way toward minimizing this impact.

# Part III

## BUILDING YOUR CHILD'S SKILLS

# CHAPTER 9

# BUILDING SELF-QUIETING SKILLS

Each day, we encounter situations that make us frustrated, anxious, or disappointed. Children also experience these feelings as they face new developmental tasks, relationships with peers, and the pressures of school and outside activities. You can teach your child to cope with such challenges by helping her develop self-quieting skills. *Self-quieting skills* are a child's ability to calm herself down in the face of an undesirable situation or outcome. Such skills can help children go to sleep alone, keep their temper when being told "no" or when their block tower falls down, remain calm when giving a speech or taking a test, and cope with being cut from a team. As you can see, self-quieting skills apply to a variety of situations that children face every day.

We have all seen children (and adults) who do not have good self-quieting skills. They are the people who have tantrums over the smallest frustration, display "road rage," or frequently give others "a piece of their mind." A toddler who kicks the remaining parts of his fallen block tower is demonstrating that he doesn't have adequate self-quieting skills to deal with a frustrating event. An adolescent without self-quieting skills who cannot get her CD player to operate may end up throwing something, kicking, or swearing. Although it's obvious that throwing, kicking, or swearing won't help the situation, such children simply don't have the skills necessary for coping with situations they don't like.

It is vital that children have good self-quieting skills if they are to benefit from any type of problem solving you might try to teach them. If your child is frustrated or upset and cannot calm down, a discussion about alternative solutions to the problem will most likely be unproductive. Further discussion on how to help your child solve problems once he is calm can be found in chapter 3 on communicating with your child and chapter 13 on aggression.

Some people are born with calm temperaments and better self-quieting skills than others. But those who do not have these skills can begin learning them in infancy with the help of their caregivers. The younger your child is when you start to teach her self-quieting skills, the easier and quicker it will be for her to learn them. This chapter will teach you how to encourage self-quieting skills in your child and how to make sure these skills are developing appropriately across childhood. We will also discuss how to deal with your child when his poor self-quieting skills affect his ability to separate from you without anxiety.

## HOW TO ENCOURAGE SELF-QUIETING SKILLS

We believe that helping your child develop self-quieting skills is one of the most important jobs you have as a parent. Although you might like to spare your child from ever feeling the hurt that accompanies frustration, anxiety, or disappointment, you simply cannot. In fact, if you do everything possible to reduce your child's frustration, rather than teach him how to deal with it, you are choosing short-term gain and long-term pain. Thus, your best option is to teach your child how to deal with life's negative situations.

## Developing Self-Quieting Skills in Infants and Toddlers

You can start to develop self-quieting skills in your infant at sleep times. Between birth and about 12 weeks of age, infants usually fall asleep while they are being fed. By about 12 weeks, they will be very tired when they finish feeding, but they will often still be awake. If you place your baby in her crib or bassinet awake but very drowsy, she will almost inevitably fall asleep very soon, although she may fuss for a minute or two first. After about one week of placing her in her crib when she is awake and drowsy, she will get into the habit of fussing briefly, and then falling asleep. That is the start of self-quieting skills.

Similarly, between birth and about 12 weeks of age, infants typically begin fussing or crying the instant they awaken. But at about 12 weeks of age, they will awaken and babble or coo before they start to fuss or cry. If you can discipline yourself to get up then and pick your baby up when he's babbling and cooing, but before he's fussing or crying, he will learn that you come to get him when he's babbling and cooing. He won't feel any need to continue to cry on awakening, because he knows you will pick him up shortly. Your child's ability to coo quietly while waiting for you to pick him up is a demonstration of a self-quieting skill.

You can also teach your toddler self-quieting skills. For example, if your toddler is playing on the floor and the toys he is playing with don't do what he wants them to do, so he starts to fuss, leave him alone. Stay in the vicinity, but try to not make eye contact or talk to him. As soon as he is calm, which, if you don't interrupt him, could take only a minute or so, move over to him. If you wish, you can also give him an unobtrusive hug or make a brief comment about what he is playing with and allow him to continue playing.

To increase the likelihood that your child is actually able to calm down under these circumstances, it's very important that you practice when he isn't very upset and that you pay attention to him, again, as soon as he has made even the slightest attempt to self-quiet. When we practice these procedures in the office, we try to engage the parents in a conversation, ever mindful of the child's whining, fussing, or pouting. As soon as the child stops whining, fussing, or pouting for as little as two seconds, we immediately motion to the parent to pay attention to her again.

Is it possible that your child won't calm down under these circumstances? Of course it's possible. But please remember that you are trying to reverse a process that you have practiced many, many times in the past. Each time, in the past, that your child was upset, you made every attempt to help him calm down. Now, all of a sudden, you are ignoring his whining, fussing, or pouting, leaving your child on his own. It will take your child a while to learn the new "rules."

It's quite common for a child, instead of self-quieting, to say something like, "Mommy, I'm quiet. I'm not upset any more, Mom." Usually, once your child tells you something like this, it's only a matter of minutes before she actually self-quiets. It's not unusual for children to get more upset several times before they actually self-quiet. If you know these behaviors are typical for most children, you will be prepared to deal with them in your child, mainly by ignoring them. If you comment on you child's comments, it will only take longer for your child to learn how to quiet herself without your help.

Are there children who cannot self-quiet? Certainly, but in our experience, they are very rare. In those few cases where a child gets very upset and will not calm down, it may be helpful later, when he is calmer, to talk with him about his feelings. What you might hear during such a discussion, however, is your child's request for you to just listen to him when he is upset. In other words, he may be rationalizing that if you just listened to him, he would not get so upset. Unfortunately, agreeing to his suggestion to listen will not build his self-quieting skills. If you practice these procedures consistently over an extended period of time, the chances of your being successful are very good. And, more important, the fact that your child will have learned such an important life skill will make all of your efforts worthwhile. Your child will also feel proud of himself as he masters this developmental milestone. Of course, you should seek the assistance of your pediatrician or a mental health professional whenever you feel too overwhelmed by your child's behavior to be effective.

### Developing Self-Quieting Skills in Young School-Age Children

Parents have a tendency, particularly with young children, to attempt to fix whatever problem upsets the child rather than simply to comfort the child. The parents of a child who falls off of her tricycle, for example, may not only comfort the child, but may also pick the bike up or even verbally "condemn" it for hurting the child! In doing so, the parents prevent the child from learning how to "fix" the situation herself. Although it is certainly all right to comfort an upset child, your child may also get the unrealistic message that her parents are available at any time to fix unpleasant situations.

Obviously, if the situation merits your immediate help, then intervention is appropriate. We're reminded of a family that brought a child in for treatment of a dog phobia. After talking with the parents, we discovered that the dog next door had bitten the child and that the dog was still living next door and allowed to enter the child's back yard. In fact, the parents brought in a picture of the dog growling at the child through the sliding glass door on their deck. Of course, in a situation like this, trying to teach the child self-quieting skills would be inappropriate. Instead, we recommended that they call their local police department. When they did so, the police ordered the neighbor to keep the dog under absolute control or it would be destroyed.

This example simply shows that you must use your common sense and address other issues along with teaching your child self-quieting skills when appropriate. Furthermore, we are aware that a child's hurt feelings or frustrations do not end simply because he has self-quieted. Thus, suggestions for helping your child problem-solve or deal with aggressive tendencies are found in chapter 13.

Many parents also try to distract their children instead of teaching self-quieting skills. For example, if a child is getting frustrated with her toys, the parent may try to get the child interested in another toy, in a TV show, or in eating something. Although the use of distraction can, at times, be a good way to deal with a child's frustration, if the parent often intervenes this way, the child never learns how to handle the situation by herself and may actually develop unhealthy coping skills, such as watching too much TV. She may also never develop confidence in her own ability to deal with difficult or frustrating situations.

So what can you do to develop self-quieting skills in your child? The best way to comfort a frustrated child is to provide physical contact, such as a pat on the arm, with or without a small amount of verbal support. For example, a parent might comfort a child who fell off his bike by rubbing his back and saying, "That must have hurt" as the child calms from crying. Your verbalizations should not imply that you can fix the problem or that the object such as the bike is to blame for whatever discomforts the child may have experienced. Reassurances, although well meaning, can also delay your child's efforts at calming down as he either argues with you ("No, it will never be better!") or simply becomes more upset as you keep talking. If you are quiet but supportive through a hug or back rub, your child will have a chance to regain his composure. You can then encourage him to approach the frustrating situation again. By going back to the situation, your child will learn that once he is calm, he can go right back to the situation that frustrated him in the first place.

Parents who do the fixing for the children are more likely to raise children who expect someone else to do the fixing and never learn to do their own fixing. Every time your child deals with a challenging situation on her own, she takes one step closer to finding that she can reduce her own discomfort with self-quieting. She takes one step closer to being more independent, which will give her positive feelings of accomplishment.

Once children learn self-quieting skills, they can use them in a number of new or unique situations. For example, children who have learned self-quieting skills at home tend to have fewer problems when they start preschool or kindergarten. A child with good self-quieting skills who is dropped off at preschool may fuss for a couple of minutes but then will stop fussing, on his own, and begin participating in school activities. The same child, without self-quieting skills, would probably end up being "helped" by one of his teachers much longer than might be expected for a child his age. Once again, your child will feel more independent and accomplished if he can quiet himself and participate in what's going on around him.

One child in our office was apprehensive about going to school. In talking to her parents, we discovered that she left Sunday school a couple of times because she "wanted to go home." She left a Girl Scout camp two days early for the same reason. She had stopped spending nights at friends' houses because she didn't want to be away from home. This pattern usually indicates that the child doesn't have the skills to manage her own uncomfortable feelings; she doesn't have self-quieting skills.

With younger children, from age 2 to 5, it is often sufficient, once you establish that a pattern exists, simply to insist that the child go to activities and remain at them until they are over. Although this is often difficult for both parents and children, younger children usually get over it quickly. But if your child simply cannot calm himself at other times (like naptimes and bedtimes, when losing at a game, and when sharing), don't expect him to be able to calm himself when he's required to separate from you.

## Developing Self-Quieting Skills in Older Children

As children grow older, many of the situations that frustrate them or hurt their feelings are situations in which their parents cannot be of much help. Much of the frustration and hurt that children in middle school experience is social in nature such as not getting invited to an important event or picked for a preferred team. Parents cannot just telephone the parents of the other children and demand that their child be included. If they did, they would end up subjecting the child to added criticism, and the child would learn nothing about the give-and-take of social relationships. The biggest difference between children who can cope with such disappointing experiences and those who cannot is their self-quieting skills.

Self-quieting skills are also vital in dealing with academics. If you've ever watched school-age children doing homework, you probably saw a big difference in how they coped with frustration. Some children who get frustrated with a difficult math problem get up, get a drink, and then calmly approach the problem again. Other children get upset and refuse to continue doing their homework unless a parent helps them or gives them the answer. The child with good self-quieting skills is more likely to get her homework done, to do it correctly, and to be able to face her homework the next time. Children without good self-quieting skills are much more likely to look for an easy way out or just give up than children with good self-quieting skills.

Allowing the school-age child to develop self-quieting skills requires a lot of self-control on your part. For example, if your child is playing basketball in the driveway, misses three or four shots in a row, and clearly starts to get upset, leave him alone. Chances are, given a little time, he can regain his composure. And when he has regained his composure, he will also gain a little independence. He'll be one step closer to being able to deal with frustration the next time it happens.

Similarly, if your daughter comes home from school and is upset about something a classmate said, instead of immediately interrogating her and offering suggestions on how she should handle the situation, leave her alone. Sure, you can console her, offer a "hmmm" or "you seem pretty upset" comment occasionally, but she needs the practice of dealing with the situation on her own if she is ever to learn the skills necessary for dealing with similar situations.

One strategy you can use is simply to restate what your child says as unemotionally as possible. For example, if your son says he got a C on his history test because he just doesn't understand history and doesn't like the history class or the teacher, you can either console him with physical comfort or say, "It sounds like the exam was difficult." Often, all a child wants is recognition that the test was hard—he doesn't want or expect you to take the test for him or to call the teacher on his behalf. A simple acknowledgement may be all that he needs. The time for teaching problem solving is not when your child is upset, but after he has calmed down.

When your older child is calm, you can teach her specific strategies, including positive self-talk, to help her develop self-quieting skills. For example, if your child often gets upset during tests when she does not immediately know the answer to a question, suggest that she skip test questions that make her worry and return to them when she has completed more of the test. Children who take tests in this way are using their self-quieting skills to avoid getting upset over the hard questions they see on the first pass through the test. Strategies for more positive self-talk that can also be used by older children are covered in chapter 5 on parent coping skills.

Other strategies you can teach your child to encourage self-quieting are visual imagery and progressive muscle relaxation.

VISUAL IMAGERY. Visual imagery involves imagining a pleasant visual scene to help oneself relax. Examples of such images are a sunny beach or a cozy fireplace. The key to making visual imagery successful in helping your child relax or self-quiet is to have him practice his images on almost a daily basis, in the absence of pressure, until he finds that he can effectively imagine a particular visual image any time he wants to. Then, when he is under a lot of stress, it will be much easier for him to use his visual imagery to calm himself down. Just practicing once or twice when your child is already in a difficult situation does not work.

Begin by sitting with your child and recalling a particularly relaxing or calm situation. If you were at the beach last summer with your child, try verbally recreating the beach with her. Ask her to see if she can think about the beach intensely enough that she can remember the sun shining on her face, arms, stomach, and legs. Go through each of the five senses with her. What can she smell as she lies there on the beach? What can she hear? What does the beach feel like on her feet or back? Are there any tastes that she associates with lying on the beach? The main goal is to get her so involved in thinking about the beach scene that her mind cannot also think about an uncomfortable situation. In other words, you will help her feel so calm that she cannot feel angry, anxious, or frustrated at the same time.

RELAXATION. Children over about 8 years of age may also benefit from learning how to do progressive muscle relaxation. In the early

1920s, Jacobson published the first research article on the benefits of progressive muscle relaxation.[1] Since that time, many adults have used these techniques and variations of them.

Classic progressive muscle relaxation involves systematically tensing and relaxing muscle groups one at a time.[2] Although the sequence of muscle groups isn't important, we usually start with the forehead muscles and progress down the body, one muscle group after another. Begin by tensing the forehead muscles quickly and relaxing them several times. Then, tense the forehead muscles and relax them while counting slowly to three so that it takes about three seconds to go from tense muscles to relaxed muscles. Children may prefer the word "stretch" instead of "tense" to help them understand what to do. You can also use more concrete images when instructing a child, such as "squeeze a lemon, then let it go" for tensing and relaxing the arm muscles.

The body sequence we usually use is as follows:

- forehead, eyes, nose, lips, tongue, jaw
- neck, chest, back
- right arm, left arm
- stomach, buttocks
- right leg, left leg

Like visual imagery, the relaxation exercises should be practiced daily until your child feels confident that he can use relaxation whenever he needs it. As his skills improve for tensing and relaxing individual muscle groups, have him practice coordinating his breathing with the relaxing so that he is taking in a deep breath and holding it while he tenses up a muscle group. As he relaxes that muscle group to a count of "one, two, three," have him slowly exhale. The combination of tensing and relaxing muscle groups with slowly breathing in and out is very relaxing to most people.

Once your child is fairly good at either visual imagery or relaxation, encourage her to use her new strategies in tense or stressful situations. For example, before midterm or final examinations, many children and adolescents worry over their preparations, which leaves them very stressed. When the day of the exam arrives, most children get anxious during the time between being seated and being told to start the test. If, at these times, your child uses the visual imagery or relaxation exercises you practiced with her, she will be better able to control the stress she feels and to self-quiet as she waits to begin her exam.

### Self-Quieting Skills Need to Improve With Age

As children grow older and encounter increasingly frustrating situations, they need to continue improving their self-quieting skills. Although you should expect a young child with poor self-quieting skills to continue riding his bike for only a few more minutes when he is frustrated, you should expect an older child to play a game of Monopoly to the end, even if he doesn't have much chance of winning. A child who always wants to forfeit a game he isn't winning is a child who doesn't have good self-quieting skills, and other children may not want to play with him very often.

The natural temptation is to stop playing games that you know are frustrating to your child, but that's probably the worst thing you can do. Such children need more practice using the strategies for encouraging self-quieting skills. If you play several different games, some that she is really pretty good at and then some that are harder, she will get the experience she needs and can progress with her self-quieting skills. It is only through practice, and with your encouragement, that she will learn how to play a variety of games that challenge her self-quieting skills.

## SELF-QUIETING SKILLS AND SEPARATION ANXIETY

Children with separation anxiety get extremely upset whenever they have to separate from their parents or leave their homes. They may think about the separation long before it occurs and worry about what will happen after they separate. There is a wide range of separation problems in children, however, most are manageable by their parents.

Some parents make every attempt to "help" their child by holding him, trying to console him and talking sweetly, which have the effect of reinforcing and confirming any anxiety the child had. These parents feel at least as much discomfort as their children. When these parent comfort their children, both parent and child feel better—and they have made the next separation even more difficult. Such parents try to figure out ways of separating less often as way of avoiding the discomfort of separating. Unfortunately, doing so just makes separation harder for both.

To minimize separation anxiety, you can show your child that separation isn't anything to worry about by modeling easy separations. Plan as many opportunities to separate as possible, even briefly. For example, run to the store, drop off your child at a friend's house, or go for a quick walk while your child stays with another adult. If you have to, pretend that the separation does not bother you by separating in a matter-of-fact fashion without numerous reassurances. Also, do not talk about pending separations. This may increase and extend your child's anxiety. Additionally, try your best to return when you say you will to show your child that he can trust that you will return. If your child has good self-quieting skills, separating is usually difficult only the first couple of times. After that, both you and your child can separate very matter-of-factly. If your child does not have good self-quieting skills, that is often the best place to start. Only after your child has developed self-quieting skills does it make sense to try to deal with separation anxiety.

Once your child has demonstrated good self-quieting skills, you can address separation anxiety by practicing frequent separations. During these separations, you have to model for your child that the separation is not something to be anxious about; in other words, act like the separation doesn't bother you. The more often you separate from your child without showing any discomfort, the faster she will learn to separate easily, trusting your message that the separation is nothing to fear.

Try to set up numerous separations so that your child gets to practice separating more often. For example, arrange to drop off your child with a relative or neighbor while you run a short errand. If there's a chance that your child will still be fussing when you return, call ahead of time to make sure he has stopped fussing before returning to pick him up.

When picking up your child, refrain from displays of emotion. The parent who can separate often and unemotionally can teach a young child to do the same rather quickly. Avoid discussing upcoming separations, as this will only give your child more time to get anxious.

If you are going on a trip or will be away for an extended period of time, it is certainly important to tell your child that you will be gone and for how long. You can also provide the child a comfort item, such as a picture or your favorite sweater. You should also talk to your child if you can while you are away. Avoid providing repetitive reassurances when you talk with your child; instead, focus the conversation on what your child has been doing since you've been away. None of these activities should increase your child's anxiety as long as your explanations and reassurances are not excessive. Once again, you must send your child the message that she is safe while separated from you.

Sometimes severe separation problems merit the diagnosis of

Separation Anxiety Disorder. A professional will arrive at such a diagnosis if the child experiences the following eight symptoms:

1. excessive distress when separation occurs or is anticipated
2. excessive worry about losing someone close to the child
3. excessive worry that something bad will happen, leading to separation (for example, getting lost or being kidnapped)
4. persistent reluctance or refusal to go places, including school, because of worry about separation
5. excessive fear of being alone at home or elsewhere
6. sleep problems when not at home or near attachment figures
7. repeated nightmares about separation
8. repeated physical complaints, such as headaches or stomachaches, when required to separate.

These symptoms must exist for a minimum of four weeks and cause significant distress or impairment in social, academic, or other important areas of functioning.

Thus, when parents speak of separation anxiety, they are most often speaking of a child who prefers to not be left with an alternative caregiver but who does not display a significant number of distressful symptoms. If, however, you suspect that your child's difficulties are as serious as the symptoms we listed, consult with your pediatrician or seek the services of an appropriately trained clinical child psychologist.

## CONCLUSION

Children, just like adults, are frequently exposed to situations that are difficult, unpleasant, or both. Thus, it is important for you to teach your child to deal with such challenging situations. The best way to teach your child self-quieting skills is to give him lots of opportunities to practice calming down with very little assistance from you. He can then develop both the skills and the confidence to approach new situations on his own. And as he approaches these new situations, his skills and confidence will continue to improve. Years of such exposure during childhood and adolescence equip children to deal with the unpleasantness that is sure to come in adulthood.

For the infant reaching for a distant toy, the school-age child who continually loses when she plays Monopoly, and the adolescent who, for the first time, is not picked for a team, frustration and disappointment are a part of life. Passing up opportunities to allow your child to deal with these situations on his own will just make it more difficult for him to learn it as he ages. If your child is to learn the coping skills she needs to minimize her own discomfort, you must stay back and allow her the opportunity to deal with unpleasant situations herself. You may need to use some of the skills we discussed in chapter 5 on parent coping skills to help you manage your own discomfort as your child learns.

# CHAPTER 10

# ENCOURAGING INDEPENDENT PLAY SKILLS

We have all met children who seem to be unable to entertain themselves, who dislike being alone, and who are frequently standing at their parents' side, on the phone with friends, or begging to go somewhere. These children are most likely missing what we call "independent play" skills. *Independent play skills* refers to a child's ability to entertain himself for extended periods of time without any help from an adult. Children with well-developed independent play skills derive enjoyment simply from their activities, with no need or expectation of the involvement of others or an external reward.

Independent play skills enable children to do long homework assignments, to work in their seats at school, to complete independent projects for school or Scouts, to read a long book, and to master a hobby or talent such as playing the piano. Some children with well-developed independent play skills will do one activity for 30 to 45 minutes, then switch to another activity, without adult help, for another 30 to 45 minutes. Others may do the same activity for hours. As such children grow older, their ability to concentrate and enjoy an activity expands to include longer periods of time and other age-appropriate activities.

In addition to developing a child's ability to concentrate, stick with tasks, and enjoy time alone, independent play skills also have other benefits for the child and her parents. Children with independent play skills usually play better with other children than those who do not. One reason may be that they have learned to derive enjoyment from playing alone and thus have less immediate need for social gratification. Furthermore, the more a child is engaged in independent play activities or homework, the less likely he is to get into trouble. Children who can play appropriately for one or two hours alone do not require much adult supervision or much discipline. Children who can play independently allow parents more time to fulfill their own responsibilities, ultimately benefiting the family by allowing more time for shared activities.

Helping their children build independent play skills is one of the most important tasks of their parents. One study demonstrated that a key indicator of how well children did over the long run was how independently they could play at 4 years of age.[1] Of course, if your child is older than 4, it is still worthwhile to teach him independent play skills. Such skills developed in childhood create adults who can be self-motivated and productive in the workplace and who can engage in fulfilling hobbies, such as reading, gardening, or running, that require the ability to enjoy one's own company.

This chapter will describe how you can encourage the development of independent play skills in your child. We provide general guidelines as well as age-specific suggestions from infancy through school age.

## ENCOURAGING INDEPENDENT PLAY SKILLS IN CHILDREN

### Make Sure Your Child Has Time

It will be very difficult for your child to develop independent play skills if he never has the chance to be or play alone. If you are always holding your infant or entertaining your toddler, she will not have the opportunity to explore activities on her own. If your school-age child is busy every moment with group activities such as Scouts, sports, and play dates, he will never know how to enjoy the time he spends alone with an activity of his choosing. Your child cannot develop independent play skills if she has no time in her day to experience them!

Watch your interactions with your child over a week. If you are constantly entertaining your child, follow the strategies in this chapter to encourage more independent play. Look at your older child's schedule and see if there are any breaks or opportunities for him to play alone. By scheduling some independent play time in your child's day, you will give him the opportunity to develop this important life skill. You will also, as he gets older, be teaching him about time management and the importance of including time for himself as he balances life's demands.

## Model Good Independent Play Skills

Chapter 1 discussed the importance of modeling the behaviors you want your child to demonstrate. Modeling is also a good way to encourage your child to develop independent play skills. Parents who are able to persevere for several hours to complete a work or home project have good independent "play" skills. Similarly, parents who persist with hobbies such as reading, gardening, or sewing demonstrate good independent play skills for their child. Some parents bring work home with them and spend part of the evening doing paperwork, such as grading homework assignments or filling out sales reports. They set a good example for their children by keeping the house quiet and modeling productive use of their time, which encourages their children to follow suit and develop good independent play skills as well. These are just some of the ways you can model independent play skills for your child. The activity really doesn't matter. Just take time for activities that you enjoy and that you engage in alone.

What if you don't have good independent play skills? Do you always seem to be busy talking on the phone, running errands, or seeking ways to avoid being alone? Or do you watch a lot of TV or even just leave the TV or radio on so it doesn't seem like you are alone? Do you have problems getting tasks done on time or meeting the deadlines you set for yourself? If any of these scenarios sound like you, you may also need some help in developing your independent play skills.

Just because you do not have good independent play skills doesn't mean you can't teach your child to have them, however. It just means that you will have to put more effort into it compared to a parent who has good independent play skills. Thus, start scheduling independent play time into your day or at least into your week. During this time, do activities in parallel with your child. Read at the same time that she is reading, or work on a quiet project, like balancing your checkbook, at the same time she is working on a project for school. The mere fact that you are working in parallel will encourage her to stay on task. Remember that watching TV does not count!

### Provide Positive Feedback

In addition to modeling good independent play skills, you can also encourage this skill development by providing your child with positive feedback when he engages in appropriate solitary activities. Nonverbal feedback strategies such as a pat on the head or squeeze of the shoulder as you walk by work best; many parents discover that when they verbally praise a child (for example, "Hey, you are doing a good job playing in there"), she will stop playing and want the parent to interact with her. It may seem that the more you try to praise your child for playing independently, particularly a younger child, the more he wants you to play with him! That is why we recommend quiet feedback instead. It is far less distracting to your child but will still communicate that you are pleased with his playing alone.

Your child's need for positive feedback will typically decrease in frequency, over a period of months, as she begins to enjoy the activities for their own sake. You can provide verbal praise to your child when she comes to show you the task she completed while engaging in independent play, such as a craft or a song mastered on the piano. Such times provide a great opportunity to ask your child about what she has been doing and how she feels about her completed activity and to praise not only the product, but her independent behavior. (Chapter 2 provides additional ideas for providing positive feedback to your child.)

## ENCOURAGING INDEPENDENT PLAY SKILLS IN INFANTS

To encourage independent play skills in your infant, start by allowing him to engage in a variety of activities until he finds one that he enjoys. Keep trying until you find one or two toys or activities that your child seems interested in. For example, if your infant is lying on the floor and exploring a rattle with her fingers and mouth, touch her briefly on her toes or head as you walk by or sit next to her doing your own task. The fact that she is getting this attention from you will encourage her to continue exploring the toy. Then when you want to interact with your child and her toy, you can start to talk and coo, which will distract her and encourage her to focus on you.

As with teaching self-quieting skills, encouraging a child to learn independent play skills is emotionally uncomfortable for some parents. I've seen parents who would not put their baby on the floor because "he doesn't like to be left alone," even when "being alone" means that the baby is lying on the floor only a couple of feet from one of his parents! If you let such fears prevent you from teaching your child independent play skills, you may end up with a child who cannot entertain herself or who will experience problems when you expect her to behave more independently in the future. Such problems are frustrating for both the parent, who wants the child to be less dependent, and the child, who lacks the necessary skills to do so.

## ENCOURAGING INDEPENDENT PLAY IN TODDLERS AND PRESCHOOLERS

Toddlers and preschoolers are at the perfect age for encouraging independent play. As your little one runs about the house, engaging in one activity after another, you should discipline yourself to provide frequent reinforcing contact without interrupting his activities. Initially, toddlers perform better at eventual independent play activities when you or another adult performs the activity with them. A child who will not play for two minutes with blocks alone may play for 30 minutes if an adult plays with him.

The secret, from your point of view, is to wait for a moment when the child seems interested in what she's doing. Then excuse yourself and say, "I'll be right back." Leave for about five seconds, just long enough to walk away about 10 feet, turn around, and return to playing with your child. After several days of playing with your child several times each day for about 10 minutes each time, leaving for 5 to 10 seconds at a time but predictably returning, your child will become less concerned about what you are doing and more interested in what she is doing. You can then stretch the length of time you're gone to 15 or 20 seconds. By very gradually extending the length of time that you're away, you can help your child gradually learn to enjoy himself without an adult present.

Be careful not to teach your child the wrong lesson by not returning when you say you will. If you and your child are playing together nicely and you excuse yourself, saying you'll be right back, but don't return, you will teach your child that whenever she plays nicely by herself, you will leave her. Your child may have no choice, then, but to become upset that you did not come back or simply to find out where you went, disrupting her independent play.

How long, realistically, should your young child be able to play independently? A toddler may be able to color with crayons for 10 to 15 minutes or more, whereas some 3- to 4-year-olds can play in a sandbox or with blocks for up to half an hour or more. You should encourage your child to play long enough to be engaged in active play that requires some thinking and exploring. For example, a child who is building a "garage" for his "trucks" is probably going to play longer than one who is simply playing with blocks. The two children may look like they are doing the same thing, but the former is more strongly motivated to keep playing.

## ENCOURAGING INDEPENDENT PLAY IN SCHOOL-AGE CHILDREN

Often, when school-age children are left alone to entertain themselves, they will either call a friend or try to go to a friend's house, almost as though they are trying to avoid having to entertain themselves. If you have been working on independent play skills since your child was young, your school-age child most likely will continue to develop these skills as he matures. If your school-age child needs your help in this area, however, you can teach independent skills in the same way you would a younger child. Spend time playing with your child, and then leave for very brief periods. Repeat this frequently, and your child will come to enjoy the activity and need your presence less and less over time.

With older children, you may have to experiment to find an activity that interests your child long enough to begin building her independent play skills. As with most other people, a school-age child doesn't want to spend a long time doing something she isn't good at, particularly if the activity makes her feel uncomfortable. Thus, it is important for you to expose her to activities that she will find rewarding and gradually show her that she can enjoy time alone without your involvement or that of her friends. You might do this by helping her find hobbies that require some continuation of tasks—for example, building a car model or sewing a bag. Once she gets started, your participation will be less, and your child's will be more. The motive of accomplishing something or completing a project makes independent play take on much more meaning than simply "playing."

For the most part, the particular activity is not important. Whether your child is playing with toys or reading a book, the important consideration is that the activity can engage him for long periods of time. There is almost no way that you can predict which independent play activities your child will enjoy, and you should be accepting of and positive about whichever one your child chooses.

With school-age children, it's often a good idea to discontinue an activity while the child is still enjoying it and before the activity becomes boring or repetitious. If a father shoot baskets with his son for 5 or 10 minutes, then stops before the boy becomes bored or says he's had enough, it may be easier to get the boy involved in shooting hoops the next time. Over time, the child will be able to spend increasingly longer periods of time before quitting. Thus, one mistake is to continue with an activity, stopping only when your child says he can't stand it any more. Obviously, if you can start to teach independent play with activities that your child really enjoys, there's a better chance of getting the child to remain involved in the activity for longer periods of time.

## HOW QUICKLY DO CHILDREN LEARN INDEPENDENT PLAY SKILLS?

Independent play skills take a long time for children to learn, perhaps as long as four to six months, but during this period you should see steady progress and your child should entertain herself for increasingly longer periods of time. The older a child is before she learns independent play skills, the longer it takes to teach her, and the harder it usually is on her parents. A child with very poor independent play skills who is 8 or 10 years old might take six or eight months to learn them. But remember, you are trying to encourage participation in activities that your child will enjoy for years to come, so the time and effort that you put into teaching these skills will be well spent.

Independent play is not an all-or-none proposition. Once your child learns to derive enjoyment from reading, he will do so for the rest of his life. And once your child learns to derive enjoyment from working in the yard, exercising, or doing crafts, he can enjoy some variation of that activity for years. So be patient, and plan to spend a lot of time helping your child establish some healthy and productive interests and habits.

## FAMILIES WITH SEVERAL CHILDREN

Whether a family has one child or three, each child needs to learn independent play skills in preparation for the time when the child goes out on her own, whether to first grade or to her first job. You

**203**

can often tell which children have poor independent play skills, because they always want a sibling to help them with their homework or their chores. We don't think it's so much that they want the company; they just haven't had enough practice doing things by themselves.

You may need to structure times when everyone in your family is expected to do something on his or her own. Younger children with fewer independent play skills can have a parent to help them learn over time. The older children can be required to go to their rooms or outside as the whole family spends some time relaxing. Although there are clear benefits to children learning how to work and play together as a group, there are also advantages to children learning to play independently. Spending the time and the effort to help each of your children acquire independent play skills means that you are helping to make your children's lives more enjoyable and more productive.


CONCLUSION

Few parenting activities will make as much difference in your child's overall development as encouraging independent play skills. Although it may take you four to six months to encourage your child to play or work on projects independently, it's clearly in your child's best interests to do so. Many challenges await him, challenges that will be much easier to face if he can function independently.

You can start to teach your child independent play skills during infancy and continue to encourage them through childhood by modeling your own independent play skills. Once your child has learned to entertain herself, there is far less need for her to be entertained by others. The need for discipline should also decrease, because your child is occupying her time in enjoyable and productive activities, leaving her less time to get into trouble. Ironically, a child's independent play skills also make him a better playmate for others, because he is able to wait for social gratification.

Thus, teaching independent play skills has wide-reaching benefits for your child. You will help to create an adult who enjoys hobbies, activities, and her own company.

# Part IV

## SPECIAL CHILD TOPICS

# CHAPTER 11

# ESTABLISHING BEDTIME

At some time, practically every parent has had problems getting a child to go to bed. Perhaps this problem is so common because infants usually have at least two or three naps in addition to night-time sleeping. That means that there are several times during the course of a day to experience problems. Several research studies have documented that sleep problems, once present, tend to persist through early childhood, with percentages ranging from 25% to 84% of children.[1] Children who had problems with self-soothing at 12 months of age still had problems at 39 months. Thus, parents who address these issues early may be able to forestall problems later.

The most common problems children and families face are bedtime resistance, nightmares, night awakening, night terrors, and sleepwalking.[2] More children have problems with bedtime resistance than with any other bedtime problem. If your child has been going to bed at approximately the same time each night, give or take 15 to 20 minutes, and she is fussing or carrying on less than 10 minutes, then you're not likely to improve much on that. If, however, your child is getting drinks, going to the bathroom, and stalling bedtime for 45 minutes or more, your child most likely has a bedtime problem that you can effectively address. This chapter will give you some guidelines on normal sleep patterns and issues for young children, followed by suggestions for preventing or managing your child's sleep problems.

## NORMAL SLEEP HABITS FOR CHILDREN

One question many parents have is, "How much sleep should my child be getting?" Although there isn't any research that answers this question, Ferber's 1985 book *Solve Your Child's Sleep Problems* provides estimates of the number of hours of sleep children need at each age from birth through adolescence (see chart).[3]

| Estimates of the Amount of Sleep Children Require | |
|---|---|
| Age | Hours of Sleep Required Per Day |
| Newborn to 6 months | 16 hours 30 minutes |
| 6 months to 12 months | 14 hours 15 minutes |
| 12 months to 24 months | 13 hours |
| 3 years | 12 hours |
| 4 years to 5 years | 11 hours (may no longer need naps) |
| 6 years to 9 years | 10 hours |
| 10 years to 14 years | 9 hours |
| 15 years to 18 years | 8 hours |

Note. From *Solve Your Child's Sleep Problems*, by R. Ferber, 1985, New York: Simon and Schuster. Copyright 1985 by Simon and Schuster. Adapted with permission.

Ferber estimated that infants should sleep almost 16 hours each day, with the amount of sleep needed gradually decreasing until about 1 year of age, when the average is about 13 hours. Ferber also reported that the average child gives up the morning nap by about 1 year of age and gives up the afternoon nap at about 4 years of age.

Most babies at about 1 year of age will awaken one or more

times during the night, look around, and maybe even cry out for you. There's nothing wrong with reassuring him by patting him on the back or stroking his hair. Usually it's best not to turn on the light, pick up the baby, or talk to him. All of that additional stimulation will make a baby who was half-awake completely awake. And, ultimately, he will have to learn how to get back to sleep on his own. Handled properly, this period of nighttime awakenings should last no more than a few weeks. If you reinforce it by turning on the light, picking her up, and talking to her, you could be establishing a ritual that lasts for months or more.

By 2 years of age, you will be seeing the results of your efforts. If you have been promoting self-soothing, then your child will probably have a minimum of problems with going to sleep and staying asleep throughout the night. If, on the other hand, you have been providing your child with a great deal of assistance with both sleep onset and night awakenings, your toddler will probably continue to have problems with both.

By 3 to 5 years of age, your child may resist going to bed, even when very tired. Children are very good at getting their parents to help them delay bedtime by allowing them to stay up until they fall asleep in their tracks, by giving "one more hug" or "one more kiss," or by checking out the room one more time for monsters and other assorted bedtime gremlins. This resistance can be even more of a problem for children with an older brother or sister who is allowed to stay up later.

If you haven't established consistent bedtime routines by now, you should certainly do so. After he has had a bath and is getting ready for bed, reading a story and saying prayers (if this is your practice) sets the stage for your child to fall asleep on his own. Say "good night," turn off the lights, and leave. Don't stay around and negotiate with him, and don't let him talk you into staying with him until he falls asleep. Avoid any form of roughhousing that tends to get him more active immediately before bedtime.

Occasionally, your child may wake up from a nightmare. Strategies discussed later in this chapter may help you and your child cope with this common occurrence. If your child hears a scary story or sees violence on TV, the images may crop up later as nightmares. Try not to watch violent programs when your child is around, and try to protect your child from unnecessary violence. Appendix G, "Raising Children to Resist Violence," in chapter 13, includes a number of valuable suggestions for reducing your child's exposure to violence in everyday life.

### DOES YOUR CHILD HAVE BEDTIME PROBLEMS?

How do you decide when you have or are starting to have a bedtime problem with your child? The best clues lie in the answers to a few basic questions: How smoothly does bedtime go? Is bedtime determined by the parent or by the child? Is bedtime consistent from day to day?

It is human nature to want to avoid unpleasant situations. If every time you tell your child to get ready for bed she immediately starts stalling or whining, you'll begin to try to avoid this situation. A common solution is to let the child stay up until she is ready to go to bed. If this is already happening in your home, then you have bedtime problems. In this instance, two of the clues are present: You're allowing the child to determine bedtime, and bedtime doesn't really go smoothly.

If your child requires your presence to be able to fall asleep, you may also have a bedtime problem. All children must learn how to go to sleep alone. This usually requires that they learn to use transition objects, which help them make the transition from being awake to being asleep. Typical transition objects for infants are a hand (he may suck on his thumb, fingers, or the side of his hand), a blanket (she may hold it against her face or suck on the edge of it), or a stuffed toy. With any one of these transition objects, the child learns to relax with the object and fall asleep.

If the transition involves a parent, however, as in feeding to sleep, rocking to sleep, or lying down with the child until he falls asleep, the adult's presence becomes essential for the transition to sleep to occur. And if the child awakens in the middle of the night, the adult must be there for the child to get to sleep again.

Similarly, if your child usually goes to sleep anywhere but in bed, then you have a bedtime problem. It is also not reasonable to expect a parent to hold and cuddle an older child to sleep unless the child is ill. This can be very disruptive to your routine and the time you need for yourself. It also doesn't foster your child's growing sense of independence, which is important to his healthy development.

## PREVENTING BEDTIME PROBLEMS

The easiest way to prevent bedtime problems is to begin placing your 3-month-old baby in bed awake but drowsy, providing her with several potential transition objects, and allowing her (that is, leaving her alone) to learn to fall asleep by herself. If your child hasn't learned to go to sleep alone, no matter how old she is, then you need to begin this teaching. The older the child, though, the more difficult this is to do. If you have ever heard horror stories about a child crying for an hour or two at bedtime, it was almost certainly an older child. A 3-month-old, with the obvious exception of a baby with colic or an illness, simply will not usually cry for that long. Rather, the horror stories come from parents who never allowed their children to learn self-transition at bedtime.

Thus, one way to prevent sleep problems is to allow your child to transition to sleep alone from the time he is an infant. Furthermore, if your child always goes to bed in his bed and is allowed to fall asleep on his own, then on those occasions when he's really fussy or crying at bedtime, you'll have a clear reason to suspect that something may be wrong. Excessive crying is unfair to the child and unfair to you as a parent. If you fail to establish a regular bedtime routine, however, it will be difficult to tell when your child is not feeling well and when he is just fussing.

Another strategy for preventing sleep problems is making sure that your child has a consistent bedtime routine. This routine should involve the same bedtime, as well as the same routine events such as bath, reading stories, getting a snack, and so on. Children will establish the best sleep habits if they are put to bed at night and awakened in the morning at the same time, seven days a week. Getting them on a schedule may also improve their eating and toileting habits as well.

Finally, you may also be able to prevent your child from having sleep problems by making sure she gets an adequate amount of vigorous exercise during the day. It is difficult for a child to sleep at night if she isn't very tired. Exercise can help her get rid of some energy and feel fatigued enough at night to fall asleep without excessive delay. Be sure the activities you choose get your child moving, such as swimming or walking, and incorporate these activities into your family routine for best success.

## Psychological Benefits of Establishing Good Bedtime Habits

Infants and young toddlers are almost totally dependent on the adults in their lives to meet their every need. As children learn to dress and undress themselves, to feed themselves, and to go to bed at night, they are becoming less dependent on their parents for these basic necessities. If you notice the expression on the face of a friend's child who goes to bed on his own, he looks comfortable and confident. He has the sense that he has accomplished something—in his small way, he can "take care of himself."

Children who depend on adults to get to sleep at night don't have this sense of accomplishment. Nor, for that matter, do they feel independent. If you look at the face of a child who is afraid or completely unwilling to try to get to sleep on her own, she typically looks worried and anxious. Children will have to go to sleep alone thousands of times during their childhoods. They have a right to the sense of accomplishment that comes only when they can comfortably go to bed on their own.

## MANAGING BEDTIME PROBLEMS

Before you try to address your child's bedtime problems, it is best to develop a plan, instead of deciding one late night that you have had enough and will now try anything. Also, if there are many stressful events going on in your life, you may wish to wait until some of the stress has cleared before tackling bedtime issues. Although there may never be a good time to address your child's sleep problems, be sure you have the energy to deal with your child's protests as you try to change what is familiar and comforting.

### Strategies for Bedtime Resistance

A critical component of getting a child to fall asleep on his own lies in his self-quieting skills, or the ability to calm himself down when he is upset. Fortunately, self-quieting skills can be taught during the day. In fact, we feel very strongly that it is unkind to try to work on self-quieting skills at bedtime, if most of the time during the day you never allow him to practice his self-quieting skills. The best and most readily available time to work on self-quieting skills is when you see a naturally occurring opportunity, such as when he is playing with a toy and the toy won't do what he wants it to do, or when he doesn't want you to leave him in a room and you have the option of leaving anyway. Each time your child quiets himself down, he is getting a tiny step closer to falling asleep on his own and to being less dependent on you and more self-assured. Before you begin to address a bedtime problem, be absolutely certain that your child is able to quiet himself during the day.

Another very convenient time to let your child practice her self-quieting skills is when you use time-out. The self-quieting skills used during time-out will be very useful at sleep times. (See chapter 9 for a more detailed discussion of self-quieting skills and chapter 4 for more information on the use of time-out.)

Begin with training in self-quieting during the day, and stay at it at least one week before you begin to work on the bedtime problem. The first night after your week of day training, start by doing whatever you usually do before bedtime—a bath, a bedtime story, a prayer, a glass of milk and a cookie—it really doesn't matter. Change one thing, though. About 30 minutes before the bedtime you've decided on, discourage roughhousing and running around the house to allow your child time to wind down before going to bed.

When bedtime comes, place your child in bed, give him a kiss, say goodnight, tell him you'll see him in the morning, walk out of the room (we also prefer closing the door, but that's optional), and *do not* go back into the room before morning for anything short of a catastrophe. The first night you can expect anywhere from 15 minutes to several hours of crying, yelling, and screaming. However, the better you do your day preparation, the easier the night training will be for both you and your child. Letting a child cry himself to sleep when he does not have good self-quieting skills can be very draining emotionally and physically for both the parent and child. Thus, we prefer that you start with day preparation, providing multiple opportunities during the day for your child to self-quiet. It is better to teach your child to master these skills during the day and continue with your previous bedtime routines than to try to implement the new strategies at night when you are tired and most vulnerable to giving in to your child. Once your child can calm down more quickly during the day, try the strategies at bedtime.

## Strategies for Night Awakenings

A slightly different bedtime problem is the child who goes to bed without many problems, but who wakes up in the middle of the night and cannot get back to sleep alone. Typically, however, these children have problems with sleep onset as well and simply need their parent's presence to fall back to sleep. Thus, be sure to review the strategies for minimizing bedtime resistance, such as having a routine and allowing self-transition, before trying to manage night awakenings. If you lie with your child until she is asleep at the beginning of the night, do not expect her to be able to wake up at night without needing your help to fall back to sleep.

Often simply leaving your child's room, after cuddling but before he's asleep, will teach him the skills he needs to get back to sleep from a night awakening. Conversely, staying with him until he's asleep prevents him from learning the self-quieting skills that will serve him well in the middle of the night. If you've done the day training for at least one week and your child has shown improvement during the day, then the middle-of-the-night training shouldn't take more than a couple of days to manage. Above all, don't start to manage night waking until you have seen your child self-quiet, during the day, on a number of occasions.

Another remedy for middle-of-the-night awakenings, after you've done the day training, is to ignore the child's crying, pleading, and moaning and allow her to learn how to go back to sleep alone. Strategies for night awakenings caused by night terrors and nightmares are found later in this chapter. If she comes out of her room, simply pick her up and carry her back to bed without saying a word each and every time she gets up. You might be tempted to explain what you are doing, but this will simply reinforce your child's behavior of getting out of bed. This time there's no kiss, no tucking in, and no saying goodnight. At first, your child may test you greatly. But even the child who holds our clinic record of getting up 72 times the first night of our intervention got up only 10 times the second night.

If your child tries to run away from you or simply gets up in the night and wanders through the house, you can use the same strategy. If you can carry your child, carry him facing away from you. Gently place him back in bed and leave the room. If your child is too big to carry, then simply lead her back to her bed holding her hand. When you get to the bed, try to limit stimulation as much as possible. Refrain from talking to her, tucking her in, or even arranging her stuffed animals. Even a small amount of interaction can awaken her more fully, making it more difficult to get back to sleep. If your child becomes confrontational during your attempts to return her to bed or you become excessively angry, you may need more specific strategies offered by your pediatrician or a mental health professional.

Some have recommended the use of rewards, during the day, when a child stays in bed at night. One example is a "star chart," on which your child earns a star for each night he remains in bed the entire night, and he can exchange stars for a reward the next day. For a star chart to be effective, the child must be able to exchange the stars the next day for an item or activity of his choice. Begin by generating a "menu" with your child of possible rewards he can earn. The list might include an extra bedtime story, baking cookies with you, or playing a game of his choice. The items do not have to cost money and in fact are more rewarding when they include time with you. The morning after the star is given, have your child choose his reward and "cash" it in as soon as possible that day or evening. If you are going to use some type of reward, remember that children's preferences can change from day to day —that's why you use stars or stickers. One day your child might want to exchange a star for an extra bedtime story, and another day he might want to exchange the star for an extra treat or sweet. Thus, plan to be flexible if you choose to reward appropriate bedtime behavior in this way. Make sure as you are putting the star on the chart that you talk to your child about why he is getting the star. Offer specific praise, such as "You must be so proud of yourself, sleeping all alone."

Another strategy is called a "bedtime pass."[4] Your child starts out each evening with one pass (see sample bedtime pass).

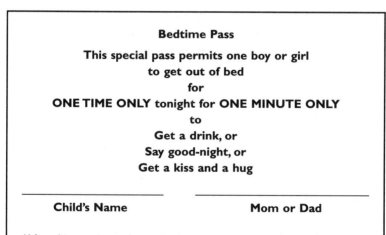

**Bedtime Pass**

**This special pass permits one boy or girl
to get out of bed
for
ONE TIME ONLY tonight for ONE MINUTE ONLY
to
Get a drink, or
Say good-night, or
Get a kiss and a hug**

_____    _____

**Child's Name**         **Mom or Dad**

(After this pass is used once in the evening, it cannot be used again until the next evening. Boys or girls who come out of their bedrooms after using the Pass will be escorted back to their room, have their bedroom door closed, and remain in their bedroom until morning. No exceptions!)

**219**

She can use the pass only one time each night. For example, she can exchange it for one more hug, a drink, or a trip to the bathroom. Often the child isn't sure whether she will "need" the pass later in the evening, so she learns to hold off using it until later, "just in case." The result is that she falls asleep while trying to determine whether it's time to use it or not. In essence, she is using her self-quieting skills while she is waiting. The bedtime pass is a nice idea because it promotes quiet contemplation instead of confrontation. What do you do if your child gets up in the middle of the night and tiptoes so quietly into your room that you do not hear him to put him back in his room? If this happens, it's usually because two things are working against you: You are a sound sleeper, and your child is a good creeper. Both can be handled with an ingenious little device available at most hardware or discount stores—a cowbell. Simply tie the cowbell above your child's or your own door so that when he opens the door to sneak into your room, the bell will swing down and make enough noise to awaken you. Carry him back to bed, facing away from you, without saying a single word. The cowbell also works for children who get up at night for other reasons, such as to go to the kitchen for a midnight snack.

Of course, it is always reasonable to discontinue your efforts to eliminate bedtime problems if your child becomes ill or experiences a traumatic event. If you have houseguests or take a trip and you all must sleep in the same room, the disruption in routine may very well make bedtime problems worse or help to create bedtime problems you haven't had before. In fact, many children who have never had bedtime problems develop them with these disruptions. Such problems are typically short term, however. If your child's sleep problems persist beyond a week or so after an illness, your return from vacation, or the thunderstorm, treat it while it's still minor with the strategies we've discussed.

Once a child is self-quieting easily and frequently, is getting lots of exercise, and is on a routine schedule, bedtime resistance and night awakenings will almost always resolve themselves. However, these strategies for dealing with bedtime problems, as with those for other problems, work best when you also follow the other guidelines offered in this book. Remember, at least half of eliminating any problem behavior is catching your child being good when he is good, which usually covers a major portion of the waking day. If you aren't working on following the other guidelines, then these bedtime remedies may not be very effective.

## Strategies for Night Terrors

Your child may have night terrors if she awakens in the middle of the night crying and cannot be consoled and if, in the morning, she does not recall having awakened or remember any of the details about what awakened her. The most thoroughly researched approach to minimizing night terrors is to record what time they occur for about one week. When you have established what time they are occurring, set your own alarm clock for about 30 minutes before you expect the night terror to occur. Get up with the alarm, and go to your child's room. Wake him gently until he is just about awake. Then, tuck him in again and go back to bed. In most cases, these scheduled awakenings will eliminate or significantly decrease the night terrors in about one to two weeks.

## Strategies for Nightmares

Nightmares are a more common occurrence than night terrors and are a normal part of child development. They can be distinguished from night terrors by the fact that the child typically awakens after the nightmare and remembers it and can tell you about it both at the time and again in the morning. Nightmares occur in about 10% to 50% of children between the ages of 3 and 6 years.[5] If your child awakens from a nightmare, hold her comfortably and pat her on the head or on the back, perhaps making soothing comments such as, "Everything will be OK." Try to avoid the temptation to discuss the nightmare at length in the middle of the night, as this will awaken your child further. Save any such discussion for the next day. The next day after you've both had more sleep, and with the nightmare a little more distant in time, you and you child are much less likely to be upset.

Treatment strategies for nightmares have focused on reducing the child's anxiety at bedtime. It is also wise to monitor your child's TV or movie watching if scary images seem to increase his likelihood of a nightmare. You may also want to try the scheduled awakenings that are effective for night terrors. There are many books on the topic of nightmares and bad dreams on the market. You may want to visit your local bookstore and read through books on nightmares, often found in the parenting or children's section of the store. Make sure that you read any such book yourself before reading it to your child to make sure it will have the desired effect of reassuring him. You don't want to find out, too late, that the content frightens him instead. As you read them to your child and discuss them with her, she'll better understand that everyone has dreams and that they need not frighten her. Most children experience a decrease in nightmares as they mature, however, with little or no intervention.

### Strategies for Sleepwalking

Sleepwalking occurs in about 1% to 6% of children, and 15% of all children experience at least one episode of sleepwalking.[6]

"Sleepwalking" includes simply sitting up in bed as well as walking. The child is often difficult to awaken and, on awakening, appears confused. Sleepwalking is most prevalent in children between the ages of 4 and 8 years and usually spontaneously disappears after adolescence. The frequency of the behavior can vary from infrequently to several times a week. Sleepwalking can be exacerbated or induced by fever, sleep deprivation, and some medications.

The only research we could locate on sleepwalking recommends using scheduled awakenings, as with night terrors. You can usually expect a decrease in sleepwalking in about one to two weeks. One other procedure that has appeared in the research literature involves awakening the child while she is sleepwalking, which can be difficult because the child is sleeping very soundly, even while walking.

A key concern with sleepwalking, unlike the other bedtime problems, is the risk factor. Because the sleepwalker is moving around the house and may even try to leave the house, the possibility of a fall or a bump into something is very real. For that reason, most sleep experts recommend childproofing the house as much as possible and making it very difficult for your child to leave the house by locking the outside doors and securing doors to the basement or to the attic. Outside doors can be secured by a double cylinder dead bolt lock, which is a large (usually at least 1 inch long) bolt that secures the door to the doorframe. Because a key is required each time the door is opened, even from the inside, it's a good idea to mount the key on a nail near the top of the door jam where a sleepy child would not be able to find it, but where any alert adult could locate it immediately. Be sure to place the key in exactly the same place by all doors so you do not have to think about where it is during an emergency. And, when you practice fire drills at home, include finding your key in the dark.

## WHEN TO SEEK PROFESSIONAL HELP

If you are having major confrontations at bedtime or in the middle of the night that persist for more than a few weeks, it might be time to talk to your pediatrician to get other strategies or to obtain a referral to a professional who is trained in the management of sleep problems in children. Your pediatrician is also the best person to determine if another factor such as diabetes is responsible for your child's frequent night awakening. The parents of the two children who hold our clinic records for getting out of bed (72 times) and crying in the middle of the night (8 hours) both required professional consultation to eliminate their respective problems.

Any time a child is getting up more than 10 times a night or crying for more than 1 hour, you may need help. In our outpatient clinic, this usually means a few clinic appointments and a number of phone calls. The clinic appointments are to make certain there aren't more serious problems, and the phone calls are to help parents stick to the treatment procedures.

You may want to try the procedures in this chapter for a month before you seek professional treatment. If they do not help, find a mental health professional who has experience working with children with sleep problems. If the professional wants to see either you or your child repeatedly for a long time, you should ask why he or she is recommending such extensive treatment. The therapist may feel that other issues requiring longer term work underlie the immediate sleep issues. Most of the time, if you follow good behavioral advice, your child's sleep problems should diminish within three weeks or so, depending on the age of your child; usually, the younger the child, the more readily sleep problems can be remedied.

Sleep problems that are a result of anxiety or a traumatic event (for example, a break-in at your home) may not resolve as quickly and may also require professional intervention. In such cases, you should consult a mental health professional who is experienced in the treatment of anxiety and anxiety-related disorders in children.

## CONCLUSION

The only real difference between sleep problems and the other problems that parents experience with their children is that they occur at night when we, the parents, are tired or even sound asleep. The most important message of this chapter is to recognize that sleep problems are best dealt with during the day or around bedtime—not in the middle of the night. As with other problems discussed in this book, you will probably need to teach your child either how to apply an old skill in a new situation or teach her a new skill such as effective self-quieting. Resolution of sleep problems can be very rewarding and often leads to resolution of other problems during the day that might be a result of a tired child or parent.

## APPENDIX C: DAY CORRECTION OF BEDTIME PROBLEMS

Many parents of young children experience problems related to bedtime. They may not be able to get their children to bed at night, or their children may wake up in the middle of the night and be unable to get back to sleep by themselves. The vast majority of these problems stem from the fact that the children do not have self-quieting skills. *Self-quieting skills* refers to children's ability to quiet themselves when they begin to get upset about something. Most children with bedtime problems have had help from their parents in quieting at bedtime. This help may consist of nursing the child to sleep, rocking the child to sleep, lying down with the child, or allowing the child to drift off to sleep in the parent's bed.

The following strategies will help your child go to sleep alone:

- Wake your child up at about the same time every morning. Be sure that you get her up while she is still playing quietly instead of waiting until she is crying.
- Put your child to bed at about the same time every night. Put him to bed alone, awake, and tired.
- Feed your child meals at about the same time every day.
- Make sure that your child gets vigorous exercise every day.
- Use time-out during the day for most misbehavior. Time-out should not be over until your child has self-quieted. Make sure that you are not avoiding any opportunities to use time-out; every time-out helps her build self-quieting skills.
- Develop a routine for the last 30 minutes before bedtime that quiets your child, and do not vary from it.
- Use time-in during the day whenever your child is engaged in an activity that you consider acceptable.
- Place several soft toys in your child's bed that can be used as transition objects.

- If you have to check on your child during the night, do not talk to him, do not turn on the light, and do not pick him up.

Once a child has developed self-quieting skills during the day and has had at least one week to practice these skills, she can usually learn to self-quiet at night within three or four nights.

*Note.* From *Beyond Discipline: Parenting That Lasts a Lifetime* (p. 127) by E. R. Christophersen, 1998, Shawnee Mission, KS: Overland Press, 1998. Copyright 1998 by Edward R. Christophersen. Adapted with permission.

## APPENDIX D: HELPING YOUR CHILD STOP GETTING OUT OF BED AT NIGHT

- Establish a reasonable bedtime or naptime, and under normal day-to-day circumstances put your child to bed at that time every day.
- About 30 minutes before bedtime, start "quiet time," during which your child should engage in quiet activities and avoid roughhousing.
- Go through your regular bedtime routine (bedtime story, kisses, drink, bathroom, and so forth).
- Have your child in bed at the established time. Tell him goodnight and that you will see him in the morning, turn off the light, leave the room, and close the door (the last is optional).
- Monitor your child very closely the first few nights to catch her getting out of bed the instant she gets up.
- When your child gets up, put him back in bed as matter-of-factly as possible. Do not talk to him or act angry. Do not tuck him in, soothe him, or even carry him in an affectionate manner.
- Continue doing this each time your child gets up. You may be surprised how often he will get up the first night or two, but don't get discouraged—he is just testing to find out whether you really mean it. Don't give up.
- In the morning, praise your child for staying in bed (if he did) and reward him with something minor, like allowing him to choose between two different-flavored foods for breakfast or access to a preferred toy. If he didn't stay in bed, say nothing.

*Note.* From *Little People: A Commonsense Guide to Child Rearing* (4th ed., p. 185) by E. R. Christophersen, 1988, Shawnee Mission, KS: Overland Press. Copyright 1988 by Edward R. Christophersen. Adapted with permission.

# CHAPTER 12

# FACILITATING TOILET TRAINING

Toilet training can be a very sensitive issue. At times, this training seems to take place on a parent–child battleground. Although many other skills that parents teach their children can be and are ignored by friends, neighbors, and relatives, this often is not the case with toilet training! Many otherwise reasonable people will put pressure on parents to toilet train their children. We marvel at the "records" we hear from parents at social functions. If one mother says her daughter was trained at 18 months, someone else in the group says his son was potty trained at 15 months. This goes on and on until one parent says her child was potty trained at 8 months. Nonsense! How can you be potty trained before you can walk to the toilet?

Parents also have some interesting ways of toilet training and various definitions of "success." For example, some parents might consider their child toilet trained if they hold her over a toilet and she happens to have a bowel movement that hits the water. Or some parents may hear their child grunt, hurry him to the toilet, take off his diaper, and set him on the toilet for a bowel movement. In both of these situations, the parents might be "toilet trained," but the child surely is not!

So how do you successfully train a child to use the toilet without creating a battleground in your home? This chapter gives some suggestions for how to tell when your child may be ready for toilet training, how to encourage the building of toileting skills, some common barriers to successful toilet training, and how to address other toileting problems.

## HOW TO TELL IF YOUR CHILD IS READY

A child is not ready to be toilet trained just because friends or relatives begin asking her parents when they're going to start toilet training. When pressed, parents need to say, firmly but nicely, "When she's ready," and drop it. An excellent book called *Toilet Training in Less Than a Day* describes how to tell when a child is ready to be toilet trained.[1] The authors describe what they call their "readiness criteria," and we know of no better ones. Their criteria address the following four points:

1. Does the child have the manual dexterity to raise and lower his pants? If he doesn't, it is too soon to completely toilet train him. When children are first toilet trained, there is only a short lag between the time they feel the urge to urinate or defecate and when they can't wait any longer. That is why your child should be able to quickly lower his pants before you begin training. And it may make training easier if you make certain the child is wearing loose-fitting underwear.

2. Does the child urinate only a couple of times a day, completely emptying her bladder, or does she still urinate a little bit many times a day? It is much harder to train a child who urinates seven or eight times a day than to train one who usually urinates four times a day because of physical maturity and larger bladder capacity.

3. Does he have vocabulary sufficient to understand the words

connected with toilet training? He must understand words such as *wet, dry, pants,* and *potty*. If your child doesn't know what you're talking about, it will be difficult to toilet train him.

4. Does your child understand and follow simple commands, such as "Please come here," "Please put that down," and "Please sit down"? Does she follow reasonable instructions when she is asked to? This criterion is the most important of the four. If, for example, your child has a temper tantrum whenever you ask him to do something, the chances of being able to toilet train him are very slim. Be careful not to be misled that your child is good at understanding and following simple commands if you have a tendency to never ask him to. Many parents who think their child is good at following directions often realize that, in reality, they rarely ask their child to do things he may not want to do.

We suggest that you wait three months after your child can successfully meet all four of the readiness criteria, which provides a safety margin in case you have overestimated your child's abilities. This also means that you most likely won't be starting to toilet train your child until she is between 24 and 30 months old. You should expect toilet training to take as long as a few weeks to a month or two. Some children do catch on and are trained in a couple of days, but that is uncommon. Also, keep in mind that most children will have at least occasional "accidents" for six months or so after being toilet trained.

How can you tell when toilet training isn't going well? If you spend a week or so on toilet training and the only difference you really see is that you and your child are at odds much of the day, we suggest that you consider stopping your efforts for at least a month or two before trying again. Also, consider whether stressful events in your household, such as a move or the birth of a baby, may be contributing to the problem, and wait for your family to stabilize before trying training again.

You may also have more success with toilet training at home if the care providers at your child's school try as well. To ensure consistency, it is best to discuss and agree with them on the procedures to be used and when the training should start. Many children seem to do better with toilet training when they are around a number of other children their age who are also in the process of being toilet trained.

## WHAT ABOUT EARLY TOILET TRAINING?

We know of very few advantages of toilet training children too early, or before the age of 18 to 24 months. There will be toilets that they cannot possibly get up on, just because they are so small and the toilets are so tall. There will also be many outfits, particularly in the winter, which they cannot put on or take off on their own. In both of these cases, the too-tall toilet and the difficult clothing, you will end up helping your child to use the bathroom —which, in essence, defeats the advantages of training him early. Certainly, some day care providers will not take a child unless he is toilet trained, but we know of only a few child care centers that would expect a 2-year-old child to be toilet trained.

On the other hand, there may be disadvantages in training too early. Probably the most important is that it can cause friction between you and your child and make the experience of toileting unpleasant. If you commit yourself to getting your child toilet trained, for example, during a two-week vacation from work, the pressure is on. You've got a limited period of time to accomplish something your child has never done before. And, ultimately, whether or not your child gets toilet trained depends, in large part, on your child, and not on your time schedule.

Finally, for children who have a predisposition to constipation, early attempts at toilet training can result in constipation or a combination of constipation and stool withholding. *Constipation* refers to difficulty or discomfort passing bowel movements, and *stool withholding* refers to the intentional withholding of stools, for example, until you put a diaper or a pull-up on the child. Both of these problems can present barriers to successful toilet training and are discussed further later in this chapter.

## PSYCHOLOGICAL ASPECTS OF TOILET TRAINING

Toilet training is probably the most difficult skill that toddlers need to learn. At no prior time in their lives have they been expected to recognize feedback from their bodies in the form of the sensation that they need to urinate or defecate. Furthermore, they must cognitively process the feedback and stop what they are doing, walk to the bathroom, partially disrobe, eliminate in the toilet or potty-chair, wipe themselves, dress themselves, and return to what they were doing. And, to further complicate the process, most of the time it is virtually impossible for an adult to tell when a child feels the urge to urinate or defecate, and children must rely on themselves to act in time. In short, toilet training is very demanding for children.

Of course, toilet training can also be very rewarding. Most children seem to take great pride in being able to independently toilet. That's why Grandma and Grandpa are usually called the first time a child eliminates in the toilet—because it is a major milestone in a child's life. The sense of accomplishment and the sense of independence can contribute greatly to a child's self-esteem.

## EARLY PREPARATION FOR TOILET TRAINING

By paying close attention to the four readiness criteria, you can begin teaching your child some of the skills necessary for toilet training before you actually begin training. The following sections describe some specific suggestions for encouraging toileting readiness.

### Raising and Lowering Pants

Begin by teaching your child how to raise and lower her pants when you are dressing and undressing her. Place your hands on top of her hands. Put both her hands and your hands on the top band of her pants. If you teach your child to place one hand in front and one hand in the back, it is much easier for her to get her pants up. Small children have very prominent bottoms; therefore, if they try to lift their pants by gripping the sides, the back of their pants can get stuck. This is why countless children come out of the bathroom holding their pants up with both hands, with the waistband caught right below their bottoms.

At first, you can pull her pants down with little or no help from her. After you have helped her a number of times, you will begin to feel when she helps to pull. Gradually do less and less of the pulling, letting her do more and more. This may take several weeks to accomplish.

### Building Toileting Vocabulary

You can start building toileting vocabulary each time you change your child's diapers. Use words consistently as you change your child's soiled or wet diaper. For example, say, "You peed in your diaper, so now it is wet." Or ask your child, "Did you go poop in your diaper?" when you smell that he needs to be changed. You can also build your child's vocabulary surrounding toileting when your child sees you using the bathroom. Children are notorious for coming into the bathroom when their parents are using the toilet. Tell him that "Mommy's going pee-pee in the potty" or that "Daddy is going potty in the toilet." Whatever words you choose to use in your family, in time your child will associate those words with toileting behavior.

Some parents worry about their child seeing them naked, or at least partially naked, when they are using the bathroom. A general rule of thumb is that you should exercise discretion about appearing naked in front of your children, but there's no need to overreact about it. It's virtually a fact of life that your children will see you using the bathroom at some point. This will not be detrimental to your young child, especially if it is handled matter-of-factly. You can develop rules of privacy for the bathroom as your child gets older.

## Following Instructions

Problems in toilet training sometimes arise because a child won't follow simple instructions. Before you start with the actual toilet training, you should be working with your child to follow instructions. Many parents, instead of teaching their child to mind, just stop asking her to do things. Parents sometimes report that their child is good at following instructions, yet when we ask them to get their child to do something, they say, "Oh, she doesn't like to do that." Getting a child to do only what he wants to do doesn't require much skill or training. Getting him to do something he doesn't want to do is the real work.

If you attempt to toilet train a child who will not follow simple verbal instructions, you stand a very good chance either of meeting with complete failure or of undertaking toilet training that lasts for six or eight stressful months. If you are having problems with your child doing what she's asked to do, you can find helpful suggestions in chapter 2 on positive feedback and chapter 4 on discipline.

## Becoming Familiar With the Potty-Chair or Toilet

Potty-chairs can be attractive to children because they sit on the floor, they're small, and they are usually relatively easy for the child to get on and off. A potty-chair that sits on the floor should be stable and should allow the child good footing to enable balance and elimination. This increases the likelihood that the child can accomplish toileting with little or no assistance, and therefore that the child will be successful.

You can put the potty-chair in the bathroom for a few weeks before you begin training to give your child a chance to get accustomed to its presence. Or as Dr. Brazelton, a well-known pediatrician and author, recommends, you can put the potty-chair in an area that the child frequents, such as the kitchen or the family room. Over time, you can encourage him to sit on the potty-chair. Some parents give their child a treat on the potty-chair or encourage him to sit on the potty-chair while they read him a story. The purpose of this exercise is to expose your child to the potty-chair enough that he's relaxed when sitting on it—obviously a prerequisite to being able to use the potty-chair for elimination.

One disadvantage of using a potty-chair is that you have to empty it into the toilet, and your child may make a mess if she attempts to copy you and empty the container herself. In addition, your child may not be able to reach the potty-chair in time if it is not located conveniently.

Instead of using a potty-chair, you may decide to use the

bathroom toilet. The obvious benefit is that you will not have to purchase the equipment to toilet train your child. In addition, toilets are found in most places that your child will be visiting, such as stores, malls, and friends' houses, and will thus look familiar to him. If you intend to use the regular toilet, however, you may want to consider purchasing a small toilet ring that fits over the toilet seat, making the opening of the toilet smaller and easier for a child to sit on. You may want to obtain a portable ring that can be folded and carried with you on outings or when going to friends' or relatives' houses. When some children get accustomed to using a toilet ring, they report that they "cannot go to the bathroom" without the ring, which can result in training problems and accidents but usually doesn't last very long.

One drawback of using the toilet is that most children of toilet-training age cannot rest their feet on the floor when they are sitting on the toilet, resulting in precarious balance and difficulty bearing down to have a bowel movement. Thus, if you decide to train your child on the toilet, get two steps that your child can use both to get onto and off of the seat and to rest her feet when using the toilet. Without such steps, getting on the toilet may be difficult or impossible, particularly when you consider that children usually wait until the very last second before heading for the toilet.

Perhaps the most important part of toilet training is consistency. Regardless of what type of toilet you choose to use, try to present your child with consistent experiences. Thus, if you're going to use a potty-chair and you have a home with several toilets, you may want to consider purchasing two or more similar or identical potty-chairs. And, when going out, you may want to take a portable toilet ring with you. Most importantly, be patient with your child if he hesitates to use a toilet that does not look like the one he has trained on.

## TOILET TRAINING YOUR CHILD

When *Toilet Training in Less Than a Day* was published in 1974, it was virtually the only book of its kind on the market. Over the years, it has sold hundreds of thousands of copies. In early 2001, it was still ranked at about 1,100 out of the 500,000+ books available through amazon.com, the world's busiest Web site for books. In the interim, there have been hundreds of books published on the topic of toilet training, some of which you may find useful.

Unfortunately, to our knowledge, there is no research that compares even two of the available books to determine if one method was better than another. Because there is no research showing which procedures work the best, you should consider the ideas we present to be just some of the many available approaches. We do not recommend, however, the use of physical punishment, criticism, or embarrassment as a part of the toilet training process. If you find that you are getting stressed out by the process and are using such tactics, you may need to wait a month or so before proceeding. Your best option is to choose the strategies that fit best with your availability and lifestyle. And remember, no method for toilet training will be successful if your child is not ready to be trained.

### Practice Sitting on the Potty-Chair or Toilet

The strategy we recommend involves making sure that your child has met each of the readiness criteria listed earlier in this chapter. Although you may not feel that working on these criteria constitutes "toilet training," it really does. Once you are comfortable that your child meets these criteria, you can have her practice sitting on the potty-chair or toilet.

If your child gives some sign that he needs to use the bathroom, such as grimacing, squatting, or pulling at his pants, a sign that in the past has been followed by urinating or defecating in his diaper, then you can suggest that he sit on the potty-chair or toilet. If you place more importance on what your child should do to use the toilet correctly while ignoring accidents as much as possible, you'll find that toilet training will be less stressful.

Instead of forcing your child to sit on the potty-chair or toilet for long periods of time, have her sit on the potty-chair many times in one day for short periods. You can even make a game out of it by sitting on the toilet yourself, then asking your toddler to sit on the toilet, then sitting on the toilet yourself again. Try to be relaxed about what you are trying to do or your toddler will realize that you are getting anxious, and the process may suffer a setback.

Try spending five minutes with your child each time he correctly has a bowel movement in the toilet, doing (within reason) something that the child has chosen to do. This helps the child learn that doing something his parents want him to do leads to doing something he wants to do. Don't, however, resort to punishment if you find that a month or two after toilet training your child starts having accidents again. (Remember: Punishment does not teach what you want the child to learn and will make your child more anxious about the whole process.) Instead, spend a little extra time with your child, teaching him the way you want things done, and when he does it correctly, spend time with him letting him know you appreciate it.

## Intensive Toilet Training

*Toilet Training in Less Than a Day* described what has come to be called an "intensive toilet training procedure."[2] The aspect of it that is "intensive" is the suggestion that parents put a lot of effort into toilet training with the hopes of accomplishing it within a week or so. The authors begin by recommending that you purchase a doll that wets to model for your toddler how to appropriately use the toilet. They recommended having the doll urinate in the potty-chair on numerous occasions on the first day. This allows you to demonstrate almost all of the procedures involved in toileting, including lowering pants, sitting on the potty-chair, urinating, wiping, raising pants, carrying the bowl from the potty-chair to the big toilet to empty it, and flushing the toilet.

Then, before starting toilet training, they recommend giving your child lots of fluids all day long to increase the number of times she urinates during the first day or two of toilet training. This way, if you encourage your toddler to do lots of "toilet sits" (just sitting on the potty-chair often, for short periods of time), she is much more likely to urinate during one of the sits. As mentioned previously, we don't know of any research that supports one toilet training strategy over another. Thus, we recommend reading through all of the ideas in this chapter and choosing the one that best fits the demands of your family's lifestyle. If the strategy does not work, take a break from training and try the strategies again or try another strategy.

## Other Strategies

Virtually all children end up toilet trained, regardless of the method their parents use. In families with 8 or 10 children, the toilet training is usually done by older siblings who have never read a book or visited a Web site on toilet training. Rather, they model appropriate toileting, and, usually well after their younger siblings are "ready," they prompt the use of the toilet.

So should you have Cheerios floating on the water where your son can attempt to "shoot" them with his stream of urine? Should you use sticker charts to track your daughter's progress?

Should you read books to your child about the various animals on this planet who all "poop"? Of course! What most of these strategies do is provide you with creative ways to address the issue of toilet training. Pick a couple of the strategies that appeal to you, and see what happens! Just remember to stay relaxed, and don't become too invested in "making" one of your strategies work.

## COMMON BARRIERS TO SUCCESSFUL TOILET TRAINING

### Pressured Training

Perhaps the bottom line in toilet training is that it's difficult, if not impossible, to make another person urinate or have a bowel movement. For that reason, children should not be pressured into being toilet trained. Pressure can come in several forms and typically results in failure. One type of pressure is trying to toilet train too early before your child is ready. Pressure can also take the form of coercive words and obvious nonverbal signs of your displeasure, such as sighing or aggressively changing your child's diaper. Early training, hurtful words, and forceful actions are a waste of your time and, even worse, will only increase your feelings of frustration, negativity, and guilt about your child. Equally important, the pressure will not help your child to relax, which is an important component of toilet training.

If your child isn't making any progress and you let him know how frustrated you are, your child will know that he has disappointed you and will feel like a failure. Feeling like a failure will do nothing to promote his toilet training. It's usually better, if you reach such an impasse, to declare a moratorium on toilet training for a least a couple of weeks, during which you don't even mention toilet training. After this cooling-off period, you can begin your toilet training attempts again.

Pressured training and the stress it causes a child can also lead to constipation and stool withholding, which can become a self-perpetuating problem. The child experiences stress when passing a bowel movement and so withholds it, and the next time she has to have a bowel movement, she holds it in. Holding it in typically results in harder and dryer bowel movements, which are more likely to produce discomfort, which makes the child even more unwilling to have a bowel movement and easier for her to hold her stools. We routinely see children who have been able to prevent themselves from having bowel movements for up to two weeks. Constipation is discussed in more detail later in this chapter.

### Toileting Refusal

"Toileting refusal" refers to a child's refusal to have a bowel movement on the toilet, even though he will readily have a bowel movement in his diaper or pull-up. In the classic case of toileting refusal, a child is playing when she feels the urge to have a bowel movement. She will hold her stool until her parent puts a diaper or a pull-up on her, at which point she very easily has a bowel movement. Toileting refusal often starts after a child has had one or more painful bowel movements. Even though the painful bowel movement may not have occurred while he was on the toilet, the child still seems to make a connection between his painful bowel movements and the toilet.

Toileting refusal can be very frustrating for parents. Because toileting refusal is frequently seen in 3- and 4-year-olds, it's difficult to get much information about why they are refusing because they lack sufficient verbal and cognitive skills. In an unpublished survey we conducted with pediatricians, they reported that about 1.5% to 2.0% of the pediatric population has problems with toileting refusal, which is a significant number of children. Despite the number of children that have this problem, there is almost no research on toileting refusal to guide its diagnosis and treatment. One publication on treating toileting refusal provides the suggestions we discuss in this section.[3]

When a child refuses to use the toilet, the first goal is to make certain she is not having large or painful bowel movements. Increasing the amount of fiber and reducing the amount of dairy products in her diet usually accomplishes this goal. After your child has gone at least one month having soft, formed stools, it is much easier to try to encourage her to use the toilet.

You can encourage your child to have his bowel movements in the bathroom, but not necessarily in the toilet, using the following steps: When your child asks for a diaper, assume that he is about to have a bowel movement. Ask him to come into the bathroom so that you can put the diaper on and he can have his bowel movement in the bathroom just like Mommy and Daddy do. Getting a child with toileting refusal to restrict his bowel movements to the bathroom is a big improvement, especially when it comes to cleanup.

If your child refuses to accompany you into the bathroom to have her diaper put on and to have her bowel movement in the diaper, you may have to settle for putting the diaper on and allowing her to have her bowel movement somewhere else in the house. The point of this step is for your child to have to respond to the "call to stool," or the feeling that she is about to have a bowel movement. If you cannot make it to this step, you probably need to schedule an appointment with your child's pediatrician.

After your child is routinely having his bowel movements in a diaper in the bathroom, encourage him to sit on the toilet, with the lid down, or on the potty-chair, with the lid down, to have his bowel movement. If you want him to use the toilet, make sure there is a stepstool to help him get on and off of the toilet and keep his balance.

Once your child is willing to sit on the toilet with the lid down, try sitting her on it with the lid up but the diaper still on. Gradually, you can loosen the tabs of her diaper so that the bowel movement will eventually fall into the toilet out of the loose diaper. Be sure to give your child positive attention for cooperating with these small steps by reading him a story, playing a short game with him, or even putting stickers on a chart that can be exchanged for special time with Mom, Dad, or a grandparent or older sibling. Once again, if you find this process overly frustrating, seek help from your pediatrician, who may also refer you to a child psychologist.

## Day Wetting

For children who have recently been toilet trained, it's not uncommon to have occasional accidents for the first six months or so. Such accidents typically do not indicate a problem unless they happen once every two weeks or more. And, even then, if your child is having an occasional accident because she is so involved in her play or because she's outside playing and did not make it to the toilet in time, just ignore it and help your child clean up.

One way to address day wetting is simply to frequently remind your child to go to the bathroom on a regular basis. If you keep track of when he has wetting accidents, you will probably find that there is a pattern. It might be when he is playing or when he is watching a favorite TV show. If you remind him to try going to the bathroom and briefly interrupt his playtime to give him the opportunity to do so, you can expect him to have far fewer accidents.

How long should you plan on keeping up these reminders? We lightheartedly tell parents to remind for at least one year. The purpose of using such a long time is to convey to parents that this is not a behavior that can be changed overnight. Rather, it may take anywhere from several weeks to several months.

## OTHER TOILETING PROBLEMS

### Constipation

Parents must be aware of constipation, its signs, and how to prevent it from interfering with full toilet training and good health as the child gets older. The most common time for a child to get constipated is when she is switched from breast milk to formula or cow's milk during infancy. Thus, a child may have a history of constipation before she even begins toilet training. If constipation begins during toilet training, however, it may be because the parent is placing too much pressure on the child to become toilet trained and therefore, the child may be holding her stools.

Although parents often think of constipation in terms of how long it has been since their child last had a bowel movement, the term "constipation" really refers to difficulty when passing stools. Classic signs of constipation include large stools, pebbly stools, and stools that are uncomfortable or painful to pass. The amount of time that lapses between bowel movements is probably the least reliable sign of constipation; some children have only three bowel movements per week and are not constipated, whereas other children can have one to three movements in a day and be constipated. It's the consistency of the stools and the ease or difficulty with which your child passes them that determine whether he's constipated.

CAUSES OF CONSTIPATION. Constipation can be caused or exacerbated by stool withholding. Some children get into a vicious cycle; they have a bowel movement that is painful or that produces dis-

**245**

comfort, so the next time they need to have a bowel movement they hold the stool rather than passing it. When a child holds her stools, the stools become harder and dryer, which makes it easier for the child to hold them. Over time, this pattern can result in the child's colon (or large intestine) actually stretching to accommodate the added amounts of stool. When the child finally passes the next stool, she is far more likely to experience discomfort, which leads her to hold her stools again, and so on.

Another common cause of constipation is the repeated postponement of the urge to go because of embarrassment about using school toilets, public toilets, or long waiting times for the home bathroom. Often, such children are modeling the behaviors of a parent. If you avoid using public restrooms, you may be unknowingly encouraging your child to avoid responding to his toileting urges as well, which may facilitate constipation if he is prone to have this problem. Thus, when you begin toilet training your child, you should also begin using public rest rooms regularly and continue doing so until well after your child is completely toilet trained.

The most frequent cause of constipation, however, is a diet that is deficient in fiber, which is found in fruits, vegetables, and whole-grain foods. Because fiber is not digested, it makes stools larger, softer, and easier to pass. Eating or drinking too many milk products also causes constipation, either directly, because such products promote constipation, or indirectly, by lessening the child's appetite for fruits and vegetables.

GETTING PROFESSIONAL HELP. Many pediatricians don't ask about constipation. Rather, they wait for you to mention a concern to them. So if your child is having problems with bowel movements, either bring it up at your next regularly scheduled office visit or schedule an office visit for the express purpose of discussing your child's bowel habits. If your child resists having bowel movements, complains about pain during a bowel movement, or actually cries out during a bowel movement, you should discuss it with the pediatrician. Several research studies have shown that the normal range for bowel movements in children is from one or two bowel movements per day to one or two days between bowel movements. If your toddler is consistently having more than two bowel movements per day or is going three or more days without a bowel movement, check with your pediatrician.

Prepare for the appointment with your child's pediatrician by summarizing, preferably in writing, the types and quantities of foods that you child eats and her bowel habits over at least one week. Whenever your child has problems with her bowel movements, it is important that you either accompany her to the bathroom or ask her to call you when she has finished so you can view the size and consistency (hard or soft) of the bowel movement before the toilet is flushed. We recommend that parents typically take care of the cleanup after a bowel movement until their children are about 6 years old, which is a good time to observe bowel movements. A 4- or 5-year-old can, however, help by getting the right amount of toilet paper off the roll, or by wiping with the parent's help. As with the other skills discussed in this book, learning how to wipe takes the physical maturity to complete the task, modeling by parents as they wipe the child, and a gradual increase in opportunities to wipe until the skill is mastered. It is best not to rely on the reports of your young child, as she may be a poor historian. Simply get as much information as you can about your child's bowel movements for your pediatrician.

In addition to considering the information you collect about your child's eating and bowel habits, your pediatrician will probably want to examine your child. By being calm, understanding, and supportive, you can help your child through this uncomfortable procedure.

If your child is constipated, your pediatrician may recommend a regimen of enemas, suppositories, or medications such as stool softeners. This regimen must accompany, and not substitute, the dietary changes needed to ensure the continued passage of soft stools. Finally, your pediatrician may also refer you to a pediatric psychologist. This type of psychologist specializes in medical disorders in children that require behavior changes to effectively manage symptoms. Such a referral does not necessarily mean that your child has mental health problems; such professionals can provide guided assistance in changing some lifestyle behaviors.

Because constipation seems to run in families, if you have had problems with constipation it wouldn't be inappropriate to share that fact with your child. Doing so will help convince her that she isn't the only person in the whole wide world who suffers from constipation. Also, many television commercials advertise products that combat constipation, so when you see one, point out to your child that there must be a lot of out people with similar problems.

## Preventing Constipation

The best way to prevent constipation is to make sure that your child gets adequate dietary fiber. Dietary fiber helps to soften your child's stools and helps to keep them moist by absorbing moisture. A task force from the American Academy of Pediatrics suggests using as a rule of thumb for the daily gram intake of dietary fiber the child's age plus 5.[4] For example, a 4-year-old child should eat 9 grams of dietary fiber each day. Children seem to have fewer problems with constipation if the fiber is divided among the three main meals. So a 4-year-old should be getting three grams of fiber with breakfast, three grams with lunch, and three grams with dinner.

By carefully reading the nutritional information provided on the packaging of food, parents can become knowledgeable about the fiber content of foods fairly quickly. Remember to check serving sizes as well. If your child is a light eater, he may not be eating the full serving size required to get the number of fiber grams stated on the product label. Appendix E lists a number of popular foods and the number of grams of fiber in each.

Getting your child to eat fiber is easier if you purchase foods that have adequate amounts of fiber and avoid foods that contain lots of sugar and little or no fiber. Most children do better with simple dietary substitutions rather than large-scale changes. For example, when purchasing Cheerios, pick the multigrain Cheerios instead of regular Cheerios.

In addition to monitoring your child's fiber, you should also watch her calcium intake from dairy products. Although children need calcium and dairy products are high in calcium, try to avoid giving your child too many dairy products if she tends to have stools that are hard to pass. Children can get all of the calcium they need from reasonable amounts of dairy products. The American Academy of Pediatrics recommends the following daily calcium intake for children and adolescents: Children 1 to 3 years of age should ingest 500 mg of calcium, those 4 to 8 years old need 800 mg daily, and children 9 to 18 years of age require 1300 mg. Many nondairy products such as orange juice are also fortified with calcium. As with other issues of this nature, always check with your pediatrician if you aren't sure whether your child is getting adequate calcium in his diet.

When you are trying to change your child's eating habits to eliminate constipation, it is important to be a good role model. You can do this by eating foods with healthy amounts of fiber, not eating unhealthy snacks between meals, and eating and drinking a reasonable amount of dairy products. If you cannot relieve constipation with fairly simple dietary changes, you need your doctor's reassurance that your child is physically all right and suggestions for preventing future constipation. Home remedies for constipation, such as suppositories, enemas, or laxatives, should not normally be given to children without a doctor's advice.

Parents who have had the most success with dietary changes have included their child in the selection and preparation of foods. Before going to the grocery store, sit down with your child and Appendix E and identify foods she is willing to try. Then, when in the grocery store, read the nutritional information with the child to decide whether a substitution should be made. In time, children prone to constipation become just as knowledgeable about the foods that are best for them as children with other medical conditions such as diabetes. And generally, children are much more compliant when they have adequate input into the decisions made in selecting foods. They may also feel proud of themselves and the contribution they are making to improve their toileting problems.

## Soiling

Some children alternate constipation with soiling. They'll go two, three, or four days without a bowel movement, soil, then go several days more with no bowel movement. The medical term for soiling is *encopresis,* which refers to having bowel movements other than in the toilet after the child reaches 4 years of age. Of children with constipation, 35% of the girls and 55% of the boys also experience fecal soiling.[5] The vast majority of encopretic children, some 90%, have a history of large or painful bowel movements.[6] Many children with encopresis have experienced constipation since infancy, and many get into the vicious cycle of discomfort, withholding, and increased discomfort.

For a number of years, encopresis has been referred to as the "hidden disease," because most parents simply do not talk about it. About two or three of every 100 children experience encopresis, which means that if a grade school has 300 students attending classes, about six children in the school have encopresis.[7] Only rarely do children—or their parents—know that other children suffer from the same disorder. Children, in particular, usually think they are the only one, which can create anxiety.

Encopresis is difficult to manage, so your child should see his pediatrician. If your child has had problems with constipation since he was an infant, make sure your pediatrician knows you are concerned about finding a long-term solution to the constipation. Long-term management usually involves both increasing the amount of fiber and decreasing the amount of dairy products in the child's diet. And, although fiber supplements are fine, initially, for getting the child to ingest enough fiber, most children with encopresis have to keep their intake of dietary fiber up for a very long time, long enough to be getting adequate amounts of fiber from the foods they eat rather than from supplements.

Although several research studies have shown that children who soil are no more likely to have behavioral or emotional problems than their same-age peers, continued problems with soiling can take their toll on a child emotionally. Beyond about 5 years of age, children who soil are likely to become the subject of teasing. Parents can take several steps to minimize psychological damage to a child who soils:

- Make certain that your pediatrician or pediatric psychologist explains to your child, in language that your child will understand, that soiling is usually a direct result of constipation and that, if your child works with you to make some changes in her diet, the constipation should improve and the soiling should get better.
- Let day care personnel and teachers know about the problem so that they can assist with its management. Parents of school-age children should request that the child be allowed to use

a bathroom in either the nurse's office or the administrative area of the school. The extra privacy will help prevent other children from knowing about the soiling, thereby decreasing the chances that they will tease your child. Also, request that the school substitute fruit juice for milk at lunch. It will be much easier to limit your child's intake of dairy products if you don't have to worry about dairy consumption at school. You should probably also keep an extra change of clothes at school in case your child has an accident there.

- Many teachers or school counselors are really good at educating children, during health discussions, about health care needs. They might, for example, teach the entire class about the benefits of dietary fiber. They might even be willing to assign a class project in which the children keep track of their diet intake, including the amount of fiber they are eating. The age plus 5 rule for children applies to all children, not just children who soil.

- All children with special needs, including children with encopresis, can benefit from private discussions with their parents, their pediatrician, and their school nurse about their needs. Children who soil usually feel quite alone with their problem. Just knowing that there are other children with the same problem can help to alleviate the stigma that they feel. Of course, the health care professionals would not point out who the specific children are, but they can say that they have worked with children with soiling problems before.

- Your child will need a lot of support and encouragement from you during and after he is treated for soiling. Children don't like medical conditions that make them different from their peers, and soiling probably has as much stigma attached to it as any condition that a child can have. Thus, encourage your child to talk to you about his concerns, and provide reassuring hugs and words that you are in it together to solve the soiling problem.

## BED-WETTING

Another major category of toileting problems is enuresis, or bed-wetting. Although very annoying for parents, bed-wetting typically is not a serious problem, and bed-wetting at a young age is not predictive of problems at an older age. Bed-wetting is usually just that, bed-wetting.

Bed-wetting usually stops as your child gradually wets the bed less and less often until she stops completely. If she's wetting twice each night, she'll start wetting only once each night. Then, she'll go from wetting every night to wetting five or six nights each week, with an occasional week when she'll be back to wetting every night. Over a period of months, once she's developmentally ready, she'll eventually stop wetting the bed.

The medical term for bed-wetting, *enuresis,* describes a very common condition in young children. There is a strong familial trait to bed-wetting. If neither parent's family had a bed-wetter in it, only 15% of their children will wet the bed; if one family had a bed-wetter, about half of the children will be bed-wetters; and if both families had a bed-wetter in them, about 77% of the children will wet the bed.[8]

At 3 years of age, almost half of all children still wet the bed if they are not wearing a diaper. By 5 years of age, slightly more than 60% of children are consistently dry in the morning. By 8 years, almost 80% are dry all night. Bed-wetting seems to be a developmental problem rather than a "defect." The vast majority of children end up having a dry bed in the morning without any intervention; the only real variation is when. If bed-wetting continues after age 8, however, or if it causes significant conflict for you or your child or is occurring in combination with other developmental concerns, a consultation with a child psychologist may be indicated.

## What Can Parents Do to Stop Bed-Wetting?

Almost half of children 3 years of age wet the bed, and most parents aren't very pleased when they do, so what can be done while waiting for a child to outgrow bed-wetting? First and foremost, punishment and bribery cannot "teach" a child to stay dry at night, any more than they would teach a toddler to climb the stairs before he is developmentally ready to do so. If you have a child with enuresis, make sure that no one in your home or your family is making him feel bad or humiliating him because of his bed-wetting. Some strategies that that may help, but do not actually stop the bed-wetting, are requiring that the child wear a pull-up or diaper at night (to absorb the urine, not to humiliate the child) and waking the child up and walking her to the bathroom late in the evening or very early in the morning.

If your child is at least 7 years old and is inconvenienced by the bed-wetting, such as being afraid to spend the night at a friend's house, other strategies may be helpful. Consider asking your pediatrician for a referral to a practitioner who has considerable experience in treating children who are bed-wetters. There are several treatments that we recommend for bed-wetting; two involve medications, and one involves time and effort.

## Medications to Reduce Bed-Wetting

The two medications, Tofranil™ (imipramine) and DDAVP™ (desmopressin), were originally marketed for completely different reasons. Imipramine has been on the market for years as an antidepressant for adults. Many adults who took imipramine found that, as a side effect of the medication, they didn't urinate very often. The same is sometimes true of children. Research studies have shown that approximately 35% of children who take imipramine stop wetting the bed. Unfortunately, when the medicine is discontinued, half of the children resume wetting the bed.

The figures for DDAVP, which has been marketed for diabetes insipidis, a disorder which causes children to drink large amounts of liquids and urinate excessively, are quite similar. While actively taking the medication, about 35% of the children stop wetting the bed, with half resuming bed-wetting when the medication is discontinued. Thus, the percentage of children who have stopped bed-wetting after the DDAVP has been discontinued is only about 17%.

The known side effects of these two medicines are potentially quite troublesome, so it is important that you discuss them thoroughly with your pediatrician. Imipramine taken in large doses (for example, if a child swallows too many pills) can be life threatening. Because DDAVP works basically by shutting down the kidneys, children should not be allowed to drink a lot of fluids when taking it. Both medications are generally effective only as long as your child continues taking the medication. DDAVP costs more than $100 per month—not a trivial consideration; children have been reported to take medication for up to three to five years. The medication, when it is effective, does help control bed-wetting while parents wait for their children to outgrow it.

### Bed-Wetting Alarms

Commercially available bed-wetting alarms, if used properly, work about 75% of the time, with almost half of the children resuming their bed-wetting after the alarm treatment is over. Reinstating the alarm eliminates bed-wetting in most children. There are basically two types of bedwetting alarms. The older type, consists of two pads made of a product that resembles extra heavy aluminum foil separated by a thin sheet of paper. The two pads are placed on the bed immediately below where the child sleeps. If the child wets the bed he wets the thin sheet of paper which serves to connect the two pads together completing a circuit, powered by flashlight batteries, that rings an alarm. The second type is worn on the child with a sensing device placed in the child's underwear so that

| Bedwetting Alarm Devices | | |
|---|---|---|
| Device | Manufacturer | Cost |
| Wet-Stop | Palco Labs<br>Santa Cruz, CA<br>800-346-4488<br>www.palcolabs.com | $85.00 |
| Nytone Enuretic Alarm | Nytone Medical Products<br>Salt Lake City, UT<br>801-973-4090<br>www.nytone.com | $58.00 |
| Potty Pager | Ideas for Living<br>Boulder, CO<br>800-497-6573<br>www.pottypager.com | $56.00 |
| Nite Train'r | Koregon Enterprises<br>Beaverton, OR<br>800-544-4240<br>www.nitetrain-r.com | $69.00 |
| Sleep Dry | The TakeCare Store<br>Seattle, WA<br>800-447-2839<br>www.take-care.com | $54.95 |

For additional information on bedwetting alarms, visit www.bedwettingstore.com or call 800-214-9605.

even a small spot of moisture will complete the circuit and ring an alarm.

Alarms generally cost about $50 to $75 and are usually available through pharmacies. Because alarm manufacturers often advertise in pediatric journals and newsletters, you can ask your pediatrician to recommend a manufacturer. Here are some mail order companies that have alarms available and the approximate cost of their products.

The following are some practical tips for using an enuresis alarm successfully based on the work of Dr. Moffatt[9]:

- Plan on using the alarm for a three-month trial.
- Keep a diary, starting at least two weeks before you start using the alarm, that includes the number of wet nights, the number of episodes per night, and the size of the wet spot.
- Do not rely on the alarm to awaken your child. You need to plan on being a part of the alarm system, because your child may not arouse on his own to the alarm initially. After a few weeks of your help, he may begin to respond on his own.
- Sit down with your child and figure out a list of rewards for both getting up with the alarm and for dry nights.
- Instead of focusing your attention on stopping bed-wetting, you need to think of decreased frequency of wet nights, decreased number of episodes per night, and decreased size of the wet spot as signs of improvement.
- Continue with the alarm until your child achieves 14 consecutive dry nights (no alarm sound for even for a spot of urine).
- After this goal is achieved, use overlearning; that is, encourage your child to drink 16 ounces of fluid before bed or, alternatively, start with 2 ounces of fluid and increase in 2 ounce increments, increasing as each step is mastered, until 16 ounces is reached.

- Continue overlearning until your child achieves 14 consecutive dry nights.
- When overlearning is completed, stop the alarm and extra drinking.
- In the event of a relapse, reinstituting the alarm program usually works.

In addition to these suggestions, parents can also use a more involved set of procedures call "dry-bed training," which incorporates the bed-wetting alarm and other procedures. Dry-bed training is effective in about 85% of children over the age of 7, with only a 15% relapse rate. Dry-bed training was originally described by Azrin, Sneed, and Foxx, who have published several research studies on bed-wetting treatment.[10] Here is an outline of the steps of dry-bed training.

---

**Dry-Bed Training Procedures**

I. Recording: Use calendar progress chart to record dry or wet for each night
   A. Plan to praise your child for each dry night
   B. Plan to encourage your child to keep working if he has wet nights
II. At bedtime, prompt your child to do the following:
   A. Feel his sheets and comment on their dryness
   B. Describe what he will do if he has the urge to urinate
   C. Describe his current need to urinate and encourage him to urinate if necessary
   D. You should express confidence in your child when you review his progress
   E. Place the alarm on the bed or on your child (depending on how it works)
   F. Connect the alarm and turn it "on"
   G. Prompt your child to go to sleep

---

*continues on next page*

*continued*

III. Nightly awakening
    A. Awaken your child once during the night
        1. Use minimal prompts in awakening him, but be sure he is awake
        2. Have him feel his sheets and comment on their dryness
        3. Praise your child for dry sheets
        4. Prompt your child to go to bathroom, urinate as much as possible, and return to bed
        5. Prompt your child to feel the sheets again
        6. Prompt your child to state what he will do if he feels the urge to urinate
        7. Express confidence to child
        8. Keep the alarm on his bed if it has not sounded before awakening
        9. If the alarm sounded more than 30 minutes before the scheduled awakening, awaken at scheduled time
      10. If the alarm sounded less than 30 minutes before the scheduled awakening, do not awaken at the scheduled time
    B. Adjust the time of nightly scheduled awakening
        1. On first night, awaken your child 5 hours before his or her usual time of awakening
        2. After your child has six consecutive dry nights, awaken him or her 1 hour earlier the next night. Continue moving the awakening time 1 hour earlier after every six dry nights until the awakening time is 8 hours before the usual time of awakening
        3. When your child is dry for 14 nights at the 8-hour scheduled awakening, discontinue the scheduled awakenings and discontinue the alarm
IV. When alarm sounds during the night, do the following:
    A. Awaken your child and tell him he wet the bed
    B. Prompt your child to feel his sheets and to comment on their wetness
    C. Prompt your child to walk to bathroom and finish urinating
    D. Prompt your child to take a quick bath
    E. Prompt your child to change into dry clothes

*continues on next page*

*continued*

> F.  Prompt your child to remove the wet sheets and place them in the laundry
> G. Prompt your child to remake his bed with dry sheets
> H. Prompt your child to feel his bed sheets and to comment on dryness
> I.  Do not reconnect alarm
> J.  Prompt your child to go back to sleep
>
> V. During the day
> A. Describe progress to relevant friends or family members
> B. Repeatedly express confidence in your child and praise him or her
>
> *Note.* Adapted from *Behaviour Research and Therapy, 12*, N. H. Azrin, T. J. Sneed, and R. M. Foxx, "Dry-bed Training: Rapid Elimination of Childhood Enuresis," pp. 147–156, Copyright (1974), with permission from Elsevier Science.

As you can see, there are many steps to this type of training. Thus, be sure you have the time and energy to devote to such training efforts, and that your child is motivated to do the same, before you start the dry-bed training procedures.

## When Is Bed-Wetting a Sign of Emotional Disturbance?

In our combined 30 years of practice, we have evaluated hundreds of children for enuresis. In that time, we have never seen a child whose only symptom was enuresis who was also moderately to severely disturbed. In other words, unless your child has other symptoms, bed-wetting is no cause for concern about your child's psychological health.

In virtually every diagnostic category of mental health problems in children, the key factor is that the disorder results in a clinically significant impairment in the child's academic, social, or vocational performance. Bed-wetting, by itself, rarely if ever results in such a significant impairment. However, if your child is a bed-wetter and has a significant impairment in one of these areas of functioning, then an appointment with her pediatrician is indicated, followed by a mental health consultation with a practitioner trained and experienced in the treatment of enuresis.

The one exception to this rule is acute onset enuresis. If your child has been dry at night for at least six months and then suddenly begins bed-wetting most nights or every night, he should be evaluated for a possible urinary tract infection or diabetes. Urinary tract infections are the leading cause of acute onset bed-wetting in children who are otherwise dry at night.

### Psychological Aspects of Bed-Wetting

Although bed-wetting is one of the most common problems among children, there has been almost no research on how to minimize its psychological ramifications. Discussions with your child about her bed-wetting and her progress with the treatment can do a great deal to minimize the isolation that she may feel. Because most children who wet the bed have a relative who wet the bed when young, you can ask that relative (often either the mother or the father) to talk to your child about his or her bed-wetting and to offer encouragement. It often helps children to know that other people have had the same problem and are willing to share their experience.

### CONCLUSION

Toilet training is potentially one of the most difficult tasks that parents face. Given the complex interplay between a child's physiology, his ability to learn life skills, and the psychological and developmental issues inherent in toilet training, it can be the first major stumbling block that parents encounter. You can make the training process much easier on your child and yourself if you pay attention to your child's development. Watch for the physical and emotional readiness skills we have discussed and for problems such as constipation. If you concentrate on the need to teach your child each of the components he has to master to independently toilet, instead of on the ultimate goal of not having any accidents, toilet training becomes much more manageable.

There are many strategies available that can encourage your child to use the toilet. Ultimately, however, your child's development and cooperation will determine when training will be successful. Most parents can take comfort in the fact that virtually all children, in due time, are toilet trained. Simply being mindful of the pitfalls of toilet training, such as training too early, putting on too much pressure, and not teaching readiness skills, can help toilet training to be an unremarkable experience.

Most older children also stop wetting the bed without much intervention, and very few day wet. This chapter also provides some guidelines for treating these problems. More serious problems, such as constipation, soiling, and bed-wetting, are discussed at greater length and may require the help of your pediatrician or a child psychologist.

The psychological ramifications of toileting problems can be profound. Children who still have toileting problems after about 5 years of age become susceptible to teasing from their peers. Although most available research has shown that toileting problems are not linked to emotional disturbances, criticism and ridicule can cause psychological problems. Keeping lines of communication open with your child, and with his teachers and school nurse, can go a long way toward minimizing the negative impact of toileting problems on your child.

## APPENDIX E: THE FIBER CONTENT OF SELECTED POPULAR FOODS

The following table may help you obtain the recommended amount of dietary fiber in your child's diet. Many new high-fiber foods are coming on the market each week. Watch for them! Check food labels for actual grams of dietary fiber per serving.

| | Serving Size | Dietary Fiber (Grams) |
|---|---|---|
| **Breads and crackers** | | |
| Fiberich bread™ | I slice | 3.2 |
| Seven grain bread | I slice | 3.0 |
| High bran "health bread" | I slice | 3.0 |
| Cornbread | I square (2 1/2") | 3.0 |
| 100% whole wheat bread | I slice | 2.4 |
| Cracked wheat bread | I slice | 2.1 |
| Whole wheat crackers | 6 | 2.0 |
| Rye crackers | 3 | 2.0 |
| Whole wheat croutons | 1/4 cup | 1.5 |
| Rye bread | I slice | 1.2 |
| White bread | I slice | .8 |
| **Cereals** | | |
| Fiber One™ | I cup | 24.0 |
| 100% bran cereal | I cup | 20.0 |
| Corn Bran™ | I cup | 8.0 |
| Cracklin' Oat Bran™ | I cup | 8.0 |
| Fruit n' Fiber™ | I cup | 8.0 |
| Granola | I cup | 7.0 |
| Shredded Wheat and Bran™ | I cup | 6.0 |
| Raisin Squares™ | I cup | 6.0 |
| Bran Muffin Crisp™ | I cup | 6.0 |
| Raisin Nut Bran™ | I cup | 6.0 |
| Grape Nuts™ | I cup | 5.3 |
| 40% Bran Flakes™ | I cup | 5.0 |
| Most™ | I cup | 5.0 |

*continues on next page*

**263**

*continued*

|  | Serving Size | Dietary Fiber (Grams) |
|---|---|---|
| **Cereals** (*continued*) |  |  |
| Raisin Bran™ | I cup | 4.0 |
| Oatmeal, cooked | 3/4 cup | 3.0 |
| Shredded Wheat™ | I biscuit | 3.0 |
| Wheat Chex™ | I cup | 3.0 |
| Ralston™, cooked | 3/4 cup | 2.7 |
| Wheaties™ | I cup | 2.0 |
| Cheerios™ | I cup | 1.8 |
| **Flours** |  |  |
| Bran (millers) | I cup | 48.0 |
| Cornmeal, stoneground | I cup | 16.5 |
| 100% whole wheat | I cup | 14.4 |
| 100% rye | I cup | 14.4 |
| Rolled oats | I cup | 12.0 |
| All purpose white flour | I cup | 1.6 |
| **Fruits (fresh, unless otherwise indicated)** |  |  |
| Figs, dried | 2 | 8.0 |
| Apricots, dried | 8 | 7.8 |
| Dates, dried | 10 | 7.0 |
| Raisins | 1/2 cup | 5.4 |
| Prunes, dried | 4 | 5.2 |
| Orange | I medium | 4.5 |
| Banana | I medium | 4.0 |
| Apple, with peel | I medium | 3.3 |
| Strawberries | I cup | 3.3 |
| Pear | I medium | 3.1 |
| Cantaloupe | 1/4 medium | 2.5 |
| Plums | 2 | 2.5 |
| Apricots | 3 | 2.4 |
| **Nuts and Seeds** |  |  |
| Brazil nuts | 10 | 5.5 |
| Peanuts | 1/2 cup | 5.5 |
| Almonds | 10 | 3.6 |

*continues on next page*

*continued*

|  | Serving Size | Dietary Fiber (Grams) |
|---|---|---|
| **Nuts and Seeds** (*continued*) |  |  |
| Soy nuts | 2 tbsp. | 3.0 |
| Sunflower seeds | 2 tbsp. | 3.0 |
| Corn nuts | 2 tbsp. | 3.0 |
| Walnuts | 1/2 cup | 3.0 |
| Peanut butter | 2 tbsp. | 2.3 |
| Poppy seeds | 2 tbsp. | 2.0 |
| Sesame seeds | 2 tbsp. | 2.0 |
| **Vegetables (fresh, raw, unless otherwise indicated)** |  |  |
| Baked beans | 1 cup | 18.6 |
| Peas | 1 cup | 11.3 |
| Corn | 1 cup | 9.3 |
| Broccoli | 2 spears | 7.0 |
| Yams, baked with skin | 1 medium | 6.8 |
| Brussel sprouts | 1 cup | 6.5 |
| Green beans | 1 cup | 3.5 |
| Spinach | 1 cup | 3.5 |
| Carrots | 1 cup | 3.2 |
| Potatoes, baked with skin | 1 medium | 3.0 |
| Tomato | 1 medium | 3.0 |
| Cauliflower | 1 cup | 2.5 |
| Cabbage, shredded | 1 cup | 1.9 |
| Lettuce | 1 cup | .8 |
| Celery | 1 stalk | .7 |
| **Miscellaneous** |  |  |
| Kidney beans | 1 cup | 20.0 |
| Chili | 1 cup | 17.0 |
| Macaroni and pasta (whole wheat, cooked) | 1 cup | 5.7 |
| Brown rice | 1 cup | 4.0 |
| Coconut, shredded | 2 tbsp. | 3.0 |
| Popcorn, popped | 1 cup | 1.0 |

*Note.* From *Childhood Constipation and Soiling: A Practical Guide for Parents and Children* (pp. 23–24), by J. Owens-Stively, 1995, Minneapolis, MN: Children's Health Care. Copyright 1995 by Children's Health Care. Reprinted with permission.

# CHAPTER 13

# DISCOURAGING AGGRESSION

Aggression in a child is one of the most disconcerting issues a parent can face. Aggressive behavior may prompt more phone calls to parents by day care centers, mothers day out programs, and preschools than any other behavior problem. Aggression in a young child may indicate an increased risk of future problems as well. In fact, young children who regularly engage in physical fighting are three times more likely to be diagnosed later with a mental health problem than children who do not engage in physical fighting.[1]

This chapter discusses some of the reasons children engage in aggressive behavior and offers suggestions for preventing or managing your child's aggressive behavior and teaching more appropriate responses to anger and frustration. You will find as you read this chapter that many of the parenting and child skills already discussed in this book are very important in reducing aggressive behavior as well.

## WHY ARE CHILDREN AGGRESSIVE?

Where does aggressive behavior come from? Why do we see it in our children? One major source of such behavior is the ways parents model behavior and treat their children. Parents who threaten, yell, and berate their children often have children who deal with frustration the same way. Parents who use physical discomfort or pain to influence their children's behavior are far more likely to have children who are aggressive than parents who don't use such methods.[2] In other words, aggressive behavior begets aggressive behavior.

Dr. James Garbarino, an expert on violence in children, has analyzed the research literature and identified a number of other factors that are correlated with aggressive behavior in children.[3] These factors include TV violence, violent video games, movies, the presence of guns in the child's social surroundings, child maltreatment, unresponsive schools, inadequate mental health services, spiritual emptiness, the use of psychoactive substances, and economic inequality.

The American Psychological Association and the American Academy of Pediatrics published a brochure, "Raising Children to Resist Violence," that discusses a number of ways to help reduce a child's exposure to violence. This brochure is reprinted in Appendix F for the convenience of the reader. No single factor alone accounts for aggressive behavior, but addressing the factors that are in your control, such as what your child watches on TV, can help you prevent or reduce aggression in your child.

## PREVENTING AGGRESSIVE BEHAVIOR IN YOUR CHILD

You can monitor, eliminate, or encourage many factors that influence aggressive behavior. The following are some suggestions for modifying your behavior and your child's environment to reduce your child's aggressive behavior.

## Model Good Anger Management Skills

Parents who model good anger management skills and who help their children learn skills for dealing with anger and angry feelings are much more likely to have children who have good anger management skills. Conversely, when parents yell at each other or physically fight when they are angry, they are modeling this behavior for their children. They are teaching their children that it is all right to handle difficult or frustrating situations with aggression.

As we discussed in chapter 1 on teaching your child what is important, your behavior, both good and bad, serves as a model for your child. If you expose your child to aggressive responses to problems such as arguing, yelling, and confrontation, he is learning to argue, yell, and confront. On the other hand, when you deal with problems in a calm, rational way, you are teaching your child to do the same when he has a problem. Try to remember that the calmer and cooler you stay, the calmer and cooler your child will be. He's learning by the behavior he sees you model!

Bear in mind that, from our knowledge of modeling and children's behavior, your day-to-day behavior is much more influential on your child than the isolated times when you have lost your temper. Despite the best of intentions, almost every parent loses his or her temper once in a while! If you are working at learning skills to help you to keep from losing your temper, your child will benefit from your efforts. Appendix G, "Controlling Anger Before It Controls You," describes several strategies for helping you deal with anger.

Specific behaviors you may want to eliminate if you would like to prevent or reduce aggression in your children include spanking, yelling and swearing, direct confrontation, roughhousing, and violent media and games. In addition, you should provide appropriate consequences for aggressive behavior and monitor the behavior of your child's friends.

## Eliminate Spanking

The first thing that comes to mind for some parents wanting to reduce a child's aggressive behavior is that the child hasn't been punished enough. Ironically, the children who are the most likely to be aggressive are the ones who have been subjected to the strongest punishment. The most common discipline strategy used by parents of aggressive children is spanking.[4] The act of spanking may actually encourage aggressive behavior. Although parents who spank usually say that the aggressive or oppositional behavior is what "causes" them to spank their child, it may be the other way around—the parent's rough handling of the child over time may help to precipitate the child's aggressive behavior. Shifting the emphasis away from punishing "bad" behavior and toward teaching appropriate behavior goes a long way toward making children less aggressive.

We have heard the argument that one swat on a child's bottom does not constitute child abuse. On the other hand, how do you make certain that it isn't too hard, especially if you are swatting when you are angry? The real issue is not whether a swat constitutes child abuse, it's really what you hope to accomplish with the swat. Most parents hope to reduce negative behavior with a swat, but in reality they may be increasing the odds that their children will act more aggressively in the future.

Parents resort to spanking their children when the real problem is that their children do not have good coping skills. Spanking cannot teach coping skills; instead, children may learn to hit when they are angry. Suggestions for other discipline options instead of spanking can be found in chapter 4 on discipline. Ideas for teaching your child coping skills are found both throughout this book and later in this chapter.

### Eliminate Yelling and Swearing

Yelling seems to have the same effect on children as spanking. In a study of over 800 parents, researchers concluded that parents who yell frequently are the ones most likely to hit frequently and vice versa.[5] We also suspect that many parents who would have spanked their children several years ago are now yelling at them instead. Yelling has become a substitute for spanking.

As with spanking, you have to ask yourself what you hope to accomplish with yelling. If what you are hoping for is that yelling will help to teach your child important life skills, it will not! It will, however, teach her to yell when she wants something.

We have observed that aggressive children also seem to swear a lot. It is difficult to determine the exact reason for this, although parent modeling may well be a factor. One explanation may be that the parents who are likely to behave aggressively toward their children with spanking or other rough physical contact are also likely to swear at or in front of their children.

Thus, your first priority is to monitor your use of yelling and swearing and work to eliminate using them in front of your child, even if they are not directed at him. The next step is to stop reacting to your child's swear words. Often, a parent busy talking on the phone or visiting with a friend or relative will ignore his or her child's attempts to get attention and then, when the child swears, immediately reprimands her. For that child, the swearing worked—she got the parent's attention for it.

Review the times when your child used bad words. You may be able to figure out how he gained from it. Try to eliminate the payoff of grabbing your attention, and come up with a plan that

**271**

allows him to gain your attention without exhibiting negative behaviors.

### Avoid Direct Confrontation

Some parent–child relationships seem to consist of one confrontation after another. Each interaction escalates to a battle of the
wills in a matter of minutes, often resulting in yelling, arguing,
threats, or physical aggression.[6] Aggressive children seem to thrive
on confrontation. Get right in their face and tell them that they
can't do something, and it immediately becomes the next thing on
their agenda. On the other hand, aggressively insist that they do
something, and it will be the last thing they intend to do for you.
If you use confrontation to get your child to do or not do something, your child will learn to do the same to get her needs met.
Thus, direct confrontation is typically not effective and teaches
your child behaviors that you most likely do not want her to display with you or with others.

You may find that if you are using the skills discussed in this
book to teach your child what is important and have good coping
skills yourself, your need for confrontations with your child may
be reduced. For example, you can point out to your child that,
although the woman at the dry cleaners was abrasive, you chose
not to become confrontational with her. Or you can point out the
person in traffic who let two cars go in front of her rather than
succumb to the temptation to be confrontational. Once your child
learns skills for managing anger, which we will discuss later in this
chapter, parent–child confrontations should also be reduced.

If you find that you engage in frequent confrontations with
your child, especially if these confrontations become physical, then
you probably need more help than we can provide in this chapter.
Several books address the specific needs of parents of defiant or

strong-willed children. Some examples are *Your Defiant Child: 8 Steps to Better Behavior*[7] and *Parenting the Strong-Willed Child: The Clinically Proven Five-Week Program for Parents of Two- to Six-Year-Olds.*[8]

If there is significant conflict in your home, you will probably need the services of a clinical child psychologist before things get better. Most often such intervention will help you develop more effective parenting strategies and teach both you and your child coping skills. You may also need a medication consultation with a child psychiatrist to determine if available medications might help you or your child cope. Your pediatrician is probably the best person to recommend a child psychiatrist.

## Provide Appropriate Consequences for Aggressive Behavior

Ignoring children's negative behaviors or responding inappropriately may teach them that aggression works. Some parents arrange their lives and their children's lives to avoid as many chances for aggression as possible. Such a parent might be reluctant to ask a child to do a chore or get ready faster or to share with his sister if he typically becomes angry and aggressive in response. Another parent might respond to a child's aggression by giving the child what she wants. For example, if two children are fighting over one toy and the aggressive child forcefully takes that toy and is allowed to keep it, the parent is actually encouraging her to be aggressive. This parental response often happens with young children; many parents will tell an older sibling, "Just give your little brother the toy" when the younger child is screaming and hitting the older child. Children who are able to get their way by acting aggressive, with no repercussions, are actually being encouraged to be aggressive.

To avoid encouraging aggression between siblings, tell them

they must share a toy in dispute. If they do not, put the toy in time-out and then encourage the children again to share the toy. Although this strategy may take a number of repetitions, your children will learn that aggression or refusing to share means the toy is removed, and sharing means that they get to play with the toy. This strategy can be varied slightly when one child has monopolized a toy and refuses to share it with a sibling or a friend. In that case, give the toy to the other child to show the first child that it is better to share the toy than to have to relinquish it.

### Reduce Roughhousing

In addition to controlling your own behaviors and responses to your child's behaviors, you can also alter your child's environment to prevent or reduce aggression. For example, aggressive children often have an older adolescent or adult who wrestles with them to the point where the aggressive child simply cannot calm down. If your child has a tendency to lose control in such aggressive interactions, it is a good idea to eliminate or minimize aggressive play and roughhousing.

If eliminating all such play results in a real improvement in your child's aggressive behavior, then clearly you should discourage aggressive play in the future. If eliminating all aggressive play does not help at all, then it is certainly your choice to allow it again, but beware of the potential for injury and the message that you approve of aggression.

### Restrict Violent Media and Games

There is no more powerful media, in our lives and the lives of our children, than TV. In most cities, there are so many channels to choose from that both violent and nonviolent programs are available virtually around the clock. Aggressive behavior is most frequently shown in professional wrestling bouts, police action programs, and some cartoons or cable shows. Thus, it is important to monitor how much time your child spends watching TV as well as what he watches.

Our suggestions for children watching TV are really pretty simple. Sit down with your child and a copy of either *TV Guide* or the TV section from the newspaper, and review which shows are on and which shows she is allowed to watch. Try to get into the habit of looking up the shows first, then turning on the TV to watch a specific show, then turning the TV set off. In this way, your child will be better able to discipline himself when it comes to watching TV. Leaving the TV on continuously increases the odds that he will see a violent show.

Similar guidelines can be followed for the movies your child watches and for the video or computer games she is allowed to play both in your home and at the homes of friends. Pay attention to violence rating systems offered by movies and video game makers. More importantly, though, watch what your child is watching or playing. You may find that even with the rating systems for movies and games, the level of violence is greater than you prefer your child to be exposed to. Supervision plays a key role in reducing violence in your child's environment.

You should also supervise the number of hours your child spends playing video or computer games, especially those with violent content. One research study concluded that reducing the number of hours children watch TV and videos and play video games results in less aggressive behavior in school.[9] This study included a school intervention that provided alternatives to TV viewing and video game playing. Thus, although it is difficult to conclude that merely limiting the number of hours your child engages in such activities will reduce aggression, such a strategy is a good place to start. Your child will be free to do other activities that involve less aggression.

## Monitor Your Child's Playmates

The children your child plays with and how they are allowed to play can also influence aggressive behavior. As a parent, you must deal with aggressive play immediately. Children should not be allowed to physically "work it out" when they have a disagreement, any more than two adults would be encouraged to "work it out" in the workplace. In fact, the only recent research we located that addresses the issue of whether acting out aggression decreases aggressive play found that it does not.[10] Thus, the old notion that children can work out their aggressive feelings by hitting a pillow or whacking a softball with a soft bat does not appear to help them deal with aggression. Of course, your child may benefit from having legitimate physical outlets for his energy, such as consistent exercise. If you are going to encourage your child to engage in sports for this physical outlet, however, try to identify a sport that does not encourage competition or aggressiveness. We have long recommended the martial arts for three reasons: (1) the main competition is oneself, (2) parents are typically not the coaches, and (3) the main emphasis is on self-control. Of course, the most effective strategy is to help children to learn effective coping and anger management skills.

The simplest thing you can do is consistently encourage your child to play with well-behaved children who exhibit very few aggressive behaviors. You can do so by inviting such children to your home to play with your child. When you invite another child over, you should, at least initially, monitor the activities of your child and his playmates. Count on spending almost the entire time that the other child is there playing with them or monitoring their interactions. You will not be able to supervise them if you send them downstairs or to the family room and out of your view. Rather, you need to think of this playtime as an opportunity for your child to learn how to play appropriately with peers. Your role should be that of teacher, not disciplinarian. Once you are confident that your child can play appropriately with another child, you can decrease your direct involvement with the play activity, but be sure to continue providing frequent supervision.

You may also want to consider establishing a rule that your child is allowed to play at a friend's house only if that friend's parent will be available for supervision as well. You should find out how that child's parents discipline their child and the child's guests (your child) should misbehavior occur. If the parents use other than nonviolent discipline strategies, your child should play with their child only at your home.

## TEACHING YOUR CHILD HOW TO COPE WITH FRUSTRATION AND ANGER

From the first couple of times that your toddler reaches for a ball that is just out of her reach until she is taunted for dropping the ball during an important game, you need to encourage your child to develop good coping skills to deal with frustration and anger. In addition to your efforts to model appropriate behavior when you are angry and to remove violence-promoting influences in your child's life, you should teach your child coping skills as well. These coping skills are often not easy to learn and will require your patience and much practice on the part of your child.

The first thing that you have to do to help your child to work on anger management skills is accept the fact that you cannot help him deal with his anger by getting angry yourself. So rather than react to his anger, you have to teach him how to deal with a situation that would make him angry—when he's not angry. You have to be proactive, not reactive. Once you have accepted the fact that anger management requires practice and the acquisition of skills, you're on your way to helping your child learn anger management.

Beginning with a child's earliest verbalizations about things not going her way, you can help your child learn to adopt helpful thoughts rather than hurtful thoughts to improve her odds of not becoming angry or aggressive. When the family pet eats her cookie, you can model statements that are helpful, such as, "I don't like it when Lassie eats your cookie, but we can always get another one," rather than saying, "If that dog keeps taking the baby's cookies he's out of here." When your child makes a hurtful statement, you can help her learn how to rephrase it as a helpful statement: "Honey, we don't need to get rid of the dog, we just need to be more careful how we handle cookies in front of him."

Over time, you will have literally hundreds, if not thousands, of opportunities to encourage appropriate verbalizations. Taking these opportunities as they naturally occur is a very effective approach to teaching good coping skills.

We have developed a five-component program to teach young children how to deal effectively with angry feelings. Our motivation for developing this program was twofold. One, anger management is one of the most common reasons parents bring children in for professional help. Two, there is virtually no published outcome research on anger management in young children. All of the programs we were able to locate were appropriate only for older adolescents and adults, primarily because they involve language and cognitive skills that young children simply have not developed yet.

Our five-component program includes the following:

1. identifying times when you as a parent deal effectively with frustrating or anger-provoking situations and pointing these out to your child

2. teaching your child to use a controlled breathing technique both at home and at school

3. rewarding your child for practicing the breathing exercises

4. encouraging your child to use the breathing exercises when frustrated

5. teaching your child problem-solving strategies to cope with angry feelings.

## Identifying Times When You Deal With Anger Effectively

Although children easily recognize when their parents become angry, it is very difficult for them to notice when parents successfully avoid becoming angry. For this reason, we encourage parents to point out to their children when they encounter a frustrating situation and deal with it effectively.

One example we use is a parent who is about to pull into a really convenient parking place when another person takes that place. If the parent deals with this calmly, he needs to tell his child what happened and how he dealt with it. So, in addition to saying, "Jeffrey, did you see that woman take my parking place?" he would also need to share his strategy, which may mean saying, "Parking places belong to whoever pulls into them first. Even though I am not happy about that, I'm going to park in the next available spot. It shouldn't take us any longer to get into the store from there."

If your dry cleaning is not ready when expected, tell your child how frustrated you are because you wanted to wear an item in the order. Then say that because the dry cleaning wasn't ready, you will go home and pick out another outfit to wear. Make sure you also talk about what cognitive strategy you used to help you to deal with the situation, such as "I told myself I have plenty of other clothes at home that I can wear." In this way, you draw your child's attention to a situation when you dealt with a potentially anger producing situation in an effective manner, and you prompt your child to observe it.

### Teaching Your Child Controlled Breathing Exercises

One helpful anger management skill to teach your child is the use of a "competing response," which can be described as a purposeful behavior that is difficult to do if you are angry. Teach your child controlled breathing by having your child practice blowing both real and imaginary bubbles. Yes, that's right, bubbles. Get a bottle of bubbles and practice blowing them, with your child, at least once every day, preferably at a time when no one is angry. As both you and your child practice blowing bubbles, first blow real bubbles, and then practice blowing imaginary bubbles by putting your finger up to your mouth and blowing.

The idea is to teach your child a skill, blowing imaginary bubbles, that he can do only by blowing gently and with controlled breathing. Try blowing too hard, and the bubble solution just blows out of the wand without producing any bubbles. Try blowing too soft, and the bubble solution stays on the wand. Only when he blows gently do the bubbles pour out of the wand. For older children, you can use the concept of blowing bubbles, blowing on hot soup, or any other image that comes to mind when you think of slow, controlled breathing.

Of course, other competing responses such as counting to 100 or shooting baskets exist that can distract a child and reduce her anger. The purpose of controlled breathing as a competing response, however, is not to distract a child from her anger, but to help her focus on her anger sensations and control them. This skill is also very portable and can be used anywhere. Ultimately, controlled breathing can provide a foundation on which to build her anger management skills.

## Rewarding the Practicing of Breathing Exercises

Because children usually are not motivated to practice breathing exercises, figure out some simple rewards that you can provide each time that your child practices his exercises. The rewards don't have to be money or expensive things. Give your child a choice between several small rewards, such as spending time with Mom or Dad playing a game, building something, or baking cookies. Identify activities that your child enjoys doing with you, and make these activities readily available as rewards. All he has to do to earn the reward is do his practicing.

Children don't seek professional help for themselves, like adults do. When adults commit themselves to working on something like anger management, they are usually motivated, or they wouldn't be doing it. Children, on the other hand, don't have the intrinsic motivation of a distressed adult, and they do much better if their parents figure out ways to reward them for their efforts.

For older children, the motivation issue may be more difficult. On one hand, we have found that many children, including adolescents, are not proud of their poor anger control and will take controlled breathing and other suggestions seriously. They may even practice on their own. Their ability to execute them when angry, however, can be limited. Thus, they need support and recognition from their parents and other adults for their efforts. On the other hand, some children enjoy being angry or, more commonly, are somehow rewarded for being angry, perhaps by getting their way. If your child is not open to these strategies despite her best efforts or yours, you may need to seek the help of a mental health professional.

### Prompt Your Child to Use His Breathing Techniques

After your child has practiced his controlled breathing for several days, prompt him to use his breathing (to "blow his imaginary bubbles") the next time he is in a situation where you know, from past experience, that he would have gotten angry. This might take a fair amount of practice, at least a week or two, before he actually attempts to use his exercises when he's upset or feels himself starting to get upset.

This component is perhaps the most important one in teaching children anger management strategies. Your child needs to practice and be prepared long before she encounters a situation that, in the past, would have resulted in an angry outburst. The first time your child appears aggravated, and before she is angry, encourage her to try blowing her imaginary bubbles or whatever image your child prefers. If she's successful, wonderful. If she's unsuccessful, then try, try again.

The ability to control anger does not come easily to many people. Thus, you can expect to have to prompt your child many times to use his strategies for calming. If for example, your child is watching TV and you want him to get ready for bed at the end of the show he's watching, you can prompt him by saying, "This might be a good time for you to use your breathing (or imaginary bubbles). As soon as this show is over, I want you to get ready for bed." Although it may take some time before your child actually uses the coping strategy without any reminders, these are strategies that can be used for years to come.

## Teaching Problem-Solving Steps

Older children (ages 8 or 9 through adolescence) can also be taught problem solving steps to help them deal with anger and conflict resolution. Now more than ever, children are expected to be able to resolve their interpersonal conflicts without resorting to aggression. The problem-solving steps discussed in the next section can help a child develop such skills.

STEP 1: WHAT EXACTLY IS THE PROBLEM? This first step encourages your child to identify and define the problem. If, for example, he is getting mad at his younger sister because she is coming dangerously close to destroying the fighter plane that he is building with Legos, he needs to identify the problem in such a way that he feels capable of doing something about it. For example, it makes infinitely more sense to build the plane on the desk in his room than to build it on the family room floor. When you encourage him to ask himself, "What exactly is the problem?" he will learn to shift from his initial thinking of "My sister has to leave my plane alone" to "I had better start building my plane in a place that is safe and out of the way of my baby sister."

STEP 2: WHAT ARE MY POSSIBILITIES? To continue with the previous example, your child has to think about *his* possibilities, instead of possibilities that involve only his sister. If he thinks about alternate locations to build his plane before starting construction, then he only has to be able to control his own behavior rather than his sister's. This step is also important when a child needs to confront a person for some reason. For example, if a friend keeps forgetting to return the child's favorite video game, she must develop a plan to ask her friend for it back without getting angry.

Children, including adolescents, will most likely need help with this step. For simple or complex problems, write down as many possible solutions to the situation as you both can think of, even if the idea seems silly. You will be showing your child that there are typically many different possibilities to solve problems encountered on a daily basis.

STEP 3: WHAT ARE MY CHOICES? What gets most children and adults into trouble is seeing situations as either black or white. A child may think, "Either my sister will ruin my work or she won't" or "My friend is going to keep my video game or get mad at me for wanting it back." A child must learn to think about the problem from the standpoint that she has choices to make and that the choice that she picks can significantly affect the outcome.

Take out the list of possibilities you and your child made in Step 3. Have your child choose a reasonable option and try it out. If it does not work well to eliminate the problem or your child's angry response, go back and choose another idea. Perhaps your child will choose to call her friend and ask politely for her game back. This will reduce her need to confront her friend when she's angry.

STEP 4: HOW CAN I PLAN AHEAD NEXT TIME? Instead of starting an activity impulsively, a child must learn to plan ahead. For example, he needs to learn that, in the past, his sister has usually ventured into almost everything that he has tried to do. Now, he needs to learn to focus on the activity he wants to engage in and explore his options before he starts construction or before the problem occurs. Once a child masters this step, he does not have to wait for problems to happen before he engages in thought about how to avoid potentially troublesome situations.

STEP 5: HOW DID I DO? This final step entails the child's checking to verify that the solution she chose took into consideration the options she actually had control over and that the option she picked was the best she had available at the time. She needs to consider whether the problem-solving process she followed was accurate and productive, or whether she made a mistake or selected a less-than-desirable solution, in which case she should be prompted to begin the process anew.

The steps discussed in the previous section can also be used to help parents and children learn how to develop mutually agreeable solutions to conflicts at home. Together they can identify a problem in the family such as how to complete chores without arguing. They can look at all of the possibilities for completing chores from hiring a maid to dividing chores evenly and having consequences for incomplete chores. The family can then choose a mutually agreed time strategy for chore completion and see how it works. If it doesn't work, the family can discuss how each person can plan ahead to avoid the problems that are occurring, such as doing the chore sooner or delivering the consequence before getting too angry and yelling. The choice can then be routinely re-evaluated for its success or for the chance to engage in the problem-solving steps again to come up with a more effective solution.

Helping your child learn anger control can be a lot of work. It will take an honest effort to teach your child controlled breathing and the steps of problem solving. Be sure to give the practicing at least a few weeks before you conclude that it won't work for your child. If you find that you just don't have the patience to help your child to work on his anger management skills, you may need to get some assistance from a mental health professional.

## CONCLUSION

Aggression in children is often a symptom of the environment the child is being raised in. When parents play rough with their children, argue with them and in front of them, approach them in a confrontational manner, and use spanking as their primary method of discipline, they often have children who are aggressive. The key to dealing with an aggressive child is to remove the elements that contribute to the child's aggression and to teach the child alternative ways of coping with her anger and dealing with life's challenges.

Throughout this book, we have emphasized the importance of teaching children important life skills such as sharing and self-quieting. The combination of reducing or minimizing violence in our children's lives and teaching them life skills should help to reduce aggressive behavior. Once your child has learned the skills in our five-component approach to dealing with anger and frustration, she can apply them to a wide variety of situations.

Developing and using these strategies takes time. It is unnecessary to impose deadlines on yourself that are unrealistic for you or your child. Your goal is ultimately to teach your child the values and skills you identified when constructing your 10-Year Plan. When you keep this goal in mind, it doesn't matter whether it takes you one day, one week, or several months to teach your child skills —he can use them for the rest of his life.

## APPENDIX F: RAISING CHILDREN TO RESIST VIOLENCE

The American Academy of Pediatrics and the American Psychological Association issued a joint report on *Reducing Your Child's Exposure to Violence.* They recommended reducing children's exposure to violence in the home, the school, the media, and the community. The text of that report follows.

## RAISING CHILDREN TO RESIST VIOLENCE: WHAT YOU CAN DO

Research has shown that violent or aggressive behavior is often learned early in life. However, parents, family members, and others who care for children can help them learn to deal with emotions without using violence. Parents and others can also take steps to reduce or minimize violence.

These guidelines are designed to help parents work within the family, school, and community to prevent and reduce youth violence.

## SUGGESTIONS FOR DEALING WITH CHILDREN

Parents play a valuable role in reducing violence by raising children in safe and loving homes. Here are suggestions that can help. You may not be able to follow each one exactly, but if you do your best, it will make a difference in your children's lives.

### Give Your Children Consistent Love and Attention

Every child needs a strong, loving relationship with a parent or other adult to feel safe and secure and to develop a sense of trust. Without a steady bond to a caring adult, a child is at risk for becoming hostile, difficult, and hard to manage. Behavior problems and delinquency are less likely to develop in children whose parents are involved in their lives, especially at an early age.

It's not easy to show love to a child all the time. It can be even harder if you are a young, inexperienced, or single parent, or if your child is sick or has special needs. If your baby seems unusually difficult to care for and comfort, discuss this with your child's pediatrician, another physician, a psychologist, or a counselor. He or she can give you advice and direct you to local parenting classes that teach positive ways to handle the difficulties of raising children.

It is important to remember that children have minds of their own. Children's increasing independence sometimes leads them to behave in ways that disappoint, anger, or frustrate you. Patience and a willingness to view the situation through the children's eyes, before reacting, can help you deal with your emotions. Do your best to avoid responding to your children with hostile words or actions.

## Make Sure Your Children Are Supervised

Children depend on their parents and family members for encouragement, protection, and support as they learn to think for themselves. Without proper supervision, children do not receive the guidance they need. Studies report that unsupervised children often have behavior problems.

- Insist on knowing where your children are at all times and who their friends are. When you are unable to watch your children, ask someone you trust to watch them for you. Never leave young children home alone, even for a short time.
- Encourage your school-aged and older children to participate

in supervised after-school activities such as sports teams, tutoring programs, or organized recreation. Enroll them in local community programs, especially those run by adults whose values you respect.

- Accompany your children to supervised play activities and watch how they get along with others. Teach your children how to respond appropriately when others use insults or threats or deal with anger by hitting. Explain to your children that these are not appropriate behaviors, and encourage them to avoid other children who behave that way.

## Show Your Children Appropriate Behaviors by the Way You Act

Children often learn by example. The behavior, values, and attitudes of parents and siblings have a strong influence on children. Values of respect, honesty, and pride in your family and heritage can be important sources of strength for children, especially if they are confronted with negative peer pressure, live in a violent neighborhood, or attend a rough school.

Most children sometimes act aggressively and may hit another person. Be firm with your children about the possible dangers of violent behavior. Remember also to praise your children when they solve problems constructively without violence. Children are more likely to repeat good behaviors when they are rewarded with attention and praise.

You can teach your children nonaggressive ways to solve problems by

- discussing problems with them,
- asking them to consider what might happen if they use violence to solve problems, and

- talking about what might happen if they solve problems without violence.

This kind of "thinking out loud" together will help children see that violence is not a helpful solution.

Parents sometimes encourage aggressive behavior without knowing it. For example, some parents think it is good for a boy to learn to fight. Teach your children that it is better to settle arguments with calm words, not fists, threats, or weapons.

Help your children learn constructive, nonviolent ways to enjoy their free time. Teach them your favorite games, hobbies, or sports, and help them develop their own talents and skills. Read stories to younger children, take older children to the library, or tell family stories about admired relatives who have made the world a better place.

### Don't Hit Your Children

Hitting, slapping, or spanking children as punishment shows them that it's okay to hit others to solve problems and can train them to punish others in the same way they were punished.

Physical punishments stop unwanted behavior only for a short time. Even with very harsh punishment, children may adapt so that it has little or no effect. Using even more punishment is equally ineffective.

Nonphysical methods of discipline help children deal with their emotions and teach them nonviolent ways to solve problems. Here are some suggestions:

- giving children "time out"—making the children sit quietly, usually one minute for each year of age (this is not appropriate for very young children),
- taking away certain privileges or treats,

- "grounding"—not allowing the children to play with friends or participate in school or community activities (this is only appropriate for older children or adolescents).

Punishment that involves taking away privileges or "grounding" should be consistently applied for realistic, brief periods.

Children need to feel that if they make mistakes, they can correct them. Show them how to learn from their errors. Help them figure out what they did wrong and how they can avoid making similar mistakes in the future. It is especially important not to embarrass or humiliate your child at these times. Children always need to feel your love and respect.

A positive approach to changing behaviors is to emphasize rewards for good behavior instead of punishments for bad behavior. Remember that praise and affection are the best rewards.

### Be Consistent About Rules and Discipline

When you make a rule, stick to it. Children need structure with clear expectations for their behavior. Setting rules and then not enforcing them is confusing and sets up children to "see what they can get away with."

Parents should involve children in setting rules whenever possible. Explain to your children what you expect, and the consequences for not following the rules. This will help them learn to behave in ways that are good for them and for those around them.

### Make Sure Your Children Do Not Have Access to Guns

Guns and children can be a deadly combination. Teach your children about the dangers of firearms and other weapons if you own and use them. If you keep a gun in your home, unload it and lock it up separately from the bullets. Never store firearms where children can find them, even if unloaded.

Don't carry a gun or a weapon. If you do, this tells your children that using guns solves problems.

### Try to Keep Your Children From Seeing Violence in the Home or Community

Violence in the home can be frightening and harmful to children. Children need a safe and loving home where they do not have to grow up in fear. A child who has seen violence at home does not always become violent, but he or she may be more likely to try to resolve conflicts with violence.

Work toward making home a safe, nonviolent place, and always discourage violent behavior between brothers and sisters. Keep in mind as well that hostile, aggressive arguments between parents frighten children and set a bad example for them.

If the people in your home physically or verbally hurt and abuse each other, get help from a psychologist or counselor in your community. He or she will help you and your family understand why violence at home occurs and how to stop it.

Sometimes children cannot avoid seeing violence in the street, at school, or at home, and they may need help in dealing with these frightening experiences. A psychologist or counselor at school or a religious leader are among those who can help them cope with their feelings.

### Try to Keep Your Children From Seeing Too Much Violence in the Media

Seeing a lot of violence on TV, in the movies, and in video games can lead children to behave aggressively. As a parent, you can control the amount of violence your children see in the media. Here are some ideas:

- Limit TV viewing time to one to two hours a day.
- Make sure you know what TV shows your children watch, which movies they see, and what kinds of video games they play.
- Talk to your children about the violence that they see on TV shows, in the movies, and in video games.
- Help them understand how painful it would be in real life and the serious consequences for violent behaviors.
- Discuss with them ways to solve problems without violence.

### Teach Your Children Ways to Avoid Becoming Victims of Violence

It is important that you and your children learn to take precautions against becoming the victims of a violent crime. Here are some important steps that you can take to keep yourself and your children safe:

- Teach your children safe routes for walking in your neighborhood.
- Encourage them to walk with a friend at all times and only in well-lighted, busy areas.
- Stress how important it is for them to report any crimes or suspicious activities they see to you, a teacher, another trustworthy adult, or the police. Show them how to call 911 or the emergency service in your area.
- Make sure they know what to do if anyone tries to hurt them: Say "no," run away, and tell a reliable adult.

- Stress the dangers of talking to strangers. Tell them never to open the door to or go anywhere with someone they don't know and trust.

### Help Your Children Stand Up Against Violence

Support your children in standing up against violence. Teach them to respond with calm but firm words when others insult, threaten, or hit another person. Help them understand that it takes more courage and leadership to resist violence than to go along with it.

Help your children accept and get along with others from various racial and ethnic backgrounds. Teach them that criticizing people because they are different is hurtful, and that name-calling is unacceptable. Make sure they understand that using words to start or encourage violence—or to quietly accept violent behavior —is harmful. Warn your child that bullying and threats can be a setup for violence.

## AN EXTRA SUGGESTION FOR ADULTS: TAKE CARE OF YOURSELF AND YOUR COMMUNITY

Stay involved with your friends, neighbors, and family. A network of friends can offer fun, practical help, and support when you have difficult times. Reducing stress and social isolation can help in raising your children.

Get involved in your community and get to know your neighbors. Try to make sure guns are not available in your area as well. Volunteer to help in your neighborhood's anticrime efforts or in programs to make schools safer for children. If there are no programs like this nearby, help start one!

Let your elected officials know that preventing violence is important to you and your neighbors. Complain to TV stations and advertisers who sponsor violent programs.

Encourage your children to get involved in groups that build pride in the community, such as those that organize cleanups of litter, graffiti, and run-down buildings. In addition to making the neighborhood a safer place, these groups provide a great opportunity for parents, children, and neighbors to spend time together in fun, safe, and rewarding activities.

## POTENTIAL WARNING SIGNS

Parents whose children show the signs listed below should discuss their concerns with a professional, who will help them understand the children and suggest ways to prevent violent behavior.

### Warning Signs in the Toddler and Preschool Child

- Has many temper tantrums in a single day or several lasting more than 15 minutes, and often cannot be calmed by parents, family members, or other caregivers;

- has many aggressive outbursts, often for no reason;

- is extremely active, impulsive, and fearless;

- consistently refuses to follow directions and listen to adults;

- does not seem attached to parents; for example, does not touch, look for, or return to parents in strange places;

- frequently watches violence on TV, engages in play that has violent themes, or is cruel toward other children.

## Warning Signs in the School-Aged Child

- Has trouble paying attention and concentrating;
- often disrupts classroom activities;
- does poorly in school;
- frequently gets into fights with other children in school;
- reacts to disappointments, criticism, or teasing with extreme and intense anger, blame, or revenge;
- watches many violent TV shows and movies or plays a lot of violent video games;
- has few friends, and is often rejected by other children because of his or her behavior;
- makes friends with other children known to be unruly or aggressive;
- consistently does not listen to adults;
- is not sensitive to the feelings of others;
- is cruel or violent toward pets or other animals;
- is easily frustrated.

## Warning Signs in the Preteen or Teenaged Adolescent

- Consistently does not listen to authority figures;
- pays no attention to the feelings or rights of others;
- mistreats people and seems to rely on physical violence or threats of violence to solve problems;
- often expresses the feeling that life has treated him or her unfairly;
- does poorly in school and often skips class;
- misses school frequently for no identifiable reason;
- gets suspended from or drops out of school;

- joins a gang, gets involved in fighting, stealing, or destroying property;
- drinks alcohol and/or uses inhalants or drugs.

*Note.* From *Raising Children to Resist Violence: What You Can Do*, by the American Academy of Pediatrics and the American Psychological Association, 1995, Washington, DC: Author. Copyright 1995 by the American Academy of Pediatrics and the American Psychological Association. Adapted with permission.

## APPENDIX G: CONTROLLING ANGER BEFORE IT CONTROLS YOU

We all know what anger is, and we've all felt it, whether as a fleeting annoyance or as a full-fledged rage. Anger is a completely normal, usually healthy, human emotion. But when it gets out of control and turns destructive, it can lead to problems—at work, in your personal relationships, and in the overall quality of your life. And it can make you feel as though you're at the mercy of an unpredictable and powerful emotion. This appendix is meant to help you understand and control anger.

## WHAT IS ANGER?

### The Nature of Anger

*Anger* is "an emotional state that varies in intensity from mild irritation to intense fury and rage," according to Charles Spielberger, PhD, a psychologist who specializes in the study of anger. Like other emotions, it is accompanied by physiological and biological changes; when you get angry, your heart rate and blood pressure go up, as do the levels of your energy hormones, adrenaline, and noradrenaline.

Anger can be caused by both external and internal events. You could be angry with a specific person (such as a co-worker or supervisor) or event (such as a traffic jam or a canceled flight), or your anger could be caused by worrying or brooding about your personal problems. Memories of traumatic or enraging events can also trigger angry feelings.

## Expressing Anger

The instinctive, natural way to express anger is to respond aggressively. Anger is a natural, adaptive response to threats; it inspires powerful, often aggressive, feelings and behaviors, which allow us to fight and to defend ourselves when we are attacked. A certain amount of anger, therefore, is necessary to our survival.

On the other hand, we can't physically lash out at every person or object that irritates or annoys us; laws, social norms, and common sense place limits on how far our anger can take us.

People use a variety of both conscious and unconscious processes to deal with their angry feelings. The three main approaches are expressing, suppressing, and calming. Expressing your angry feelings in an assertive—not aggressive—manner is the healthiest way to express anger. To do this, you have to learn how to make clear what your needs are, and how to get them met, without hurting others. Being assertive doesn't mean being pushy or demanding; it means being respectful of yourself and others.

Anger can be suppressed and then converted or redirected. This happens when you hold in your anger, stop thinking about it, and focus on something positive. The aim is to inhibit or suppress your anger and convert it into more constructive behavior. The danger in this type of response is that if it isn't allowed outward expression, your anger can turn inward—on yourself. Anger turned inward may cause hypertension, high blood pressure, or depression.

Unexpressed anger can create other problems. It can lead to pathological expressions of anger, such as passive–aggressive behavior (getting back at people indirectly, without telling them why, rather than confronting them directly) or a personality that seems perpetually cynical and hostile. People who are constantly putting others down, criticizing everything, and making cynical comments haven't learned how to constructively express their anger. Not surprisingly, they aren't likely to have many successful relationships.

Finally, you can calm down inside. This means not just controlling your outward behavior, but also controlling your internal responses by taking steps to lower your heart rate, calm yourself down, and let the feelings subside. As Dr. Spielberger notes, "When none of these three techniques work, that's when someone—or something—is going to get hurt."

### Anger Management

The goal of anger management is to reduce both your emotional feelings and the physiological arousal that anger causes. You can't get rid of, or avoid, the things or the people that enrage you, nor can you change them, but you can learn to control your reactions.

### Are You Too Angry?

There are psychological tests that measure the intensity of angry feelings, how prone to anger you are, and how well you handle it. But chances are good that if you do have a problem with anger, you already know it. If you find yourself acting in ways that seem out of control and frightening, you might need help finding better ways to deal with this emotion.

### Why Are Some People More Angry Than Others?

According to Jerry Deffenbacher, PhD, a psychologist who specializes in anger management, some people really are more "hot-headed" than others are; they get angry more easily and more intensely than the average person does. There are also those who don't show their anger in loud spectacular ways but are chronically irritable and grumpy. Easily angered people don't always curse and throw things; sometimes they withdraw socially, sulk, or get physically ill.

People who are easily angered generally have what some psychologists call a low tolerance for frustration, meaning simply that they feel that they should not have to be subjected to frustration, inconvenience, or annoyance. They can't take things in stride, and they're particularly infuriated if the situation seems somehow unjust: for example, being corrected for a minor mistake.

What makes these people this way? A number of things. One cause may be genetic or physiological: There is evidence that some children are born irritable, touchy, and easily angered, and that these signs are present from a very early age. Another may be sociocultural. Anger is often regarded as negative; we're taught that it's all right to express anxiety, depression, or other emotions but not to express anger. As a result, we don't learn how to handle it or channel it constructively.

Research has also found that family background plays a role. Typically, people who are easily angered come from families that are disruptive, chaotic, and not skilled at emotional communications.

### Is It Good To "Let It All Hang Out"?

Psychologists now say that this is a dangerous myth. Some people use this theory as a license to hurt others. Research has found that "letting it rip" with anger actually escalates anger and aggression and does nothing to help you (or the person you're angry with) resolve the situation. It's best to find out what it is that triggers your anger, and then to develop strategies to keep those triggers from tipping you over the edge.

## STRATEGIES TO KEEP ANGER AT BAY

### Relaxation

Simple relaxation tools, such as deep breathing and relaxing imagery, can help calm down angry feelings. There are books and courses that can teach you relaxation techniques, and once you learn the techniques, you can call on them in any situation. If you are involved in a relationship where both partners are hot tempered, it might be a good idea for both of you to learn these techniques.

Here are some simple steps you can try:

- Breathe deeply, from your diaphragm; breathing from your chest won't relax you. Picture your breath coming up from your "gut."
- Slowly repeat a calm word or phrase such as "relax" or "take it easy." Repeat it to yourself while breathing deeply.
- Use imagery; visualize a relaxing experience, from either your memory or your imagination.
- Nonstrenuous, slow yoga-like exercises can relax your muscles and make you feel much calmer.

Practice these techniques daily. Learn to use them automatically when you're in a tense situation.

### Cognitive Restructuring

Simply put, cognitive restructuring means changing the way you think. Angry people tend to curse, swear, or speak in highly colorful terms that reflect their inner thoughts. When you're angry, your thinking can get very exaggerated and overly dramatic. Try replacing these thoughts with more rational ones. For instance, instead of telling yourself, "Oh, it's awful, it's terrible, everything's ruined," tell yourself, "It's frustrating, and it's understandable that I'm upset about it, but it's not the end of the world and getting angry is not going to fix it anyhow."

Be careful of words like "never" or "always" when talking about yourself or someone else. "This !&*%@ machine never works," or "you're always forgetting things" are not just inaccurate, they also serve to make you feel that your anger is justified and that there's no way to solve the problem. They also alienate and humiliate people who might otherwise be willing to work with you on a solution.

Remind yourself that getting angry is not going to fix anything and that it won't make you feel better (and may actually make you feel worse).

Logic defeats anger, because anger, even when it's justified, can quickly become irrational. So use cold hard logic on yourself. Remind yourself that the world is "not out to get you," you're just experiencing some of the rough spots of daily life. Do this each time you feel anger getting the best of you, and it'll help you get a more balanced perspective. Angry people tend to demand things: fairness, appreciation, agreement, willingness to do things their way. Everyone wants these things, and we are all hurt and disappointed when we don't get them, but angry people demand them, and when their demands aren't met, their disappointment becomes anger.

As part of their cognitive restructuring, angry people need to become aware of their demanding nature and translate their expectations into desires. In other words, saying, "I would like" something is healthier than saying, "I demand" or "I must have" something. When you're unable to get what you want, you will experience the normal reactions—frustration, disappointment, hurt—but not anger. Some angry people use this anger as a way to avoid feeling hurt, but that doesn't mean the hurt goes away.

## Problem Solving

Sometimes anger and frustration are caused by very real and inescapable problems in our lives. Not all anger is misplaced, and often it's a healthy, natural response to these difficulties. There is also a cultural belief that every problem has a solution, and it adds to our frustration to find out that this isn't always the case. The best attitude to bring to such a situation, then, is to focus not on finding the solution, but rather on how you handle and face the problem.

Make a plan, and check your progress along the way. Resolve to give it your best, but also not to punish yourself if an answer doesn't come right away. If you can approach it with your best intentions and efforts and make a serious attempt to face it head on, you will be less likely to lose patience and fall into all-or-nothing thinking, even if the problem does not get solved right away.

## Better Communication

Angry people tend to jump to—and act on—conclusions, and some of those conclusions can be very inaccurate. The first thing to do if you're in a heated discussion is slow down and think through your responses. Don't say the first thing that comes into your head, but slow down and think carefully about what you want to say. At the same time, listen carefully to what the other person is saying, and take your time before answering.

Listen, too, to what is underlying the anger. For instance, you like a certain amount of freedom and personal space, and your "significant other" wants more connection and closeness. If he or she starts complaining about your activities, don't retaliate by painting your partner as a jailer, a warden, or an albatross around your neck.

It's natural to get defensive when you're criticized, but don't fight back. Instead, listen to what's underlying the words: the message that this person might feel neglected and unloved. It may take a lot of patient questioning on your part, and it may require some breathing space, but don't let your anger—or a partner's—make a discussion spin out of control. Keeping your cool can keep the situation from becoming a disastrous one.

## Using Humor

"Silly humor" can help defuse rage in a number of ways. For one thing, it can help you get a more balanced perspective. When you get angry and call someone a name or refer to them using some imaginative phrase, stop and picture what that word would literally look like. If you're at work and you think of a coworker as a "dirtbag" or a "single-cell life form," for example, picture a large bag full of dirt or an amoeba sitting at your colleague's desk, talking on the phone, going to meetings. Do this whenever a name comes into your head about another person. If you can, draw a picture of what the actual thing might look like. This will take a lot of the edge off your fury, and humor can always be relied on to help unknot a tense situation.

The underlying message of highly angry people, Dr. Deffenbacher says, is "things oughta go my way!" Angry people tend to feel that they are morally right, that any blocking or changing of their plans is an unbearable indignity, and that they should *not* have to suffer this way. Maybe other people do, but not them!

When you feel that urge, he suggests, picture yourself as a

god or goddess, a supreme ruler, who owns the streets and stores and office space, striding alone and having your way in all situations while others defer to you. The more detail you can get into your imaginary scenes, the more chances you have to realize that maybe you are being unreasonable; you'll also realize how unimportant the things you're angry about really are. There are two cautions in using humor. First, don't try to just "laugh off" your problems; rather, use humor to help yourself face them more constructively. Second, don't give in to harsh, sarcastic humor; that's just another form of unhealthy anger expression.

What these techniques have in common is a refusal to take yourself too seriously. Anger is a serious emotion, but it's often accompanied by ideas that, if examined, can make you laugh.

## Changing Your Environment

Sometimes it's our immediate surroundings that give us cause for irritation and fury. Problems and responsibilities can weigh on you and make you feel angry at the "trap" you seem to have fallen into and all the people and things that form that trap.

Give yourself a break. Make sure you have some "personal time" scheduled for times of the day that you know are particularly stressful. One example is the working mother who has a standing rule that when she comes home from work, for the first 15 minutes "nobody talks to Mom unless the house is on fire." After this brief quiet time, she feels better prepared to handle demands from her kids without blowing up at them.

## Some Other Tips for Easing Up on Yourself

TIMING. If you and your spouse tend to fight when you discuss things at night—perhaps you're tired, or distracted, or maybe it's just habit—try changing the times when you talk about important matters so these talks don't turn into arguments.

AVOIDANCE. If your child's chaotic room makes you furious every time you walk by it, shut the door. Don't make yourself look at what infuriates you. Don't say, "Well, my child should clean up the room so I won't have to be angry!" That's not the point. The point is to keep yourself calm.

FINDING ALTERNATIVES. If your daily commute through traffic leaves you in a state of rage and frustration, give yourself a project —learn or map out a different route, one that's less congested or more scenic. Or find another alternative, such as a bus or commuter train.

## DO YOU NEED COUNSELING?

If you feel that your anger is really out of control—if it is having an impact on your relationships and on important parts of your life—you might consider counseling to learn how to handle it better. A psychologist or other licensed mental health professional can work with you in developing a range of techniques for changing your thinking and your behavior.

When you talk to a prospective therapist, tell him or her that you have problems with anger that you want to work on, and ask about his or her approach to anger management. Make sure this isn't only a course of action designed to "put you in touch with your feelings and express them"—that may be precisely what your problem is.

With counseling, psychologists say, a highly angry person can move closer to a middle range of anger in about 8 to 10 weeks, depending on the circumstances and the techniques used.

## WHAT ABOUT ASSERTIVENESS TRAINING?

It's true that angry people need to learn to become assertive (rather than aggressive), but most books and courses on developing assertiveness are aimed at people who don't feel enough anger. These people are more passive and acquiescent than the average person; they tend to let others walk all over them. That isn't something that most angry people do. Still, these books can contain some useful tactics to use in frustrating situations.

Remember, you can't eliminate anger—and it wouldn't be a good idea if you could. In spite of all your efforts, things will happen that will cause you anger, and sometimes it will be justifiable anger. Life will be filled with frustration, pain, loss, and the unpredictable actions of others. You can't change that, but you can change the way you let such events affect you. Controlling your angry responses can keep them from making you even more unhappy in the long run.

## APPENDIX H: STRATEGIES FOR TEACHING CHILDREN HOW TO DEAL WITH THEIR ANGER

Teaching children strategies for dealing with their anger can be challenging because feelings of anger often are not predictable. So the best time to practice coping strategies is in calmer times when they are more likely to respond to your suggestions. Therefore, you have no choice but to use the time between outbursts or meltdowns as much as possible.

There are six components to implementing the treatment strategies. All six are important.

1. You will need to practice self-calming exercises such as blowing real and imaginary bubbles every day. Prompt your child to blow his imaginary bubbles when he's mad.

2. Sit down with your child and identify some rewards that she can earn by practicing her breathing exercises (on a daily basis) and by using her exercises when she is frustrated or angry. Don't skip the rewards—rewards are essential to the success of anger management in children.

3. Try to identify times when you deal effectively with your own stressors and point these out, very briefly, to your child. Share your coping strategy with your child to give him an example of how he could deal with a similar situation. If you feel like you're about to lose control, do your breathing exercises.

4. When your child starts to get upset, briefly encourage her to practice her breathing exercises, and then stay out of the situation completely. The sooner you prompt her, the easier it will be for her to try it. If you wait until she loses it, the exercises probably will not help. Don't allow your dread of a meltdown to prevent you from enforcing your discipline. It's especially important that you address your child in a quiet, matter-of-fact manner.

5. In general it's best to avoid heated confrontation, but sometimes it's unavoidable. Teach your child how to appropriately and constructively express feelings when they seem justified. Try to stay with whatever disciplinary strategies you've agreed to use. Don't allow yourself to get drawn into negotiations. Doing so only makes it harder for you to avoid getting angry yourself.

6. Practice the problem-solving techniques with your child in "easy" situations 30 days or evenings in a row. Go through the steps: What exactly is the problem? What are my possibilities? What are my choices? How can I plan ahead next time? How did I do?

Because these skills are difficult to learn and they are so important, practice is critical. And remember, the sooner a child notices that he is starting to get angry, the easier it is to do his exercises, and the more effective the exercises will be.

The more you concentrate on teaching these skills, and the less you react when your child is angry, the quicker she will learn to deal with her own anger. Once she has learned to deal with her own anger, she won't need nearly as much help with it.

*Note.* Copyright 2001 by Edward R. Christophersen. Adapted with permission.

# CHAPTER 14

# COPING WITH WHINING AND TANTRUMS

One of the most common complaints that parents have about their children is "whining." Whining can take many forms. For example, a child who keeps repeating, "Mommy, I want a cookie" is whining. So is a child who says, "I don't want to go with Grandma." Whining may start with a whimper, an insistent demand, or a certain tone of voice that every parent recognizes with dread—your child is starting to whine, and if you don't respond properly you may have a full-blown tantrum or argument on your hands or, at least, continued whining. Kids of all ages know that whining works—that's why they whine.

And that, in fact, is the main reason children whine—because it works. If your child asks for something nicely, you ignore him or you say no. If he asks repeatedly, he knows that you are more likely to give in. So what are you teaching him? You're teaching him to whine. In families where the parents don't give in to whining, the children don't whine. They may complain briefly, but they've learned that whining doesn't work.

How does whining ever get started in the first place? Infants have one main way of communicating with us—they cry. If they are hungry, they cry. If their diaper is wet and it bothers them, they cry. If they are bored and want to be picked up, they cry. And if they are bored and want to be allowed to go to bed, they cry. Parents' job is to try to figure out what each different cry means. Unfortunately, they don't have any training in recognizing different types of cries, so they make a lot of mistakes and, often, come to the rescue for every cry. Sometimes their rescuing is built on guilt: They think that they must meet every cry and demand.

Unfortunately, knowing that children cry only when they want something and knowing what they actually want are completely different. For example, if you are holding your baby and she's crying because she's tired, how are you supposed to know that she would actually like to be placed in bed so that she can go to sleep? Many parents would not think a crying child wants to be left alone, but it can certainly be true! Babies may cry because they have an unmet need, but unless their parents have some way of telling what it is that they want, they still don't know what to do.

So what can you do to respond to your child's cries but prevent whining and tantrums? This chapter will provide you with some guidelines on preventing or managing whining and tantrums in your child.

## PREVENTING WHINING AND TANTRUMS

It's probably easier to prevent whining in the first place than it is to stop it or reduce it once it is well established. Infants and toddlers have few means of communication available to them. If they cry and they get their needs met, they are more likely to cry in the future. Yet it seems unfair to not go to them when they are crying. What, then, are a parent's options when dealing with an infant?

Between birth and about 12 weeks of age, you simply do not have any choice but to respond to your infant's cry. Infants eat until they are full, and then they fall asleep. After your infant has fallen asleep, you can place him in his bed, crib, or bassinet. However, somewhere around 12 weeks of age, many infants will still be awake, at least slightly, when they are finished feeding. If your infant is tired and has just finished eating, you can place him in his bed, on his back, and leave him alone and without any disruptions, and he will drift off to sleep. Even if he fusses a little, it won't be for long. At this age, infants also begin to wake up and often babble, coo or play with their feet or hands before crying. If you go in and pick up your baby when she is quiet, she will learn that if she babbles and coos, someone will pick her up. If you only come when she is crying, she will learn that this is how to get your attention. Thus, the infant version of whining and tantrums presents itself quite early if not handled properly by parents. More information on establishing appropriate sleep habits for infants can be found in chapter 11.

## HOW TO STOP YOUR CHILD FROM WHINING

In chapter 4 on effective discipline, we discussed the need to teach your child appropriate behaviors as well as to discourage inappropriate behaviors. You need both of these strategies to make any kind of a change in your child's behavior, including the behavior of whining.

To begin with, it takes a lot of effort for a child to whine, particularly for children who whine a lot. They wouldn't keep up the whining unless it worked. It's their job. They whine, and their parents give in. You most likely will never see your child alone out in the back yard whining, unless, of course, he knows that you can hear him and, more importantly, respond to him from your location.

There are two things you have to do to reduce whining: (1) ignore it and don't encourage it or give in to it, and (2) teach your child an alternative to whining. Within reason, if you want the whining to stay at a greatly reduced level, you should consider, whenever possible, teaching your child alternative ways of attracting your attention and of getting what she wants.

## How to Ignore Whining

If we recommended that you just give in to everything your child wanted, you'd say that we'd lost our minds. But often that's what whining amounts to—your signal to give your child everything he wants. You child wants some milk and he whines, so you give him milk. He wants to get up at bedtime and he cries out, so you get him up. He wants you to dress him and fusses, so you dress him. Whining is how your child gets what he wants.

The opposite of responding to such whining is to ignore it completely. What does "ignoring" mean, exactly? It means that you don't look at your child. That you don't talk to her. That you don't talk about her. It means that you don't respond to her. So if you start out ignoring her and then tell her that you aren't going to answer her as long as she is whining, you aren't ignoring her. If you try to redirect her by suggesting that she find something to do, you aren't ignoring her. If you give her any verbal instruction at all, you aren't ignoring her.

Why is it so important that you ignore a whining child? Children whine because their parents respond to their whining. You're responding if you try to redirect him, or tell him you aren't going to respond to him, or tell him that you can't help him right now. If you completely stop responding to him when he whines, he will stop whining.

But before they stop whining, most children will actually increase their whining. Because whining worked before, your child will whine a little louder to get it to work this time. Or she will pull on your arm and whine, or get in your face and whine. She is trying to make whining "work." Only after a period of time with you truly ignoring her will she give up and leave you alone.

## Keeping Calm While Ignoring Whining

While you are learning to ignore whining, you may need to use some of the parent coping skills discussed in chapter 5. One of the biggest factors in whether or not parents give in to whining and tantrums is whether the parents can deal with the discomfort they feel when listening to the whining or witnessing the tantrum.

Thus, make sure you have good coping skills in place. For example, if while listening to whining you say to yourself, "I can't stand it when he whines all the time," you are likely to give in to the whining. But if you can change your self-talk to, for example, "I don't like it when he whines, but I know that I can stand it," you'll probably make it through the episode. It is your responsibility to stay calm when your child is whining. Statements to your child such as "Well, you must like to see me mad, because you whine even though you know it upsets me" place the blame on the wrong person. You must control your emotional response to your child's whining, or any other behaviors that you find to be irritating or anger producing.

## Alternatives to Whining

Probably the easiest alternative to teach your daughter when she whines is to ask you in her "big girl" voice or to ask you without whining. Teach her the alternative of expressing her grievance constructively, and praise her when she does. She will soon learn that you are more likely to respond positively when she asks in this way. In chapter 1, we discussed how to teach your child the skills of sharing and taking turns by pretending, practicing, prompting, and praising. The same procedures can be used for teaching alternatives to whining. Take the time to pretend with your child that you are asking for something in a calm, pleasant voice, instead of whining. Practice the calm, pleasant voice with your child and encourage him to practice with you. Point out to your child when someone (a customer in a store, a person on a TV show, or someone in a book you are reading) is whining and when he or she is asking nicely. When you suspect that your child is about to enter a situation where she would have whined in the past, suggest that this would be a good time to use her "big girl" voice. And, when she does use her big girl voice, make sure you praise her for her efforts.

Some children (usually the ones who don't whine much to begin with) just need this gentle reminder, and they are fine. If you find that your daughter usually whines first, then asks without whining after your prompt her, you can ask her to ask without whining at other times. You can tell her how much you appreciate it when she uses her big girl voice. However, for the majority of children who are whiners, it's going to take more than just prompting more appropriate speech.

If your son wants you to pick him up, probably all he has to do is whine and you'll do it. But, each time you pick him up when he's whining, you are teaching him that whining is a good way to communicate. Now, a lot of people will say that the only way he can communicate is by whining. Most toddlers, however, are perfectly capable of raising both of their arms up into the air to communicate that they want to be picked up, and most adults understand that a toddler standing in front of them with his arms stretched high wants to be picked up. You can encourage your child to raise his arms, telling him, "If you want to be picked up, you should raise your arms like this," and demonstrating by raising your arms high above your head. For further discussion of whining, how it gets started, and how to reduce it, read the book *Whining: 3 Steps to Stopping it Before the Tears and Tantrums Start.*[1]

### Make a Plan and Stick to It

If you want to encourage your child to use an alternative to whining, sit down in the evening, when she's in bed, and map out her alternatives to whining and the steps you will take to encourage them. For example, if she wants to be picked up, she has to stretch her arms in front high above her head. You might plan to demonstrate this once each morning by raising your arms in that fashion and telling her to raise her arms when she wants to be picked up.

It's not a bad idea to also give yourself a time frame. Plan that you are going to demonstrate by putting your arms up once each morning, and picking your daughter up when she raises her arms, for the next two weeks. At the end of the two weeks, you can review how well you've been following your plan and how your daughter is responding to it.

Remember, each time you succeed in not giving it to her demands, and each time she uses your preferred mode of communication, she is one step closer to knowing how to behave when she wants to be picked up and one step closer to whining a lot less. Alternatively, each time that you give in to her, you are encouraging her to break all of your rules and then whine to get you to let her.

### What Role Does Sympathy Play?

There's nothing wrong with you being sympathetic with your child, as long as it is not in response to whining. If you are in the middle of changing the baby and your son raises his arms high above his head, as you have taught him to, you can't just stop changing the baby. Rather, you can tell him, "I know it is hard to wait, but Daddy is in the middle of changing Emily's diaper, and he'll pick you up in a minute." Thus, you can be sympathetic to your child's needs, but you do not need to give in to whining to meet those needs.

## HOW TO MANAGE YOUR CHILD'S TANTRUMS

Just as every parent knows a whine when they hear one, every parent knows the signs of a tantrum and dreads their occurrence. Perhaps no behavior is more unsettling to parents that a full-blown temper tantrum, particularly if it involves screaming, hitting or kicking, or negative words.

The response of many parents to tantrums is almost to have a tantrum themselves. When children throw a tantrum, some parents yell at them, grab their arm, or spank them. The yelling, grabbing, and spanking are the adult equivalent of a tantrum. What the child is saying is, "You better give me my way or I will scream and kick until you do," and what the parent is saying is, "You had better give me *my* way and not scream or kick, and I'll yell at you until you do!"

Do tantrums indicate that your child has a significant behavior problem or that you have failed as a parent? No, all a tantrum means is that the child has lost all reason—she has gotten so upset that she doesn't know what she's doing. When you see a child fall down on the floor in a grocery store crying, flailing her legs around, and demanding something, it just means that she hasn't gotten her way and is pulling out all the stops to get it. Rarely is it anything more than that. Most children rarely throw a tantrum when they are alone in the back yard or in their bedroom. So a tantrum is not something gone amiss in a child's nervous system, but something she uses to encourage a parent or someone else to give her what she wants.

As we know, it often works. In the simplest cases, the parent gives in to the child and the tantrum stops immediately. For example, a child wants a candy bar immediately before sitting down for dinner, the parent says no, and the tantrum starts. The parent, fearful that he or she will be an ineffective parent, gives the child the candy bar, "just this one time." Parents often use such rationalizations. They may say that a tantrum started because the child was "tired," "missed his nap," or "was in a strange store" or because "Mommy had to work late." Regardless of the rationalization, most parents are interested in knowing how to reduce or eliminate their child's tantrums.

Over the years a number of remedies have been posited for tantrums, including throwing water on the child, telling the child how much the tantrum upsets you, and the ultimate, "If you keep that up, I'm really going to give you something to cry about." Usually when a child has an extensive tantrum, it means that her parents have not been very good at ignoring it and that it worked somehow. Tantrums are also maintained when parents aren't using their coping skills and children aren't being taught to use their self-quieting skills and to use an alternative mode of communication. In addition, parents model "tantrum" behavior if they become out-of-control themselves, and they may not be spending enough time providing their child with positive feedback. Thus, although tantrums can reach the point where they seem to be unprovoked, it is more often the case that the parent–child system of interaction has simply come to support frequent tantrums, with few skills for ending them effectively. Fortunately, there are effective options for parents to manage tantrums in their child.

To deal effectively with temper tantrums, parents will need virtually all of the skills that we've discussed in this book. We recommend that you start out with a written analysis of the temper tantrums that you have witnessed over the past several weeks. Start out by answering the following questions for each tantrum:

- Where was the tantrum?
- What was the tantrum about?
- What was my child doing in the 15 minutes immediately preceding the tantrum?
- What did I do in the 15 minutes immediately preceding the tantrum?
- What did I do when the tantrum started?
- What did I do as the tantrum progressed?
- What did my child do as the tantrum progressed?
- When did the tantrum subside?
- What happened after the tantrum subsided?
- Have you taught your child an alternative strategy for getting her way?

Let's answer a few of these questions for a simple tantrum: The child wanted something, the child threw a tantrum, the parent was visibly upset, the parent gave in, and the child got what he wanted. He may well have gotten more than he wanted, including a spanking or a lecture, but he got what he wanted. Even if a parent does not actually give in and allow the child to have the desired outcome, that parent's full attention, even in the form of yelling or spanking, is often what the child really wanted in the first place.

After you have analyzed your child's tantrums, you will inevitably see that tantrums do serve a purpose. The purpose may be to obtain a toy, a snack, a chance to stay up late, or perhaps your total and undivided attention. Armed with the strategies described and discussed throughout this book, you should have the skills necessary to manage your child's temper tantrums. You might need to implement several of the strategies, including the following, but not necessarily in this order:

- Encourage your child to use self-quieting skills (see chapter 9).
- Encourage your child to use anger management skills such as blowing bubbles (see chapter 13).
- Use good parent coping skills (see chapter 5).
- Refrain from modeling behaviors that are components of tantrums.
- Be certain that you don't pay attention to your child during a tantrum and that you don't give in to the demands voiced during the tantrum.
- Establish an alternative means of enabling your child to communicate with you.
- Give your child an alternative way to obtain what he wanted to obtain by his tantrum.
- Spend a significant amount of time with your child giving positive feedback (see chapter 2) and encouraging independent play skills to help her occupy her time (see chapter 10).
- Use time-out immediately when your child starts to have a tantrum, but think of time-out as you ignoring him until he self-quiets, not as punishing him so that he won't have another tantrum (see chapter 4).

If you notice, the one strategy that we didn't mention for dealing with temper tantrums was discipline. For discipline is often what can make tantrums worse. Trying to "discipline" a child in the middle of a tantrum is futile and may well escalate her negative behaviors. Instead, you must deal with tantrums using this list of strategies.

Temper tantrums are a clear sign that you need to do your homework—that you need to be learning some skills yourself and teaching your child some skills. With some consistency and effort on your part, your child may prefer to give up his tantrums.

## WHEN TO SEEK PROFESSIONAL HELP

If you have followed the recommendations in this chapter and your child is still whining and throwing long or violent tantrums on a daily basis, or if you find yourself getting really angry at your child, you should probably talk with your pediatrician to discuss your child's behavior and your reactions to it. Likewise, consult your pediatrician if your child is pulling her hair out during tantrums or is otherwise hurting herself, such as biting her hand or banging her head. Your pediatrician may recommend some strategies for you to try, or he or she may refer you to a clinical child psychologist for additional assistance.

## CONCLUSION

Whining and tantrums are typical experiences in a child's development. As a parent, however, they can be annoying and very disruptive to your interactions with your child. Whining and tantrums are a child's way of communicating her displeasure with her parents or with a situation. They are maintained by attention and by helping the child get her way. To reduce whining and tantrums you must help your child build the skills she needs to communicate without resorting to such behaviors, as well as teach her how to cope with her frustration when she does not get her way, or when her whining or tantrums are ignored. A key aspect of reducing whining and tantrums is your ability to stay calm and be consistent in your efforts to teach more appropriate behaviors. This chapter describes a plan for systematically analyzing your child's tantrums to help you see them for what they are—your child's attempts to get her way—so that you can respond in a calm, consistent way that works best for reducing her negative behaviors. Of course, you should seek the help of a child psychologist if your child continues to have violent tantrums despite your best efforts. A professional may be able to better guide you in the parenting strategies needed to manage your child's behavior.

# FINAL THOUGHTS

Living with children is a continuous teaching and learning process for both children and parents. Almost everything a child learns during the first few years is dramatically influenced by his interactions with his parents. The important thing, which has been emphasized throughout this book, is that parents are teachers, not on selected occasions or during certain times, but during most of the time they spend interacting with their children. The manner in which a parent handles any single interaction, whether pleasant or unpleasant, in not nearly as important as how the parent interacts with the child on a whole.

You can make a significant difference in the way that your children turn out. If you want to raise children who read a lot and derive a lot of enjoyment from reading, you can encourage reading by reading to your children, from infancy on, having them read to you as soon as they are able, and talking to them about what they read. You can also show them the value of reading by regularly looking things up in books instead of always just answering questions from memory.

If you want a child who has good coping skills, you can begin early and help them to make positive self-statements and model positive self-statements to them. You can also talk to them about situations you encounter that are challenging and share how you coped with them. You can listen when they talk about situations that were challenging or frustrating to them, hear how they problem-solved, and help them with further problem-solving ideas.

A good way to help yourself to stay on course, as we've discussed several times in this book, is to decide what skills you would like to see your child have in 10 years and ask yourself, periodically, if what you are doing is helping him meet the 10 goals that you have decided are important.

You can also be judicious about what you allow your children to watch on TV, the activities that they participate in, and the people with whom they participate. You can choose to emphasize participation in activities (which is obviously more desirable) or winning in activities.

Child rearing gives thousands of pleasant, memorable experiences to parents, even though most adults have little formal or informal training in parenting. They just handle each day as they encounter it, hoping that somehow everything will work out right. Most of the advice they receive is corrective. Relatives or friends often tell you what you should have done to avoid a situation that has already occurred. No matter how superb you are as a parent, you will have some disappointments that may lead you to question what you are doing. We're advocating that you start right off working toward a pleasant, educative interaction with your child. Ignore minor setbacks. Concentrate your efforts on positive ways of building useful, pleasant behavior in your children. Treating them as adults, as little people, is the best way to do this.

Successful parenting is the most rewarding experience a person can ever expect to enjoy. The love you share with your child is a love that can't be experienced in any other way. Every day you should do everything you can to encourage, understand, nurture, and enjoy that love.

# NOTES

## CHAPTER 3. COMMUNICATING WITH YOUR CHILD

1. N. J. Blum, G. E. Williams, P. C. Friman, and E. R. Christophersen, "Disciplining Children: Verbal Instructions and Reasoning." *Pediatrics,* 96 (1995): 336–341.

## CHAPTER 4. DISCIPLINING YOUR CHILD EFFECTIVELY

1. D. Hemenway, S. Solnick, and J. Carter, "Yelling: Child-Rearing Violence." *Child Abuse and Neglect,* 18 (1994): 1011–1020.
2. A. M. M. Dedmon, E. R. Christophersen, and K. L. Campbell, "Parent-Child Activities and Preschoolers' Aggressive Behavior," manuscript submitted for publication.
3. See note 1.
4. T. W. Phelan, *1-2-3 Magic* (Glen Ellyn, IL: Child Management, 1995).

## CHAPTER 5. BUILDING PARENT COPING SKILLS

1. I. J. Barrish and H. H. Barrish, *Managing and Understanding Parental Anger* (Kansas City, MO: Westport, 1989).

## CHAPTER 7. GETTING THE MOST OUT OF TOYS, GAMES, AND SPORTS

1. *Injury Prevention and Control for Children and Youth*, 3rd ed., (Elk Grove Village, IL: American Academy of Pediatrics, 1997).
2. H. R. Quilitch, E. R. Christophersen, and T. R. Risley, "Evaluation of Children's Play Materials." *Journal of Applied Behavior Analysis*, 10 (1977): 501.
3. T. N. Robinson et al., "Effects of Reducing Children's Television and Video Game Use on Aggressive Behavior: A Randomized Controlled Trial." *Archives of Pediatric and Adolescent Medicine*, 155 (2001): 17–23.
4. American Academy of Pediatrics, *Sports and Your Child*. Available at http://www.aap.org/family/sports.html/ (2001).
5. See note 4.
6. See note 4.
7. K. D. Allen, "The Use of an Enhanced Simplified Habit-Reversal Procedure to Reduce Disruptive Outbursts During Athletic Performance." *Journal of Applied Behavior Analysis,* 31 (1998): 489–492.

## CHAPTER 8. DEALING WITH DIVORCE

1. M. G. Neuman and P. Romanowski, *Helping Your Kids Cope With Divorce the Sandcastles Way* (New York: Random House, 1999).

## CHAPTER 9. BUILDING SELF-QUIETING SKILLS

1. E. Jacobsen, "Progressive Relaxation." *American Journal of Psychology,* 36 (1925): 73–87.
2. H. Benson, *The Relaxation Response* (New York: Avon, 2000).

## CHAPTER 10. ENCOURAGING INDEPENDENT PLAY SKILLS

1. R. G. Wahler and J. J. Fox, "Solitary Toy Play and Time Out: A Family Treatment Package for Children With Aggressive and Oppositional Behavior." *Journal of Applied Behavior Analysis*, 13 (1980): 23–39.

## CHAPTER 11. ESTABLISHING BEDTIME

1. E. E. Gaylor, B. L. Goodlin-Jones, and T. F. Anders, "Classification of Young Children's Sleep Problems: A Pilot Study." *Journal of the American Academy of Child and Adolescent Psychiatry,* 40 (2001): 61–67.
2. J. A. Mindell, "Sleep Disorders in Children." *Health Psychology,* 12 (1993): 151–162.
3. R. Ferber, *Solve Your Child's Sleep Problems* (New York: Simon and Schuster, 1985).
4. P. C. Friman et al., "The Bedtime Pass: An Approach to Bedtime Crying and Leaving the Room." *Archives of Pediatric and Adolescent Medicine,* 153 (1999): 1027–1029.
5. See note 2.
6. See note 2.

## CHAPTER 12. FACILITATING TOILET TRAINING

1. N. H. Azrin and R. M. Foxx, *Toilet Training in Less Than a Day* (New York: Pocket Books, 1974).
2. See note 1.
3. M. C. Luxem et al., "Behavioral–Medical Treatment of Pediatric Toileting Refusal." *Journal of Developmental and Behavioral Pediatrics,* 18 (1997): 34–41.
4. C. L. Williams, M. Bollella, and E. L. Wynder, "A New Recommendation for Dietary Fiber in Childhood." *Pediatrics,* 96 (1995): 985–988.
5. E. R. Christophersen and P. C. Purvis, "Toileting Problems in Children," in *The handbook of clinical child psychology,* 3rd ed., eds. C. E. Walker and M. C. Roberts (New York: Wiley, 2001).
6. See note 4.
7. See note 4.
8. See note 4.
9. M. E. Moffatt, "Nocturnal Enuresis: A Review of the Efficacy of Treatments and Practical Advice for Clinicians." *Journal of Developmental and Behavioral Pediatrics,* 18 (1997): 49–56. Reprinted with permission.
10. N. H. Azrin, T. J. Sneed, and R. M. Foxx, "Dry-Bed Training: Rapid Elimination of Childhood Enuresis." *Behavior Research and Therapy,* 12 (1974): 147–156.

## CHAPTER 13. DISCOURAGING AGGRESSION

1. R. Loeber et al., "Physical Fighting in Childhood as a Risk Factor for Later Mental Health Problems." *Journal of the American Academy of Child and Adolescent Psychiatry,* 39 (2000): 421–428.
2. B. Weiss et al., "Some Consequences of Early Harsh Discipline: Child Aggression and a Maladaptive Social Information Processing Style." *Child Development,* 63 (1992): 1321–1335.
3. J. Garbarino, "Violent Children: Where Do We Point the Finger of Blame?" *Archives of Pediatric and Adolescent Medicine,* 155 (2001): 13–15.
4. M. A. Straus, D. B. Sugarman, and J. Giles-Sims, "Spanking by Parents and Subsequent Antisocial Behavior in Children." *Archives of Pediatrics and Adolescent Medicine,* 151 (1997): 761–767.
5. D. Hemenway, S. Solnick, and J. Carter, "Child-Rearing Violence." *Child Abuse and Neglect,* 18 (1994): 1011–1020.
6. G. R. Patterson, *Coercive Family Process* (Eugene, OR: Castalia, 1982).
7. R. A. Barkley and C. M. Benton, *Your Defiant Child: 8 Steps to Better Behavior* (New York: Guilford Press, 1998).
8. R. Forehand and N. Long, *Parenting the Strong-Willed Child: The Clinically Proven Five-Week Program for Parents of Two- to Six-Year Olds* (Chicago: Contemporary Books, 1996).
9. T. N. Robinson et al., "Effects of Reducing Children's Television and Video Game Use on Aggressive Behavior: A Randomized Controlled Trial." *Archives of Pediatric and Adolescent Medicine,* 151 (2001): 17–23.
10. B. J. Bushman, R. Baumeister, and A. D. Stack, "Catharsis, Aggression and Persuasive Influence: Self-Fulfilling or Self-Defeating Prophecies?" *Journal of Personality and Social Psychology,* 76 (1999): 367–376.

## CHAPTER 14. COPING WITH WHINING AND TANTRUMS

1. A. Ricker and C. Crowder, *Whining: 3 Steps to Stopping It Before the Tears and Tantrums Start* (New York: Simon & Schuster, 2000).

# INDEX

# ABOUT THE AUTHORS

**Edward R. Christophersen, PhD,** is a staff psychologist at Children's Mercy Hospital in Kansas City and a professor of pediatrics at the University of Missouri at Kansas City School of Medicine. He received his PhD in developmental and child psychology from the University of Kansas in 1970 and held faculty appointments in pediatrics at the university's Medical Center and at the Department of Psychology and the Department of Human Development in Lawrence.

Dr. Christophersen is certified in clinical psychology by the American Board of Professional Psychology. In 1998 he was elected Fellow (honorary) of the American Academy of Pediatrics (AAP) for his unique and substantial contributions to child health. In 2001 he received the Dale Richmond Award from the AAP. Dr. Christophersen has appeared on over 300 television and radio interviews and has been quoted in over 180 print interviews. He has given lectures for parents throughout most of North America.

**Susan L. Mortweet, PhD,** is a staff psychologist at Children's Mercy Hospital in Kansas City and an assistant professor of pediatrics at the University of Missouri at Kansas City School of Medicine. She received her PhD in developmental and child psychology from the University of Kansas in 1996. Dr. Mortweet currently provides psychological care for children with various emotional and learning needs. She is also the primary psychologist at Children's Mercy Hospital for children with diabetes and other endocrine disorders. Dr. Mortweet has published in the areas of cultural diversity, effective teaching strategies for children with mild mental retardation, and effective treatments for managing common childhood disorders.